This book examines an increasingly important phenomenon for competitiveness and innovation in industry: namely, the growing use of scientific principles in industrial research. Industrial innovation still arises from systematic trial-and-error experiments with many designs and objects, but these experiments are now being guided by a more rational understanding of phenomena. This has important implications for market structure, firm strategies, and competition. *Science and innovation* focuses on the pharmaceutical industry. It discusses the changes that the notable advances in the life sciences in the 1980s have brought to the strategies of drug companies, the organization of their internal research, their relationships with scientific institutions, the division of labor between large pharmaceutical firms and small research-intensive suppliers, the productivity of drug discovery, and the productivity of R&D.

Science and innovation

Science and innovation

The US pharmaceutical industry during the 1980s

Alfonso Gambardella
University of Urbino

CAMBRIDGE
UNIVERSITY PRESS

Published by the Press Syndicate of the University of Cambridge
The Pitt Building, Trumpington Street, Cambridge CB2 1RP
40 West 20th Street, New York, NY 10011-4211, USA
10 Stamford Road, Oakleigh, Victoria 3166, Australia

First published 1995

Printed in Great Britain at the University Press, Cambridge

A catalogue record for this book is available from the British Library

Library of Congress cataloguing in publication data applied for

ISBN 0 521 45118 3 hardback

SE

To Anjana

Contents

List of figures	*page* x
List of tables	xi
Preface	xii
List of abbreviations	xvi
1	Introduction	1
2	Science and innovation in pharmaceutical research	18
3	Economic implications of greater scientific intensity in drug research	42
4	In-house scientific research and innovation: case studies of large US pharmaceutical companies	82
5	Scientific research and drug discovery: an econometric investigation	106
6	A model of the innovation cycle in the pharmaceutical industry	124
7	Complementarity and external linkages: the strategies of large firms in biotechnology	146
8	Conclusions	161
	Notes	168
	References	179
	Index	195

Figures

2.1 Stages in the development of new drugs   *page* 19
2.2 Number of new drugs commercialized worldwide,
    1987–91   40
4.1 Smithkline's R&D/sales ratio, 1959–88   96
4.2 Scientific papers published by company scientists:
    Smithkline, Eli Lilly, and Merck, 1964–88   97
6.1 Estimated lag structure of R&D   138
6.2 Growth rate of market value   141

Tables

2.1	US drug development costs by stage	*page* 20
2.2	Top ten pharmaceutical products in 1991	24
3.1	Agreements and other relationships (in biopharmaceuticals) between large US pharmaceutical firms and universities or other research institutions in the 1980s	49
3.2	Ciba-Geigy's network of agreements	63
3.3	Hoffmann La Roche's network of agreements	66
3.4	Merck's network of agreements	70
3.5	Pfizer's network of agreements	73
4.1	1986 pharmaceutical sales and 1983–88 average R&D/ sales ratio of the eight firms in the case studies	84
4.2	Merck: major new drugs in the market or in the pipeline, late 1980s	85
4.3	Eli Lilly's drugs with 1989 sales of at least $100 million	89
4.4	Eli Lilly's research alliances in the early 1990s	91
5.1	Descriptive statistics: levels	113
5.2	Descriptive statistics: logs	113
5.3	Estimated parameters, equations (7)–(8)	115
5.4	Estimated parameters, equations (7)–(8) with structural differences in parameters, 1968–79 and 1980–91	116
5.5	Hypothesis testing	118
6.1	Descriptive statistics: levels	135
6.2	Descriptive statistics: growth rates – log (y_{it}/y_{it-1})	135
6.3	Estimated parameters, equations (3), (5), (6), and (7)	136
6.4	Estimated lag structure of R&D	137
6.5	Estimates of the shock parameters and shock variances	139
6.6	Growth rate of market value	140
7.1	Definition of the variables used in the empirical analysis	153
7.2	Descriptive statistics	153

7.3   Results from negative binomial estimation of AWF,
      AWU, PRL, and PRM   156
7.4   Correlations among the standardized residuals from
      negative binomial estimation of AWF, AWU, PRL, and
      PRM in table 7.3   157

Preface

This book deals with an important feature of technical change in industry towards the end of the twentieth century. The relationships between science and innovation are as old as the beginnings of capitalism, if not older. Yet, the 1980s and early 1990s have witnessed a considerable increase in the use of abstract, scientific conceptualization in the "for-profit" research sector. Moreover, impressive developments in computational power and software-based simulation have improved significantly the technology of experimentation. Altogether, these advances are bringing about prominent changes in the nature of industrial research and the innovation process.

Although in different ways and to different degrees, this trend is affecting all high-tech industries. But in order to provide extended evidence of this pattern, one would have to deal with the many idiosyncratic features that characterize and distinguish the relationships between science and innovation in different sectors.

This is why, in this book, I decided to focus on the pharmaceutical industry, wherein, for several reasons, the 1980s attested a clear shift from largely empirical industrial research processes (based on trial and error of many compounds) to a more rational search for innovation, based on effective use of scientific knowledge and computerized research technologies. I shall emphasize several times that the pharmaceutical industry is special. Nonetheless, it could well exhibit, in ways that are more apparent than elsewhere, evolutionary patterns that are important in other high-tech (and non high-tech) industries as well. If so, we could be on the verge of notable transformations in the "technology of technological change," with related implications for competition, division of labor, relationships with non-profit scientific institutions, and the like. While I do not address these broader questions here, I leave them for speculation by the reader, and to future economic research.

There are many people I would like to acknowledge. I am especially indebted to Nathan Rosenberg, who made me discover the subtleties of the economics of innovation, encouraged me to pursue the topic of this work, and provided many insightful comments. Along with Nate, I want to mention Rina's dear and warm friendship.

Tim Bresnahan and Paul David have been sources of many valuable suggestions. Paul is an economic historian with, uncommonly, a technical background, whilst Tim is a technical economist with a marvelous sense of economic history. Among other things, their versatility was of tremendous help in finding a technical basis for historical facts, and in giving historical meaning to technical results.

I have now developed such close personal and professional linkages with Ashish Arora that it was extremely difficult to disentangle things that I had not discussed with him or worked out in previous papers with him, or that we shall work out together in the future. Although I refer to our work in the text, his influence on my thinking about these issues extends to many other parts of the book. Moreover, chapter 7 is based upon joint work with him. Ed Steinmueller provided penetrating comments both in writing and in discussion. His deep understanding of technologies, and his attention to economic implications, have constituted a model that I have tried to imitate. Gianni Cozzi and Sergio Vaccà, along with Barbara Di Bernardo and Enzo Rullani, have greatly influenced my way of approaching the study of firms, technologies, and industries.

I learned many things about the pharmaceutical industry and the broadly defined chemical sector from Ralph Landau. Bronwyn Hall provided useful comments on an earlier draft of chapter 6, and kindly supplied me with the data from the NBER–Compustat File. I also discussed topics related to this work with Shane Greenstein, Roger Noll, John Pencavel, Geoffrey Rothwell, Roland Sturm, and Frank Wolak. Among my Italian friends and colleagues, I have benefited from discussion with Salvo Torrisi and Antonello Zanfei, and with Franco Malerba, Luigi Orsenigo, and Alina Rizzoni. Paolo Barbanti, Nicoletta Buratti and Raffaella Della Valle helped me in improving my understanding of the pharmaceutical industry. Francesco Della Valle, a top manager and now an entrepreneur in this industry, deserves a special mention. He discussed and shared many views expressed in this book, and made me aware that they were in accord with the "pragmatic" expertise of some drug industry executives. Italy needs many more entrepreneurs like him.

I wish to thank Steven Gass of the Terman Engineering Library at Stanford University, and Wanda Cantarello of Lifegroup SpA, for conducting the on-line search of the 1980–91 pharmaceutical patent data, and Francis Narin and Steven Kimberly of CHI/Computer Horizons Inc. for providing me with data on the scientific publications of pharmaceutical companies. Amanda Feuz patiently went through my manuscript to smooth out my crunchy English.

My wonderful wife and companion in life, Monica, and my family have been sources of endless encouragement. The book is dedicated to my daughter.

I gratefully acknowledge financial support for this research from: the Technology and Economic Growth Program, Stanford University, USA (1988–89); the Lynde and Harry Bradley Foundation, USA (1990); the Italian Ministry of Scientific Research (MURST), which funds 60 percent of the University of Urbino, Italy (1991–93); the Centro Nazionale delle Ricerche (CNR), Progetto Finalizzato "Processi di Internazionalizzazione delle Impresse," contract no. 92.02634.PF73-115.10801, Italy (1992); the EC-DG XII Program "Human Capital and Mobility," contract no. ERISCHRXCT920002 (1993–94).

Abbreviations

AHP   American Home Products
FDA   Food and Drug Administration
IND   Investigational New Drug Exemption
NBER National Bureau of Economic Research
NDA   New Drug Application
OTC   over the counter

1   Introduction

Science and innovation in industrial research

In the *Wealth of Nations*, Adam Smith stated that "improvements in machinery" are sometimes made by "philosophers and men of speculation," "who ... are often capable of combining together the powers of the most distant and dissimilar objects" (Smith, 1982 [1776], p. 114). Marx, in chapter 15 of *Das Kapital*, and more recently Kuznets (1966) emphasized that a major peculiarity of capitalism is the application of science to problems of industry. This is consistent with general historical evidence. Thermodynamics supplied the scientific basis of the First Industrial Revolution (Landes, 1969). The works of Faraday and Maxwell on electricity and magnetism, and Hertz's discovery of radio waves, laid the ground for the electricity-based industries and the Second Industrial Revolution (Landes, 1969 and 1991). In this century, Wallace Carothers and William Shockley clarified important theoretical aspects about polymer chemistry and solid-state physics which spurred the growth of the synthetic fiber and electronics industries (Nelson, 1962; Braun and MacDonald, 1978; Smith and Hounshell, 1985; Hounshell and Smith, 1988).

But, in spite of these (and other) examples, science, as a body of "generic" and systematized knowledge, has rarely offered more than a general and indirect framework for innovation. Most innovations and productivity improvements in industry have stemmed from highly empirical procedures based on trial-and-error experiments. Moreover, innovations have relied on fairly "old" science, and the application of fundamental knowledge to problems of industry has occurred with relatively long time-lags (Rosenberg, 1985; Mowery and Rosenberg, 1989).

The empirical character of industrial research reached its climax with the institutionalization of R&D in large corporations during the postwar years of this century. As Schumpeter taught us, big firms could afford the high

1

set-up costs of large in-house research laboratories. They were able to test several modifications of product and process design, and carry out a great many experiments in routine and efficient ways.

The hit-and-miss nature of business research arose from the fact that companies could make only limited use of knowledge to *scale up* and *transfer* experimental results. There was a great deal of uncertainty about whether experimental results obtained for "small" prototypes or in the laboratory would hold for larger objects or at larger scales. Similarly, it was difficult to relate the results of a given test to other experiments and phenomena (David, Mowery, and Steinmueller, 1992; Arora and Gambardella, 1993a and 1994b). Hence, industrial scientists and engineers had to carry out many careful and systematic experiments each time they wanted to evaluate the properties and performance of a certain device, and each time they wanted to scale up an object or process from smaller-scale tests.

In aeronautics, for example, engineers for many years have used wind tunnels to simulate the flight of airplanes. Wind tunnels have enabled them to observe the performance of various modifications of a specific design. Because of the lack of a general theory of aerodynamics, long and costly experiments have been the only reliable way to develop and improve aircraft (Mowery and Rosenberg, 1982; Rosenberg, 1982; Vincenti, 1990). Similarly, chemical engineers have lacked a comprehensive theory of the relationships between catalysts and chemical reactions. In the chemical and petrochemical industries, the development of new catalysts has rested on laborious experimentation with a large number of molecules to find the few that could satisfactorily raise the efficiency of a certain reaction (Cusumano, 1992). In manufacturing, production engineers have lacked a thorough understanding of how production processes work. Most process improvements have stemmed from intentional, methodical variations of process parameters (pressure, temperature, etc.) to seek more efficient combinations of the parameters themselves, or to determine how a process that works at a small scale could function at larger scales as well (Mansfield *et al.*, 1977; Steinmueller, 1987).

An important thrust of this book is to argue that this state of affairs is changing. This is largely related to spectacular developments in many scientific disciplines, along with impressive progress in computational capabilities and instrumentation. While many of these advances originated around the Second World War, or even earlier, they accelerated considerably during the 1970s and, especially, the 1980s. In addition, the lags between scientific discoveries and industrial applications appear to have shortened.[1]

Important advances in theoretical chemistry, life sciences, particle and solid-state physics, to name a few, are enhancing our understanding of phenomena that occur at the level of "nano"-structures, or in inappreciable fractions of time (e.g., chemical reactions that take less than one-millionth of a second). Scientists and engineers can then study the "causes" of many events that could not be comprehended without understanding the behavior of the infinitesimal components of objects and systems. They can examine the aggregation of micro-structures to form materials with desirable properties, or they can study optical and electrical conductivity to generate major advances in electronics, information systems, and in many other technologies. Relatedly, advances in computational capabilities, computer science, and corresponding theoretical tools (e.g., chaos theory, genetic algorithms, neuronal networks, and artificial intelligence) are making it possible to understand very complex problems, like the flight of airplanes, the dynamics of mechanical and electro-mechanical systems, or even biological systems.

These developments in theory owe a great deal to complementary advances in the technology of research. New and more powerful instruments have enabled scientists and engineers to "observe" infinitesimal objects. Using X-ray crystallography, nuclear magnetic resonance, the scanning electron microscope, laser, and other new magnetic- or optical-based techniques, they can "look" at the arrangement of atoms and molecules in exceptionally small clusters (De Solla Price, 1984; Lederman, 1984; Rosenberg, 1992). This is important, as the geometry of atoms and molecules governs the properties of matter (CSE&PP, 1983; Baker, 1986; PSI&TA, 1986). Also, using advanced instrumentation techniques – like ion implantation or, more recently, synchroton radiation – they can intervene at atomic and sub-atomic levels to obtain selected alterations of matter, and hence control specific properties of materials like strength or conductivity (PSI&TA, 1986; Steinmueller, 1987; David, Mowery, and Steinmueller, 1992).

The possibility of observing and intervening on microscopic objects has significantly helped the development of theories. Not only can theories be tested, but, more importantly, they can be perfected and corrected from observation. This is not a novel feature of either industrial or scientific research. However, because one can now observe things that could not previously be observed, it is possible to improve theories that could not be supported by visual inspection. Empirical observation also reveals new "facts," issues and problems that, in turn, stimulate the progress of theories.

In addition, advances in computer power (both hardware and software) are making it possible to perform efficient simulations of experiments, with implied time and cost advantages over physical experiments. One can model the behavior of infinitesimal objects or highly complex systems, and observe them on computers. Computer simulation is now widely used in aeronautics, automobiles, chemicals, and – as we shall see in this book – pharmaceuticals. For instance, it may take only a few minutes to test the resistance of a new material in car crashes. The computer simulates the crash, and measures the deformation of the body at different strengths of collision. It may even elaborate the data, and suggest directions for improvements (e.g., which parts of the body need to be reinforced). Moreover, like instrumentation, computer models hint at issues and problems that suggest directions for new developments of basic knowledge.

In short, theoretical advances, combined with powerful instrumentation and computational capabilities, are encouraging the diffusion of a new approach to industrial research. Instead of "blind" (physical) experiments to find what may work, industrial scientists and engineers increasingly test hypotheses using sophisticated instruments, and simulate processes on computers. This is not to imply that industry can now do without physical experiments. The latter are still necessary because the complexity of many phenomena cannot be fully comprehended using theory or simulation. Also, the new trend does not imply that innovation now follows a linear, "cascade" model, from basic research to development and commercialization. It still depends on complex feedbacks among different stages of the innovation cycle (Kline and Rosenberg, 1986). However, relevant information for innovation, from whichever sources it arises (research, production, markets), can be cast in more general frameworks. Furthermore, the blend of new powerful theories, instruments and simulation, helps in designing more efficient physical tests. Scientists and engineers can exclude from the physical experiments a number of objects and events that are inconsistent with *a priori* hypotheses (Arora and Gambardella, 1994b).

The literature on science as a source of economic value

Private appropriability of scientific research

The increasing use of fundamental knowledge and of the tools of experimental science in industrial research poses important economic questions. Is the trend just described a widespread one in industry, or is it confined to very few firms at the frontier of science and technology? What implications are there for the organization of company R&D? And for the size of the innovating firms? How is it going to affect the relationships between companies and external parties (research institutions, other companies, etc.)? What is the role of public knowledge and scientific institutions? What implications are there for competition and market structure?

Before addressing these issues in the context of the pharmaceutical industry, it may be useful to review the economic literature on the relationships between science and innovation. This will help in focusing our discussion, and in structuring our questions more carefully.

The seminal contributions of Nelson (1959) and Arrow (1962) are a natural starting point. Their well-known conclusion is that profit-seeking agents invest less than optimally in scientific research. Basic research produces information. But information is a peculiar commodity in that it can be re-produced at zero cost. Any buyer of the information, or anyone who happens to have it, can become a producer of it. This destroys the monopoly of the rent-seeking agent who invested in producing the information. Patents and intellectual property rights restore, in part, the incentives to perform fundamental research. However, the low appropriability of basic science and technology explains why the bulk of this activity is carried out by institutions not motivated by economic profits (universities, government research centers, etc.), and why it has to be sustained by public funds (Mowery, 1983).

The low appropriability of science has been criticized on various grounds. Many authors have argued that scientific research, and particularly the ability to utilize knowledge for industrial purposes, depend on tacit skills, learning, and organizational routines.[2] These are firm-specific factors that cannot be easily transferred between companies. Firms with better research skills and assets, and possibly with better downstream resources for commercialization, can then secure more effectively the benefits of their investment in basic science and technology, and they have greater incentives to perform fundamental research.

The growing application of scientific and technological principles to industry further weakens the low appropriability argument. As basic knowledge exhibits more direct effects on innovation, and shorter application lags, companies can embody more thoroughly and more rapidly their research outcomes in new products and processes. To the extent that they can appropriate innovations through patents, first-mover advantages or downstream assets, they can also shelter more productively their investments in basic science and technology.

But the incentives of private firms to invest in fundamental research do not depend only on the possibility of appropriating and utilizing one's own research outcomes. Another important reason is that in-house scientific and technological capabilities are critical for monitoring and utilizing external knowledge. Rosenberg (1990) argued that, although a public good, science is by no means a *free* good. (See also Pavitt, 1991.) The ability of firms to exploit public science will be greater if they perform similar research themselves. Investments in research are thus necessary to comprehend and evaluate external information. (See also Arora and Gambardella, 1994a.)

Cohen and Levinthal (1989) argued that R&D has two "faces." Apart from generating innovations, it helps in absorbing knowledge generated by others. If the second face of R&D is important, variables that affect the ease with which firms learn from the pool of outside knowledge ought to influence their technological opportunities and appropriability conditions. In turn, this would influence their incentives to invest in R&D.

Cohen and Levinthal developed a model of the accumulation of knowledge capital. They assumed that the knowledge capital of firms depends on the pool of outside knowledge, and on technological opportunity and appropriability factors. They used data from the Federal Trade Commission's Line of Business Program on business-unit R&D expenditures. They found that the influence of technological opportunity factors and appropriability conditions on R&D spending is affected by variables that influence the ease of learning. This suggests that the second face of R&D is important in encouraging firms to invest in research.

Although they used data on total R&D expenditures, Cohen and Levinthal speculated about the incentives of firms to perform basic research.[3] Their analysis leads to predictions about the incentives for firms to conduct scientific research. Factors affecting the firms' opportunities of learning ought to influence investments in in-house basic research. In this respect, the acceleration of scientific developments, and the more rapid application of science to industry, ought to encourage private outlays in science as a means of absorbing the rising external opportunities.

The educational and research functions of universities

As industrial research depends more substantially on formalized knowledge, the educational function of universities will become more important. Gibbons and Johnston (1974) used a sample of 30 innovations and 887 "units" of information relevant to generating the innovations. They classified the units of information according to their source (trade literature, technical literature, scientific literature, personal contacts with scientists, customers, suppliers, etc.) and content (theories, design-based information, information about materials, etc.). They found that people with university education adopt a more general approach, solve more general problems, and rely on a wider pool of information drawn largely from sources external to their company. People without university education solve more specific problems, and rely primarily on knowledge and experience gained within their company. The need to tackle problems from a more universal perspective, and to take advantage of external information implies, therefore, that companies will hire more people with a solid academic background.

Using data from a questionnaire survey with 650 R&D managers in various industries, Nelson (1986, 1988, and 1994) studied whether the business community places greater value on the research or the educational function of universities (see also Levin *et al.*, 1987). The R&D managers were asked to rank the relevance of various fields of basic and applied science to technical change in their line of business. They were also asked to rank the relevance of university research in those fields. Almost every field of science received a high score. In contrast, the scores on university research in each field were significantly smaller. Nelson interpreted this result as evidence that, whilst university training is important, industry is less keen on academic research. Computers, drugs, and new materials were notable exceptions in that R&D managers in these industries gave high scores to university research as well.

A recent report which summarized interviews with seventeen senior US company officials in a number of industries reinforces Nelson's conjecture (GUIRR, 1991). The officials emphasized the importance of university training. They also stated that universities provide in-depth understanding of new scientific and technological ideas. However, they remarked that, apart from a few cases, such as biotechnology, academic research provides little contribution to the vast and important downstream development activities that lead to commercially useful innovations.

This is not contradictory to the argument that science is playing a more important role for innovation. The point is not whether science, and particularly academic research, generates straight commercial applications, but whether it produces new technological opportunities. Nelson (1986) regressed industry R&D intensity against the contribution of university research to innovation and other variables. He measured the contribution of university research by the score given by the R&D managers in his sample to the importance of university research. He found that this measure is positively correlated with R&D intensity. However, when regressing measures of technical progress against R&D intensity and the university research score (and other variables), R&D showed a positive and significant effect, whilst university research did not. This suggests that university research enhances technological opportunities and the productivity of private R&D, which in turn induces greater R&D spending in industry.

Jaffe (1989) and Mansfield (1991) also examined the importance of university research for innovation and industry R&D. Using US data, Jaffe found that university research has a positive and significant effect on corporate patents and industry R&D. The latter result reinforces Nelson's conjecture that university research influences innovation through industry R&D. Jaffe also found that geographical proximity increases the strength of the effect of university research on corporate patents. The contribution of university research is greater if industry and university scientists can interact more easily.[4]

Using a sample of innovations from seventy-six large US firms in seven industries (information processing, electrical, chemicals, instruments, drugs, metals and oil), Mansfield found that, in the period 1975–85, about 19 percent of the new products and 15 percent of the new processes could not have been developed without substantial aid from recent academic research. He also found that the average time-lag between academic discoveries and industrial applications was seven years. Finally, although based on conservative assumptions, Mansfield estimated a high social rate of return of academic research (28 percent). Both Mansfield and Jaffe found that the effects of academic research are greater in the drug industry than in the mechanical and electrical industries.

The scientific and technological communities

Increasing scientific intensity of technical progress calls for a more rigorous economic investigation of the nature and behavior of academic institutions. In his early study of the transistor, Nelson (1962) had already pointed out that "[t]he incentives of the scientists are much more complex than the incentives of the entrepreneur of economic theory . . . The furthering of a reputation . . . and the satisfaction of intellectual curiosity are certainly as important . . . dimensions of the research worker's goal as are financial advance and status within an organization" (Nelson, 1962, p. 573; see also Nelson, 1982). In later works, Nelson (1988 and 1990) further discussed the importance of universities and research institutions in the diffusion of knowledge, and their contribution to the rising "socialization" of knowledge and research in modern capitalism.

Nelson and Rosenberg (1993) studied the origins and development of American universities. They showed that, initially, American universities performed very applied research tasks. They were suppliers of research services to local industry (e.g., chemical tests and the development of special techniques). On some occasions, they developed entirely new engineering disciplines to serve special industry needs (e.g., chemical engineering at MIT between the two wars – see also Landau, 1990). Only after World War II, with the growth of Federal funding to universities, did American academia move significantly into basic research. Nelson and Rosenberg's work is important in that it reminds us that the contribution of many universities to technical progress does not take the form of fundamental discoveries, but of more applied research tasks and experiments.

Following previous works in the sociology of science, Dasgupta and David (1987 and 1994) offered a comprehensive economic investigation of the different social behavior and institutional construct of the scientific community compared with those of rent-seeking "technologists."[5] Well before the beginnings of capitalism, scientists needed "patrons" who could support their activities. But in order to gain visibility so as to be employed in the courts of kings and princes, they had to publicize their abilities (see also David, 1991). This prompted the social organization of science that we observe today, which encourages disclosure of findings. Today's scientists diffuse their results to raise their public recognition and peer-group esteem. Apart from personal satisfaction, reputation increases their ability to raise funds for future research (both from government and industry), which in turn enhances their research skills (and hence human capital), as well as their salaries and prestige. Public reputation also enables them to obtain personal consultancies from companies, with implied pecuniary rewards.

In contrast, the technological community seeks to appropriate the rents that can be derived from research. Disclosure would undermine their opportunities to gain such rents. Firms then encourage secrecy and appropriation of findings through patents and other means. Dasgupta and David (1994) also investigated several economic aspects of scientific institutions, such as the mechanisms for allocation of funds, co-operation and competition among scientists, the interactions between scientific institutions and companies, and the effects of industry funding on academic research.

The distinction between scientists and technologists raises some questions. For one, can we really associate the technological community with firms and the scientific community with universities and other non-profit research institutions? Companies like IBM, General Electric, and Du Pont maintain some in-house research facilities that are organized in ways that are similar to academic departments. They employ scientists who publish, participate in conferences, and behave almost like their colleagues in universities. (Some of them even win Nobel prizes!) Many small innovative firms in high-tech sectors (e.g., electronics, software, and biotechnology) thrive largely because of their informal research organizations and academic linkages. At the same time, as suggested earlier, many universities perform very applied research. They normally produce research services and consultancy to local industry rather than purely academic publications. They sometimes restrain diffusion to preserve confidentiality for their clients. A good fraction of their activities feed the domain of research controlled by agents who seek appropriation of rents and secrecy rather than public knowledge.

Dasgupta and David's distinction, however, provides a useful framework for our discussion. The issue is precisely whether the growing applicability of science to industry, and the corresponding greater interdependence of firms and the scientific community, could affect the ways in which the two institutions have conducted their research for many years. Will the need for greater scientific creativity and more intense linkages with external science lead to greater openness of company research? As public research budgets shrink, and universities seek more funds from industry, will industry push for greater secrecy in academic research, with implied restrictions on the socially desirable circulation of knowledge? Will companies force academia to shift from "generic" research towards more narrow, business-oriented goals?

The possibility of greater restrictions on academic research is especially intriguing. Dasgupta and David discussed this issue in a historical perspective. Open science predated capitalism. It was made possible by the social organization of science based on the patronage of kings and princes. This furthered the evolution of modern industry by ensuring widespread diffusion of knowledge. In our own day, governments are the patrons of science. They have chosen to support science through public funds in recognition of the fact that the long-run social benefits of open science could conflict with the short-run goals of private companies. But if public support to science diminishes, firms may become the new patrons of science. Because of their short-run, private objectives, they may impose restrictions on diffusion, thereby undermining the very same factor that has encouraged their long-run growth.

The distinction between scientists and technologists hints at another important difference between research in academic institutions and firms. (See also Arora and Gambardella, 1993b and 1994b.) Scientific prestige and academic careers typically depend on the ability of researchers to identify the few "essential" elements of a phenomenon. In other words, academia tends to prize the ability of individuals or research groups to characterize phenomena in general forms, and to abstract from the complexity of particular events, objects, or systems. Even when they perform very applied research tasks, researchers in non-profit institutions have fewer incentives to perfect the use of their research outcomes, as the latter are less likely to be employed for practical purposes without further developments and modifications, especially on a large scale. In short, the prestige and careers of academic scientists do not depend on whether and how their results work in reality.

In contrast, in order to gain rents from their research, industrial scientists and engineers have to come up with products and processes that work satisfactorily (and not necessarily optimally) in practice, and that satisfy user needs. They cannot be content with understanding problems in general and abstract forms. They have to deal with the complexity and idiosyncratic features of the particular applications of knowledge (i.e., of particular phenomena, and of related objects and systems), which are typically ignored by abstract representations. And this implies greater reliance on trial and error and experimentation. (See also Rosenbrock, 1988.)

Science as a guide to search

A number of studies have looked at the economic returns of scientific research. Griliches' work on hybrid corn pioneered this field (Griliches, 1957, 1958, and 1960). Research on how a cross between genetically different plants produces a plant with higher yield dates back to Mendel and Darwin. Its scientific development took place during the first thirty years of this century. Griliches found high public and private returns to R&D expenditures on hybrid corn in the USA during the period 1930–50.

Following Griliches, various studies estimated the impact of basic research expenditure in firms on innovation and productivity (Mansfield, 1980 and 1981; Link, 1981, 1982, and 1985; Griliches, 1986). Using industry- and firm-level data, they found a positive and statistically significant effect of basic research on productivity growth. While this is an important result, as it establishes the existence of a positive correlation between scientific research and performance, the purely empirical nature of these works has offered little clue about the factors that link scientific research to innovation and productivity.

Some authors have suggested that the contribution of scientific research to innovation can be framed in the context of search theory. Search models originated from Stigler's (1961) article about the economics of information. Nelson (1961), Evenson and Kislev (1975 and 1976), David and Stiglitz (1979), Dasgupta and Stiglitz (1980), Nelson (1982), and Nelson and Winter (1982) laid down the framework for applying search models to problems of innovation. Basic research produces information that guides applied R&D towards trajectories that are more likely to generate successful outcomes. It *focuses* the search for innovation in the downstream stages, thereby raising the productivity of applied research and development. Applied research successes are like draws of balls of a given color from urns that contain balls of different colors. Basic knowledge supplies information about the urns that are more likely to contain a larger proportion of balls of the desired color. Thus it helps the researchers to make more informed choices about the urns from which they want to draw their samples (David, Mowery, and Steinmueller, 1992).

The formal specification of these models posits that innovation takes place in two stages. At the first stage, researchers study a number of techniques (urns). They then determine the yields of the techniques that were examined. At the second stage, they employ the technique with the highest yield to develop the innovation.

Assume that $(X_1, X_2, \ldots, X_N)$ is the vector of yields ("values") of the N techniques that have been examined. $F(X)$ is the distribution function of the X's, which are independent and identically distributed (i.i.d.), and are defined on a closed interval; C is the (constant) marginal cost of experimenting with a new technique. The problem boils down to determining the optimal N; this is the N that maximizes the expression E $\max(X_1, X_2, \ldots, X_N) - CN$, where E is the expectation operator. The distribution function of $Y(N) \equiv \max (X_1, X_2, \ldots, X_N)$ can be obtained from the distribution functions $F(X)$ of the X's. One can then compute the expected value of $Y(N)$. Under fairly general assumptions about $F(X)$, E $Y(N)$ increases with N at a diminishing rate. Hence, using a continuous approximation, the expression $d(\text{E } Y)/\delta N = C$ determines the optimal N. The latter is a function of the marginal cost parameter C, and the parameters of $F(X)$.

Basic knowledge implies that innovators conduct their search within a set of more productive techniques. Suppose that $F(X, \Theta)$ is a family of distributions such that $F(X, \Theta)$ decreases with Θ for all X's different from the boundaries of its support. Greater Θ implies a greater probability of higher yields (first-order stochastic dominance), i.e., researchers search for the best "urn" within a "better" set of techniques. This implies a higher expected value for the best technique. Nelson (1982) showed that if dominance is additive, viz. $G(X + \Theta) = F(X)$, with $\Theta > 0$, the optimal N under $F(\cdot)$ and $G(\cdot)$ does not change. If it is multiplicative, viz. $G(X \cdot \Theta) = F(X)$, with $\Theta > 1$, the optimal N increases.

Along these lines, Arora and Gambardella (1994a) developed a model that distinguishes between different components of the knowledge-base of firms. The model distinguishes between *ability to utilize* and *ability to evaluate* scientific and technological information. Firms receive a signal y correlated with the true economic pay-off X of an innovation project. Given the signal, firms decide whether to perform applied research and development. The expected profit-maximization problem boils down to the choice of a threshold value y^* for the signal y. The firm will carry out applied research and development at cost K if and only if $y > y^*$. Given the prior distribution of y, a higher threshold implies that, *ex ante*, firms are less likely to perform a project with signal y.

It was assumed that the conditional distribution of X on y depended on two parameters, γ and θ. The former controls for the degree of first-order stochastic dominance. Given y, as γ increases, higher values of X occur with greater probability. Firms are more likely to extract higher value from a given technology y, which would typically stem from better experimentation and development capabilities – "ability to utilize." The parameter θ controls for second-order stochastic dominance (in the sense of Rothschild and Stiglitz, 1970). With greater θ, firms predict X given y with lower error. They have greater "ability to evaluate" innovation projects before conducting applied research and development, i.e., they have greater ability to predict the "true" value of the innovation project. It would be natural to think that the latter ability depends on the stock of scientific knowledge available to the firm: science enables researchers to predict the outcome of experiments with greater precision.

The model shows that the threshold y^* is non-increasing in γ. Other things being equal, greater ability to utilize implies that firms will carry out projects at lower signal levels as well. The intuition is that with better experimentation and development capabilities, a given firm can derive an acceptable pay-off even from projects with relatively "bad" priors. *Ceteris paribus*, with greater θ, y^* is non-decreasing. Firms focus on projects with better signals. The intuition is that their predictive capability makes them more certain that good signals are associated with good pay-offs. Hence, they focus on the latter. Put differently, they can discard, with greater confidence, projects that appear to be less appealing.[6]

The pharmaceutical industry

The drug sector is a distinctive example of the changes in industrial research discussed in the first section of this chapter. For many years industrial discoveries of new drugs have rested on empirical tests of a great many molecules in the laboratory to assess their chemical and biological activity. The approach was termed "random screening" or "molecular roulette" to emphasize that the entities to be tested were chosen on the basis of scanty *a priori* knowledge about their action (Schwartzman, 1976).

Many economic studies and technical reports have discussed the changes that molecular biology and genetic engineering are exerting on pharmaceutical research.[7] They have highlighted the expansion of technological opportunities, and the opening of largely unexplored areas of research. However, most of these studies have not really deepened the mechanisms through which these advances translate into greater research productivity.

This book will argue that molecular biology and genetic engineering, together with important developments in computerized drug design and instrumentation, are offering the opportunity to extend the applicability of a "scientific" method of drug research. Industry scientists can increasingly make use of fundamental knowledge about human metabolism and the action of drugs, and they can employ advanced experimentation technologies. This enables them to select more carefully and more rationally the molecules to be tested in applied laboratory research. It is the guide-to-search nature of science that matters here, along with the ability to perform the search more efficiently using new experimentation technologies.

The book then looks at the implications of such changes for competition, strategic behavior, and market structure. The focus on upstream research is justified by the fact that innovation in the drug sector presents some important peculiarities. The generation of new drugs depends in large measure on activities that occur at the outset of the R&D process. Early research stages play a more meaningful role than in other industries, and they are the most creative steps of the drug innovation cycle.

This is not to argue that other factors are unimportant. After discovery, firms perform long clinical trials to assess the safety and efficacy of new compounds before commercialization. Clinical trials command significant outlays of resources. From an economic point of view, they are a formidable barrier to entry into the research-intensive ethical drug business. But clinical trials are somewhat routine activities. They produce "yes-or-no" information about the performance of new products. In order to make effective use of information from clinical trials to improve products, companies would need to go back to basic analyses of molecular structures and laboratory tests. This implies that feedback cycles are longer and more costly than in other industries, which reduces the economic advantages of exploiting information from downstream development.[8]

Moreover, the tempo and organization of clinical trials are governed by fairly standardized regulatory procedures, which leaves little room for action on the part of companies. A good organization of clinical trials certainly influences the ability of firms to bring new products into the market. But they tend to determine second-order differences in the competitiveness of innovative drug firms, especially if compared with differing abilities in earlier research stages.

The length of feedback cycles also explains why learning by using is less effective than in other industries. In fact, market diffusion of new drugs generates important information. Undesired effects that occur with tiny probabilities, and that are insignificant at the scale of clinical trials, may become sizeable when the drug is administered to a much larger number of patients in the market. However, like clinical trials, the market supplies dichotomous information about product performance. Unlike, say, an electronic device, drugs cannot be rapidly improved better to suit user needs. Companies would need to go back to research and long regulatory tests. Sometimes users provide information about new and different applications of drugs. This is an increasingly important phenomenon. However, as we shall see in later chapters, the ability of firms to differentiate product applications, or to utilize information about side-effects or new uses of drugs from clinical trials, also depends to an important extent on their scientific expertise, and their knowledge about the basic structure of drugs and their biochemical action.

Finally, in this industry, production is not a critical competitive factor. New compounds do not require extensive process modification. They are manufactured using fairly established technologies (US DoC, 1984; ADL, 1988). Moreover, the market of individual drugs, including important ones, is not very large. Unlike bulk chemical products, the size of the market does not justify conspicuous investments in chemical engineering to build big plants and attain large economies of scale. Also, new drugs that improve traditional remedies for a certain disease exhibit fairly inelastic demands. They are sold under patent, and hence under monopolistic conditions. This implies that, with constant returns to scale in production, companies have fewer incentives to pay the fixed cost to achieve a given reduction in manufacturing costs, as this would generate only modest increases in profits.[9]

Another important reason that justifies emphasis on upstream research is that this study focuses on a group of firms with very similar characteristics, viz. the large US drug manufacturers. They all have financial capabilities to conduct extensive clinical trials, and to meet stringent regulatory requirements. They also have large distribution assets. They are similar in many respects, but not in the extent to which, in the 1980s, they focused their strategies on the accumulation of internal scientific capabilities, and on investments in scientific research. They form a sort of natural experiment to assess the competitive potential of in-house scientific research in industry, as they allow one to abstract, in part, from other assets that are normally important for innovation-based competition.

The book will address a number of questions suggested by the economic literature on science and innovation. It has already been stressed that research in the drug industry epitomizes the guide-to-search nature of science. With increasing scientific intensity of pharmaceutical research, we can also look more deeply into the incentives for rent-seeking agents to conduct research of a more fundamental character. Cohen and Levinthal (1989) and Rosenberg (1990) emphasized the use of basic research to monitor external science. Yet, one has still to produce more compelling evidence. In addition, one has to dig into the mechanisms by which in-house scientific capabilities raise the opportunities of absorbing public knowledge.

Related to this is another point. If internal knowledge favors better exploitation of external findings, then, with increasing external scientific opportunities, the positions of leadership in the market are likely to strengthen. Firms with better in-house research can utilize outside knowledge more effectively to develop innovations. Better innovative performance will raise profits. Innovators would then enjoy a better financial position to carry out further investments in research, which would augment their opportunities of exploiting public science. Contrary to what one would expect, advances and diffusion of public knowledge may magnify, rather than diminish, differences in the ability of firms to innovate.

The book will also address questions about the changes in the way companies and scientific institutions conduct their research. Among other things, it will discuss whether the need for greater scientific creativity, and the linkages with the scientific network, are altering the attitude of drug firms towards secrecy. It will also discuss whether companies tend to restrict diffusion of academic research.

It has already been remarked that, for a number of reasons, research and innovation in the pharmaceutical industry exhibit important peculiarities compared with other high-tech sectors. One must thus be very careful in generalizing and extending the conclusions of this book to other industries. In no other sector are the changing nature of industrial research, the adoption of a "scientific" approach, and the related economic implications, probably as clear and apparent as in the drug sector. Nonetheless, the question which is intentionally left unanswered here is whether the pharmaceutical industry is so unique that no reasonable generalization is possible, or whether it points to some important transformation in industrial technical progress.

Plan of the book

The following chapter describes the changing nature of drug research and innovation. It shows how advances in genetic engineering, molecular biology, computers, and instrumentation are producing a wealth of new information which "guides" applied research towards families of molecules that are more likely to accomplish a certain therapeutic action.

Chapter 3 discusses three implications of this trend. First, it examines some implications for the organization of research in pharmaceutical companies. It argues that the increasing need for scientific creativity and for absorption of public knowledge is encouraging greater openness of company research. Second, it discusses implications for the relationships between drug companies and universities. Among other things, it looks at whether more intense relationships between drug makers and universities imply greater restrictions on the diffusion of academic research. Third, it examines the growing division of labor between large drug firms and small or medium-sized research-intensive biotechnology companies. It argues that, with greater applicability of science in pharmaceutical research, relevant information for innovation can be cast in fairly general frameworks, which reduces the costs of transferring it across organizations. With suitable contracts and intellectual property rights, this encourages specialization and division of labor among agents with different resources and comparative advantages in the various stages of innovation.

Chapter 4 develops case studies of eight large US drug manufacturers. The case studies show that, in spite of the public nature of science, firms with better in-house scientific expertise, and that organized their research in more open and "liberal" ways, obtained greater benefits from utilization of external knowledge, and they could translate it more effectively into competitive advantages.

Chapters 5, 6, and 7 present three empirical studies of the economics of pharmaceutical research and innovation. Chapter 5 develops a model of drug discovery. The model is estimated using data for the fourteen largest US pharmaceutical companies between 1968 and 1991. Among other things, the empirical results show that the productivity of laboratory research in pharmaceutical companies increased considerably in the 1980s. This suggests that, apart from advances in the technology of experimentation, greater use of scientific knowledge has made the search for candidate drugs more effective.

While chapter 5 looks at discovery, chapter 6 focuses on drug development and commercialization. It presents a model of innovation and competition in the industry. The model is estimated using data for the same fourteen US drug companies during the period 1968–91. The empirical results highlight a number of features about innovation, competition, and profitability in the US drug sector. A notable result is that, other things being equal, in the 1980s the productivity of the R&D expenditures of the largest drug companies increased relative to previous decades.

Chapter 7 examines the propensity of drug and chemical manufacturers to develop external linkages with other parties in biotechnology. Using data on eighty-one large US, European and Japanese drug and chemical corporations, it estimates the demand for different types of co-operative linkages between these firms and other parties (mainly universities and small–medium biotech companies). The empirical results show that, from the point of view of large firms, these different linkages represent complementary strategies. The empirical results also show that firms with greater in-house capabilities in biotechnology display greater propensity to enter into external alliances.

Chapter 8 concludes the book, and speculates on policy implications and future trends in the pharmaceutical industry.

2 Science and innovation in pharmaceutical research

Introduction: the drug innovation cycle

Drug innovation is composed of fairly standardized steps, which are designed in the main by regulatory authorities. At each step compounds are tested for particular properties or characteristics. Only a fraction of the compounds that enter a certain stage are considered viable, and they are moved to the next stage. Figure 2.1 synthesizes the typical sequence in the drug innovation process.

New drugs stem either from organic chemical synthesis or from the separation of compounds produced by natural micro-organisms (Wardell, 1979; ADL, 1988; FDA, 1988). In recent years, biotechnology drugs have stemmed from the fermentation of genetically engineered micro-organisms or cell fusion (monoclonal antibodies) (OTA, 1984). There is probably no other industry wherein the impact of scientific research, whether basic research or experimental science, is as direct as in the drug sector.[1] Scientific knowledge in organic chemistry, microbiology, biochemistry, physiology, pharmacology, and, more recently, molecular biology and genetic engineering, has provided the framework for drug discovery from the early decades of this century.

Pre-clinical research consists of laboratory screening of molecules (bioassays and animal tests) to evaluate their therapeutic potential and toxicity. Scientists test a great many compounds before finding some that look promising for clinical trials:

Sometimes, scientists are lucky and find the right compound quickly. More often ... hundreds or even thousands must be tested. In a series of test tube experiments ... compounds are added one at a time to enzymes, cell cultures or cellular substances grown in a laboratory. The goal is to find which show some chemical effect. Some may not work well, but may hint at ways of changing the compound's chemical structure to improve its performance. The latter process alone may require testing dozens or hundreds of compounds. (FDA, 1988, p. 9.)

18

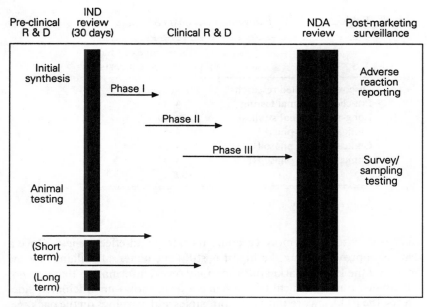

Fig. 2.1. Stages in the development of new drugs. The FDA stages are shown in black. Average time from initial synthesis to NDA approval is approximately 100 months. (*Source:* FDA, 1988.)

Before clinical trials, in the USA firms have to apply to the Food and Drug Administration (FDA) for an Investigational New Drug Exemption (IND). The FDA can reject IND applications if there is insufficient evidence that the new compounds can be safely tested in human beings.

Clinical trials comprise three stages. Going from stage I to stage III, a new compound is administered to an increasing number of patients. While stage I focuses on the toxicity of the product, stages II and III focus on its effectiveness. Typically, stage II and especially stage III involve a large number of patients, and they take place over a long period. This is to prepare an accurate profile of the drug, define its dosage, and evaluate side-effects that occur with small probabilities or that reveal themselves only after several months.

In the USA, once a new compound has passed the clinical tests, companies have to present a formal request to the FDA to market the drug – the New Drug Application (NDA). The FDA can accept or reject the application or, alternatively, require that the new medicine undergo further

Table 2.1. *US drug development costs by stage*

	Percentage of total development costs
Discovery/applied research	8–24
Pre-clinical animal testing	4–5
Long-term animal studies	8–10
Clinical testing phase I	4–5
Clinical testing phase II	24–33
Clinical testing phase III	33–42
	100

Source: US DoC (1984).

clinical tests to assess more carefully its safety and effectiveness. Once a drug is approved for marketing, it is still kept under surveillance by the firms and the FDA. Market diffusion may reveal information that was not anticipated during clinical trials. When a drug shows unanticipated side-effects, the FDA may require that companies add warnings on the package. If side-effects or toxicity are severe, the FDA can even withdraw the product from the market.

Drug innovation is a long, costly, and risky process. The development of new drugs, from applied research to commercialization, takes on average eight to nine years (Figure 2.1). If one includes the time spent on fundamental investigation of the pathology and the properties of the compounds, it may well rise to fifteen to twenty years. Moreover, development times can vary considerably across drugs.

Drug development is very costly. Development costs grew considerably over the seventies and eighties. In the USA, during the early 1970s, the cost of developing one new drug (including the costs of unsuccessful projects) was estimated to be 54 million dollars (Hansen, 1979). Around the early 1980s, it was estimated to be between 70 and 90 million dollars (US DoC, 1984). In 1986, it rose to about 125 million dollars (Wiggins, 1987), and in 1990 to about 231 million dollars (Di Masi, 1991).[2] Table 2.1 reports the breakdown of pharmaceutical development costs, and shows that the later stages of clinical trials represent by far the largest fraction of drug R&D.

Finally, drug development is very risky.[3] Recent studies indicate that only 1 out of 5,000 compounds synthesized during applied research eventually reaches the market (Halliday, Walker, and Lumley, 1992). Other estimates indicate that of 100 drugs for which INDs are submitted, about 70 complete clinical testing phase I, 33 complete phase II, and 25–30 clear phase III (FDA, 1988). Halliday, Walker, and Lumley (1992) also found that two-thirds of the drugs that enter phase III are marketed. This suggests that attrition rates are especially severe in earlier research stages. Compounds that overcome clinical trials phase II have a relatively good chance of becoming new drugs. However, as phase III is the more costly R&D stage, one failure out of three products may still imply a considerable loss of resources.

Drug discovery in industry: from chemical screening to discovery by design

Chemical screening and the origins of drug discovery in industry

In one of the most comprehensive economic studies of pharmaceutical innovation in the postwar period, Schwartzman (1976) argued that pharmaceutical research is largely an experimental process. Using several examples of drug innovations, he showed that, since the 1930s, large firms have specialized in extensive chemical modification of basic compounds, and they are responsible for the introduction of most new drugs in this century.[4] Large firms possessed the resources to perform systematic laboratory search for new molecules, conduct clinical trials, and market new drugs on a wide scale. Moreover, the expected rents in the search for new compounds were sufficiently high to justify considerable investments in this activity.

The formation of large research-based pharmaceutical companies, and their motivation to perform systematic screening of molecules were spurred by the growth of information about the properties of various classes of molecules during the early twentieth century. This was brought about by a complex blend of scientific knowledge and experimental observation. At the turn of the century, the German bacteriologist Paul Ehrlich postulated that specific sites on the surface of bacteria cells could form bonds with chemical agents (Ehrlich's affinity theory). He then observed that synthetic dyes could kill or inhibit pathogenic protozoa without affecting mammalian cells. This led, in 1910, to the discovery of Salvarsan, an arsenic compound for treating syphilis, and one of the first man-made drugs (Schwartzman, 1976; Ganellin, 1989). Ehrlich synthesized 606 compounds before finding Salvarsan. The discovery of Salvarsan, and Ehrlich's affinity theory, encouraged large chemical companies to carry out systematic examination of hundreds of synthetic chemicals to seek drugs against venereal diseases.

Not surprisingly, large-scale manipulation of molecules originated in Germany, which already featured an established chemical industry, particularly in the dyestuff sector, and already had some large chemical companies. Vast screening of the sulfonamide derivatives of the red azo dye led Gerhard Domagk at IG Farbenindustrie to discover, in 1931, that sulfamidochrysoidine had a strong antibacterial action in mice. Prontosil, the first really effective drug against bacterial infections, was marketed in 1935. Following Domagk's discovery, Daniel Bovet and other researchers at the Institut Pasteur in France clarified, in 1932, that the active site of the drug was not the azo dye, but sulfanilamide, a fragment metabolite of the sulfamidochrysoidine molecule. Many firms, in various countries, began screening several modifications of sulfanilamide. This encouraged development of a host of new products including hypotensives, anticonvulsants, diuretics, and antidiabetics (Schwartzman, 1976; Achilladelis, 1991).

Many sulfa anti-infectives have now been replaced by antibiotics. However, Prontosil, sulfanilamide and their immediate descendant, sulfa-pyridine (commonly known as MB 693, and marketed in 1938), are the products that gave rise to the modern chemical-based drug industry. Since then, large-scale modification of basic chemicals, within the laboratories of large research-based corporations, has become the predominant mode of innovation in this sector.

Antihistamines, penicillins, alpha and beta blockers, and many other drugs, present remarkably similar stories.[5] In all such cases, scientific knowledge, experimental observations, and the systematization of these observations supplied information to assess the chemical and therapeutic properties of certain molecules. This prompted large firms to engage in extensive applied research screening to develop new drugs via manipulation of the basic compounds.

The development of beta blockers is a notable example of how complex interactions between scientific knowledge and experimental observation produced information that focused laboratory screening on specific classes of molecules. In 1895, two scientists observed that a body hormone, adrenaline, injected into cats increased their blood pressure. In 1905 an English pharmacologist, Henry Dale, systematized that observation, and showed that adrenaline had different effects on different tissues. In 1947, Raymond Ahlquist clarified the action of adrenaline on different tissues, and postulated two types of adrenergic receptors: alpha and beta. This led to the search for specific compounds via modifications of the basic adrenaline molecule. The search was restricted to compounds that either stimulated or inhibited the alpha and beta receptors. Scientists developed an array of alpha and beta stimulants against asthma, and for controlling blood pressure. In the 1960s, they introduced several new drugs that blocked either the alpha or beta action of adrenaline (alpha and beta blockers) (Wardell, 1979).

The rise of discovery by design

In the 1950s and 1960s, knowledge about the properties of the compounds that could be used to synthesize new drugs was still blurred. This implied limited ability to select the substances to be tested in laboratories. More importantly, using customary techniques of organic chemistry, scientists could synthesize an immense array of chemical entities at low cost. They could generate a great many new molecules whose chemical properties, let alone linkages with physiological and pathological conditions, were unknown. As a result, not only was vast screening of chemicals the predominant approach to drug discovery in industry, but on many occasions company scientists did not even attempt to conceptualize *a priori* the activity of their compounds.

It is important to recognize that this was a deliberate economic decision of firms. As also discussed in Arora and Gambardella (1993b and 1994b), in order to invest in fundamental knowledge, firms need to have some expectation that they can comprehend problems in generalized forms. But when problems are very complex, the costs of comprehending them in general forms can be enormous. Trial and error is then economically more advantageous, even though it yields only localized knowledge. In the postwar years, with little knowledge, and particularly with little public knowledge, about human metabolism and the action of drugs, the "private" costs of understanding problems in general terms were considerable, especially if compared with the relatively low costs of producing a great many compounds for hit-and-miss experiments. Companies then approached drug research through "blind" chemical screenings, and made little effort to understand the basic properties of their molecules.

The 1960s and 1970s witnessed the growth of basic knowledge about the properties of many compounds, and about physiological and pathological conditions. This raised the economic pay-off of investments in the fundamental understanding of drugs, and gradually enhanced the applicability of a rational method of drug research. Companies could build on a more solid basis of public knowledge. They had better prospects of being able to understand organic disorders and the action of drugs at reasonable costs and in reasonable time. They then began approaching problems by looking at the general properties of molecules, and the pathology they wanted to cure.

Since then, "discovery by design" has gradually gained momentum. With discovery by design, scientists use knowledge about the causes of human disorders, the properties of drug compounds, and their action in the human organism, to conceptualize the structure of an "ideal" molecule that

Table 2.2. *Top ten pharmaceutical products in 1991*

Rank	Drug	Indication	Company	Sales ($m)	Growth (percent)
1	Zantac	Ulcer	Glaxo	3,023	10.5
2	Vasotec	Hypertension/CHF	Merck	1,745	14.1
3	Capoten	Hypertension/CHF	BMS	1,580	7.5
4	Voltaren	Arthritis	C-Geigy	1,185	5.1
5	Tenormin	Hypertension	ICI	1,180	1.7
6	Adalat	Angina/hypertension	Bayer	1,120	12.6
7	Tagamet	Ulcer	SB	1,097	(2.2)
8	Mevacor	Hyperlipidemia	Merck	1,090	43.4
9	Naprosyn	Arthritis	Syntex	954	10.3
10	Ceclor	Infections	Lilly	935	11.3

Source: FT (1992a).

is expected to restore the altered equilibrium. The ideal molecule is then given to the laboratory chemists, who search for substances whose molecular structures match as closely as possible the theoretical model.[6]

Clearly, discovery by design does not eliminate the need for bioassay and animal tests. Very often the ideal molecule fails in initial laboratory trials. The latter may suggest ways of improving its design. The entity then returns to bioassay and animal tests. In most cases, despite numerous iterations between theory and experiments, the project is abandoned. On a few occasions, long iterations produce a molecule that can be submitted for clinical trials.

Discovery by design does not however imply that information about the properties of molecules now springs from basic research. Theoretical compounds and the knowledge about pathological processes still depend upon information flows and feedbacks between basic conjectures and experimental observation. But discovery by design raises the efficiency of the feedbacks and interactions between theory and experiments. Experiments become more informative, as observations can be interpreted using better theoretical frameworks; researchers can associate observations about different phenomena, or they can relate observations to more general classes of phenomena. In turn, this often helps in perfecting and refining theories.

Tagamet, Capoten, and Mevacor, three among the ten top-selling drugs in 1991, are major examples of discovery by design (Table 2.2). Tagamet, the first H2-antagonist anti-ulcer drug, was approved for marketing in the mid-1970s.[7] Previous remedies against ulcers were based on antacid treatments, like milk of magnesia. In the event of severe complications patients underwent surgery. Sir James Black, the scientist responsible for the discovery of Tagamet, knew that ulcers are generated by over-production of gastric acid in the stomach, and that the cells responsible for secreting the acid are triggered by histamine, a chemical agent in the human body. He conceptualized a compound that blocked the acid-secreting cells by inhibiting action of the H2 histamine receptor. Although Black was looking for a compound with a specific structure and capable of a specific action in the human body, the Tagamet project took about ten years and he synthesized about 700 compounds before coming up with the final molecule.[8]

Capoten was approved for marketing in the early 1980s. Its discovery hinged upon scientific knowledge of the chemicals in the human body that are responsible for regulating blood pressure. Renin, a chemical produced by the kidneys, releases angiotensin I, which in turn produces angiotensin II. Overproduction of angiotensin II raises blood pressure and causes hypertension. Squibb combined this information with basic pharmacological knowledge. Squibb's scientists designed atom by atom a compound that inhibited overproduction of angiotensin II, thereby blocking the rise in blood pressure (*WSJ*, 1987b).

Merck spent decades studying how the body produces cholesterol. Early studies showed that cholesterol, a wax-like substance naturally produced by the human body, can clog the arteries that deliver blood to the heart, and cause heart attacks. During the 1970s, Merck's scientists isolated an enzyme (HMG-CoA) which is responsible for starting the production of cholesterol. This directed pharmacological research to designing a drug that could either inhibit HMG-CoA or prevent the cells from using it. In 1978, Merck's scientists isolated lovastatin, the Mevacor compound, which blocks the production of cholesterol (*BW*, 1987; FDA, 1988).

Discovery by design has also spurred more rational approaches to the quest for diverse applications of drugs. The search for diverse uses of compounds has been common in this industry for many years. Information about new uses of drugs has typically arisen from observation of side-effects in clinical trials or in the market. For instance, minoxidil, a drug that treats high blood pressure, also stimulated hair growth. Upjohn used this information to develop Rogaine, a hair restorer. Similarly, Naltraxone, approved against heroin addiction, proved to be active against Kaposi's sarcoma, a form of cancer associated with AIDS (FDA, 1988). But now new applications can be made less dependent on fitful and fairly casual observations. As scientists know how a certain drug acts, they can rationally plan ways of modifying the compound, and redesign it to perform different activities.

Aspirin, the most common medicine in the world, is a good example. It was introduced by Bayer in 1899. Since then, it has shown several therapeutic effects. Among other things, it proved to be an efficacious remedy for all sorts of pains, from simple headache to painful disturbances produced by tumors. However, the lack of basic knowledge about its action had prevented companies from developing aspirin-based medicines for many years.

Only over the past twenty years have scientists gained more solid knowledge about the chemical and biological function of aspirin. Studies have shown that aspirin produces an anti-thrombogenic agent that inhibits the formation of blood clots in arteries, an important cause of heart attacks. Blood clots are caused by undesired agglomerations of blood cells, platelets, which stick together. The anti-thrombogenic agent produced by aspirin keeps platelets separate. Since the mid-1980s, doctors have prescribed aspirin in combination with heparin, another drug, to cure or prevent strokes (W. Smith, 1991; *WSJ*, 1992).[9]

Knowledge about the function of aspirin has also encouraged researchers to develop more potent medicines that prevent blood clots by hindering the agglomeration of platelets. In 1987, a group of scientists at the University of California, San Francisco, isolated the gene that contains information about the molecular structure of platelet receptors. As we shall see in the next section, knowledge of receptor structure is critical in the design of drugs that conform to receptor sites, and correct unwanted behavior of cells. Publication of the gene prompted many companies – both large companies like Merck and Smithkline, and small biotech firms like Cor Therapeutics – to invest in the development of "super-aspirins," i.e., medicines that could act on platelets more effectively than the common aspirin compound (*WSJ*, 1992).

The spread of discovery by design

Scientific advances that spur discovery by design: cell receptors and receptor technology

The applicability of discovery by design has expanded considerably during the 1980s. Like Salvarsan and the sulfa drugs, information about the properties of new compounds stems from complex interactions between scientific knowledge and experimental observations. But now theoretical tools cover a broader number of cases, and they are clarifying increasingly complex phenomena. Moreover, advanced instruments, and greater computational power, have enabled scientists to examine complicated molecular structures, and to control their chemical reactions.

Discovery by design has benefited from important developments in the field of cell receptors.[10] Scientific research on receptors dates back to Ehrlich's affinity theory, and the development of beta blockers. Receptors are proteins on the surface of cells. They activate or block the functions of cells, i.e., the production of chemicals or other proteins. Human pathologies often result from the abnormal functioning of some cells: cells are inactive when they should be active or they are active when they should be inactive. Drugs bind to receptors. They can cause an inactive cell to respond (the drug is an agonist), or they can stop the undesired activity of a cell (antagonist).[11]

By studying the structure of receptors, scientists can design a molecule that binds to receptor sites, and activates or inhibits cells. Receptors have particular geometrical configurations, and the geometrical shape of the drug has to match the receptor like a key fits a lock. Moreover, electrical charges of drug molecules must be complementary to the atoms of receptors. Positively charged atoms of drugs must face negatively charged atoms of receptors, as two equal charges would repel each other. Drug compounds must also be stable. They must not decompose until they develop sufficiently tight bonds with the proteins. Finally, drugs must have a consistent dynamic activity. After they bind to an enzyme, they must produce chemical reactions that switch receptors on or off in desired ways.

Proteins are sequences of amino acids. The genes in human chromosomes contain the codes to identify the sequence of amino acids. In turn, the sequence of amino acids contains information to determine the molecular structure of proteins. Scientists have isolated some human genes, and they have obtained information about the sequence of amino acids. Using genetic engineering techniques, they have been able to clone genes, and produce large quantities of a given protein. This has supplied sufficient material to study the proteins, and identify their molecular structure. Moreover, complex theories and experimental techniques in molecular biology have revealed the existence of a number of new receptors in the human body, and they have helped in identifying the structure of some of them.

Molecular biology and genetic engineering have also given a great impetus to the possibility of predicting and controlling side-effects. Scientists have found that many receptors in different human organs have similar structures. Thus, drugs that are designed to bind to a certain receptor may also bind to similar receptors in other parts of the body, thereby causing side-effects. If scientists could devise the specific regions of the receptor molecules that differentiate otherwise similar receptors, they would be able to design drugs that fit uniquely the target receptor sites.

Similarly, advances in the knowledge of cell receptors have enhanced the opportunities of rational search for differentiated uses of drugs. Scientists have discovered that many new biotechnology drugs have different effects. With detailed knowledge of their action and molecular structure, researchers can select their activities. For instance, the human growth hormone was first commercialized by Eli Lilly and Genentech in 1985 to treat children affected by dwarfism. Scientists knew that dwarfism is caused by the failure of the human body to produce the growth hormone. They also knew that the production of the hormone slows down with aging. Lilly tested its hormone against some effects of age, and found that it has reinvigorating effects. The human growth hormone also helps in building lean muscle mass. Unfortunately, this has encouraged a black market among athletes. The same effect, however, has spurred research into using the hormone against obesity (*NYT*, 1990g; *BW*, 1990b).[12]

As discussed in the previous section, observation of the side-effects or new uses of drugs in clinical trials or in the market has been common in the pharmaceutical industry for many years. However, with limited knowledge about the properties of compounds, it was very costly just to acquire more solid evidence about the effects noted in clinical tests or in the market. Companies had to spend a great deal of time back in the laboratory, and they faced high risks that the observed effects were ephemeral. Costs and risks were not significantly lower than alternative projects "starting from scratch" or arising from other information (like evidence of effects produced by other compounds in laboratory assays). As a result, firms did not exploit systematically information gained during the development or commercialization stages.

But now companies have better prospects of being able to comprehend and plan new applications of drugs at the outset of the research process. This is economically more advantageous than pursuing "casual" observations from clinical trials or the market. Firms can take advantage of the increasing returns that will naturally arise when research and experimentation about a given compound produce information that can be used for different applications. Moreover, they can select applications on a logical basis, which raises their likelihood of success. As a matter of fact, many firms are now investigating the diverse effects of their molecules (see, for instance, *BW*, 1990b). Relatedly, with increasing knowledge about protein receptors, and more rational approaches to drug research, we can expect greater significance for learning and first-mover advantages in specific therapeutic areas.

The limits of discovery by design

Although encouraging, the new advances should not disguise the immense difficulties that still persist in drug design. Scientists have found the sequence of amino acids of only a few human proteins, and they have worked out the molecular structure of only a very small fraction of them.[13] Geometric shape, electrical charges, and, to some extent, stability pertain to the statics of drug representation. The dynamics of drugs, i.e. their chemical and biological activity inside the human body, is even more complex. Theoretical knowledge and experimental techniques in this area present ample room for improvement (*CW*, 1987a; *NS*, 1988).[14]

Moreover, the problems associated with similarity of receptors and multiple activities of drugs still dominate their advantages. Receptors are often so similar that it is extremely difficult to design drugs that bind to one receptor and not to others. In addition, many receptors are unknown. Hence, the likelihood of side-effects remains high. Biotechnology drugs still have too many effects, and the ability of scientists to rationally select them is very limited.

These remarks simply confirm that the complexity of problems in industry can be so high that the guidance offered by fundamental knowledge is typically very incomplete. This is especially true of the pharmaceutical industry, which deals with a system, the human body, that is far more complicated than mechanical or electronic systems. There are so many and complex receptors, functions, and biochemical reactions in the human organism that drug design will rely for a long time on speculation in situations with a great deal of uncertainty. Clearly, this also implies that drug discovery will never do without long trial-and-error experiments in labs, and, of course, without clinical trials.

It would nonetheless be unreasonable to deny that important progress has been made since Salvarsan and the sulfa drugs. When looking at advances in science we are often struck more by the fact that discoveries open new and wider areas of our "ignorance" than by the solution to problems that then become commonplace. Yet, it is precisely where science unravels at least part of the complexity of problems, and problems become more customary and less appealing from a scientific point of view, that industry looks for new product opportunities.

The pharmaceutical industry has been no exception. For instance, in the early 1980s, scientists thought that advances in molecular biology and genetic engineering would pave the way to the development of drugs with very complex molecular structures, and capable of actions as complex as human proteins. By knowing the structure and function of human proteins, scientists believed they could replicate such structures and functions to design complex protein-based pharmaceutical products, based on "large" molecules. But in the course of the decade, it became clear that the economic usefulness of the advances in the life sciences did not rest on the possibility of developing complex protein-based drugs. More pragmatic opportunities arose from the possibility of increasing the efficiency of the discovery of "traditional" chemical products. Knowledge of protein structures and their function has supplied useful models of cell receptors to which drugs can bind. This has facilitated rational design of "conventional," non-protein drugs, thereby giving a notable impetus to research in this area.

Frontier scientific research in top academic institutions and other research centers still focuses on complex molecular structures, and the development of complex protein-based drugs. This is important, as scientific institutions are very active in the discovery of new receptors, and in clarifying their three-dimensional shapes. But many companies are now using the advances in the life sciences primarily to produce non-protein drugs and protein-mimetics based on small molecules. From an economic point of view, chemical drugs have many advantages over protein-based products. Their molecular structure is much simpler, which simplifies rational design. Moreover, biological drugs have complicated delivery systems. They cannot be swallowed, as pills are destroyed by enzymes in the gut and do not get into the bloodstream. Biological drugs are also much more expensive to manufacture. Finally, disputes about legal protection of natural substances have not yet been resolved, and the patenting of biological material still faces a great deal of uncertainty.[15]

Serotonin drugs

Many companies are developing drugs via analysis of their molecular structure and linkages with specific receptor sites using molecular biology and genetic engineering techniques. Some of these drugs are under regulatory approval for marketing, and some of them have already been commercialized.[16]

The family of serotonin-based compounds is a notable example of drugs developed via molecular design.[17] The market of serotonin drugs is expected to tap a few billion dollars in the mid-1990s. Serotonin is a chemical secreted by the brain. It regulates a number of activities. According to where it deposits in the body, it can increase or decrease blood pressure, suppress headache, influence appetite and sexual activity, control anxiety, depression, memory, drug addiction, schizophrenia, and aggressive behavior. Serotonin was first isolated in 1948. Yet, systematic research on this molecule started only in the mid-1970s, and it was greatly spurred by advances in cell receptors.

Different actions of serotonin depend on the receptors to which it binds, and therefore on the cells it activates or inhibits. For instance, activating serotonin receptors in the brain and certain blood vessels stops migraine headaches, whereas blocking them moderates anxiety and depression. The discovery of new receptors and the visualization of their structure enables scientists to identify the cells responsible for various activities of the chemical. Researchers can then design drugs that fit the target receptors, and select different activities of the molecule.[18]

Research on serotonin drugs has already scored some successes. In 1986, Bristol-Myers obtained FDA approval for a serotonin-based anti-anxiety drug which is also being investigated as an anti-depressant. In 1987, Eli Lilly obtained market approval for Prozac, an anti-depressant. Prozac is the most important commercial success in this field so far. It is expected to reach one billion dollar yearly sales in the 1990s. In 1989, Ciba-Geigy obtained approval for a serotonin compound against compulsive disorders, which cause people to repeat obsessively a certain action (like hand-washing). In 1990, Glaxo introduced a drug that prevents vomiting in chemotherapy patients, and it is waiting for FDA approval of a drug against migraine headaches. Glaxo's drugs are especially noteworthy, as they are opening important new research trajectories in this area. Unlike Prozac, which simply increases serotonin levels, they mimic the effects of serotonin on cells. Many other companies are developing serotonin drugs to treat disorders like cardiovascular diseases, schizophrenia, drug and alcohol addiction (*BW*, 1988a and 1992a; *NYT*, 1990b).

The discovery of Prozac is another important example of drug design. Scientists showed that when serotonin, which is produced by the brain, is re-absorbed too quickly by nerve cells, it triggers depression. They realized that by slowing down the absorption of serotonin, they could improve mood. Eli Lilly's researchers rationally designed a compound that retards absorption of serotonin. Prozac was also designed in a fairly selective way to match specific receptors, and hence minimize side-effects. Reports indicate that Prozac seems to have fewer side-effects than traditional non-serotonin anti-depressants. However, clinical analysts also warn that Prozac has not yet reached the cumulative volume of sales of previous remedies, and hence unforeseen side-effects may show up in the future (*NYT*, 1990c).

Prozac also appears to have other effects. Lilly's researchers have observed that it reduces weight, and they are studying it to treat obesity (*BW*, 1988a). Other serotonin drugs have shown diverse effects. Glaxo's drug that prevents vomiting in chemotherapy patients targets a receptor that is present both in the gut, where the drug acts, and in the brain. The brain receptor controls various neurological conditions. Glaxo's researchers are thus studying how to use the compound to treat anxiety and schizophrenia.

Development of serotonin-based medicines still encounters several diffi-culties. The discovery of new serotonin receptors facilitates detection of other effects. However, it also points to side-effects that, although not yet observed in patients, can be rationally anticipated. For instance, Glaxo's drug against migraine acts on receptors on blood vessels around the brain. This suggests that the drug may generate cardiovascular problems. For this reason, the FDA is delaying its approval, even though the drug has not yet shown such effects in patients. More generally, as more serotonin receptors are discovered, scientists realize that they are so similar that it will be extremely hard to design drugs that act selectively on desired targets (*BW*, 1992a).

These difficulties suggest that a notable contribution of the new scientific discoveries is the prediction of *failures* rather than successes. Prediction of failures is important. Firms can save time and costs by ignoring research lines that are anticipated to be sterile. Unfortunately, the present scientific advances do not seem to be as effective in telling scientists *what to do*. And this implies that, in searching for what to do, companies still have to rely, to a good extent, on trial and error and somewhat "blind" experiments.

Scientific instruments and computers in drug research

Advances in experimentation technologies

X-ray crystallography and nuclear magnetic resonance are the two spectro-scopic techniques normally employed in drug research to "observe" molecular structures.[19] Drug researchers have used X-ray crystallography for many years. This technique is based on the analysis of the diffraction of X-rays passing through protein crystals. The diffraction pattern reveals the spatial distribution of electrons, and the location of the atoms of the molecule. The analysis of the molecule then depends upon theoretical knowledge of how X-ray diffraction is linked to the density and spatial distribution of electrons. Relatedly, the effectiveness and precision of X-ray crystallography has benefited from advances in the science of crystals, and the development of theoretical models about atomic units and how they arrange to form molecular masses.

This is important as it suggests that, although scientists try many molecular structures before finding one that satisfactorily pictures the three-dimensional shape of a protein, experimental research is strictly related to more fundamental understanding of phenomena. Theories are critical because observations of infinitesimal phenomena, like proteins, cannot be made by the naked eye (and neither can they be made by powerful microscopes). Hence, phenomena have to be deduced from theoretical relationships among objects and variables. In other words, scientists perform a great number of hit-and-miss experiments. But when the latter are made using advanced instruments, they depend upon complementary progress in theories.

Nuclear magnetic resonance (NMR) has recently emerged as an alternative approach for inspecting molecular structures. Molecules are exposed to radio waves in magnetic fields. Atoms respond by emitting their own radio waves. The frequencies of the radio waves produced by atoms can be interpreted to devise the approximate distance between atoms. This, combined with known chemical properties of the molecule, helps in determining the position of atoms. Again, experimental observations are not made by the naked eye, but are deduced from theoretical principles.[20]

Mathematical analysis of how the diffraction of X-rays or the frequencies of atomic radio waves transform into three-dimensional structures of molecules, is performed by computers. Computers elaborate the data. They also visualize the protein structure on screen. In the 1950s and 1960s, researchers examined X-ray crystallography data through charts, oscilloscopes and photographs, and they built brass or plastic models of molecules. With limited computational capabilities and visualization techniques, they could analyze only very small molecules. The impressive growth of computational power in recent years has made it possible to inspect incredibly complicated compounds. This has furthered considerably the growth of discovery by design by providing models of complex cell receptors which can be used to design drugs that match given receptor sites.

The productivity of X-ray crystallography and NMR has increased considerably during the past twenty years. Eberhardt *et al.* (1991) estimated that using today's X-ray crystallography instruments it takes one-tenth of the time, one-twenty-first of the cost, and one-tenth of the labor hours needed twenty years ago to perform the same baseline experiments. Apart from conventional X-ray crystallography, synchroton crystallography, which uses more powerful synchroton radiation sources, has developed at an even faster speed. Time reduction, cost reduction, and labor-hour reduction of synchroton crystallography have been of the order of 1:14, 1:39, and 1:15. The same ratios for NMR are, respectively, 1:9, 1:7, and 1:8 (Eberhardt *et al.*, 1991).

In spite of these advances, the analysis of protein structures is still a very complicated task. In the first place, basic knowledge about how to relate X-ray diffraction or frequencies of atomic radio waves to protein shapes is incomplete. As suggested earlier, computational chemists have to perform systematic trial-and-error tests to find a reasonable solution of a protein shape. They normally run different models of how a protein could be generated from crystallography or NMR data, and they produce many protein structures all consistent with the given data. Long and tedious work is needed before they can come up with one protein shape from a given amino acid sequence.[21]

Moreover, the cost of instruments has increased with their capabilities. Eberhardt *et al.* (1991) estimated that, on a current-dollar basis, the capital cost of today's instruments is about the same as the capital cost of the same instrument twenty years ago. However, their life is much shorter. This implies that today's scientists have to carry out far more experiments per unit of time to achieve the same cost per hour of effective use of the instrument. Finally, scientists need to perform more complex experiments (i.e., determination of far more complex molecular structures). Thus, even though time and cost reductions have been significant when compared with the same milestone experiment twenty years ago, researchers approach problems that require longer experimentation time and greater costs compared with the 1970s.

Advances in screening technologies

Advances in instrumentation are also influencing the productivity of laboratory screening of compounds. The most important developments in this area are related to the growth of knowledge about cell receptors. Researchers can increasingly assess the affinity of compounds to specific receptors via laboratory assays rather than administering the substance to animals. The great advantage of *in vitro* over *in vivo* techniques is that experiments can be performed on a much larger scale, and in less time. With animal tests, scientists have to wait for the metabolization of the compound within the animal body, whilst *in vitro* tests provide more rapid indications of whether the compound binds to the receptor or not. (Moreover, *in vitro* tests are ethically more acceptable.) Novascreen, an *in vitro* receptor screening system developed by Nova Pharmaceuticals,(a medium-sized biotech firm), in the 1980s, enables laboratory technicians to screen about 1,200 compounds against a receptor in a week. It takes about a month to screen the same number of compounds in animals.[22]

Of course, receptor technology is not a complete substitute for animal tests. Test-tube experiments do not reproduce all the environmental conditions that are encountered when receptors are inside the human organism. Scientific knowledge cannot yet fully explain why, on some occasions, compounds that block or activate a receptor *in vitro* do not produce the same effect *in vivo*.[23]

Nonetheless, receptor screening technology is moving at a rapid pace. Some university institutions and biotechnology companies have developed very powerful techniques.[24] In 1990, George Smith of Washington University in St. Louis, Missouri, and three biotechnology companies, Chiron, Cetus and Affymax, made a first important breakthrough. They devised a method of creating and examining vast libraries of biological, protein-based compounds ("peptides") to check for potential therapeutic action. The method is based upon genetic manipulation of a virus, called *filamentous phage*, which attacks bacteria, and makes them produce a large number of different peptides. The latter are immersed in a solution containing a target receptor. Researchers can then determine whether any of the peptides produced by the bacteria binds to the receptor. Typically, scientists cannot use the peptides they isolate as potential new drugs, because biological material, unlike chemical drugs, is destroyed by enzymes in the gut. However, they can use the peptides as models to design chemical drugs.

The main limitation of this method is that it can test only biological material, i.e. material produced by live organisms such as viruses and bacteria. This implies that the method can only produce drug models based upon the twenty naturally occurring amino acids. This rules out the countless chemical compounds that can be produced synthetically. Two biotech companies, Houghten Pharmaceuticals and Selectide, have developed alternative receptor screening methods that can test vast libraries of chemical compounds against specific cell receptors. Both methods hinge upon the following idea. Human proteins (enzymes, receptors) are composed of chains of twenty different amino acids. Drugs are approximately the size of a six-amino-acid chain. Six-amino-acid chains, called hexamers, are normally sufficiently small to sneak into bigger molecules, like human enzymes, and influence the way they work. Organic chemists have created more than 150 synthetic amino acids. They can then produce billions of different hexamers by simply combining the natural and synthetic amino acids six at a time.

Houghten and Selectide have devised methods to test quickly the reaction of a huge number of hexamers against a given receptor. For instance, it may take just one week to test all 64 million possible hexamers that can be obtained by combining the twenty natural amino acids six at a time. The two methods consist of immersing millions of hexamers in a solution containing a target receptor. Radioactive material makes the reacting hexamers turn a different color. They can be isolated, and their amino acid sequence can be identified. The sequence can then be used as a model to design drugs.

Many other companies, which include, apart from biotech firms, software companies, are trying to develop even quicker peptide screening methods. A few of them are trying to automate the screening process by using robots that work twenty-four hours a day and seven days a week to test peptides against an array of different receptors. This is likely to have important effects on future opportunities for drug discovery. High-speed and very efficient screening methods could provide vast libraries of drug models which are known to react against certain receptors. These would be like libraries of "prototypes" which could be used as "ideal" compounds to design new drugs.

Efficient screening methods may give a new impetus to extensive trial and error in drug research. In fact, as suggested earlier, the new methods arose primarily from a basic understanding of the function and structure of cell receptors. Moreover, as hexamers are not candidate drugs themselves, researchers still have to perform chemical drug designs, which rely upon rather fundamental knowledge about the properties of drugs and their action inside the human body.

More importantly, some analysts have suggested that a major limitation of the new screening methods is that researchers have little ability to extract useful information from such huge libraries of peptides (*ECON*, 1991). Greater scientific understanding is needed in order to utilize more selectively the enormous number of peptides that can be generated in this way. Relatedly, even though researchers can efficiently screen a great many hexamers against various receptors, it would be practically impossible, even with the most sophisticated technologies, to perform blind screening of peptides against the massive number of receptors in the human body. Researchers need some guidance about the pathology they want to attack. They also need guidance to restrict the number of receptors to be examined.

Put differently, efficient screening technologies will be more valuable when applied to areas where basic knowledge offers an indication of potential opportunities. Once again, it is the complementarity, rather than substitution, between basic understanding and improved experimentation technologies that drives the prospects for successful research, and for commercially useful innovations.

Computers: the fundamental tools of drug design

Computers have become critical instruments for drug research. We have already seen that, armed with impressive computational power, scientists can now approach the complicated mathematical equations that are necessary to work out the molecular structure of very complex human enzymes from X-ray crystallography or NMR data. Sometimes, computational chemists attempt to determine protein structures without using information from X-ray crystallography or NMR. Purely computational models rely solely on basic theories of quantum chemistry about the density of electrons and the position of atoms. However, fully theoretical models are typically forced on researchers by the difficulties of collecting data from experimental observations. Researchers then simplify equations using arbitrary assumptions. At present, the most effective (and feasible) models are those that use "realistic" information from X-ray crystallography and NMR to approximate immensely complicated quantum chemistry equations (*NS*, 1988; *Science*, 1992).[25]

Computers also convert the solution of protein models into three-dimensional images. Three-dimensional visualization is of the utmost importance for comprehending the intricacies of molecular shapes. In the past, molecules were represented using balls, sticks and wires. Physical visualization presented various problems. For instance, the physical structures of complex molecules composed of thousands of atoms, such as proteins, could collapse under their own weight. With computers, scientists can easily rotate images, and observe them from different angles. Computerized images can also be very helpful in detecting regions of receptor structures where drugs can bind.

Computers are also used to design drugs that match target receptors.[26] The drug industry has used computers for this purpose since at least the end of the 1970s, and it was one of the first industries to employ computers to design molecular structures (*Science*, 1992).[27] At present, most applications are static representations. Typically, given the topography of a receptor, researchers design drugs whose geometrical configuration matches suitable spaces of the enzyme. Apart from rotating the image, and observing it from different angles, they can easily add or eliminate atoms to experiment with different models of drugs. Moreover, computers perform various calculations about atomic charges, size, and other aspects of the chemical interaction between drug molecules and receptors.

Static representations can rarely predict potentially effective drugs with great precision. An important reason is that they ignore dynamic aspects about the action of compounds inside the enzyme. However, they can be very useful, as researchers can eliminate many drug candidates simply because their geometrical configuration or atomic charges are inconsistent with the target receptor. Cost savings can be substantial as companies can exclude from animal tests and clinical trials a number of compounds that will not bind to specific enzymes.

Dynamic simulations are still in their infancy. But some applications already offer the possibility of simulating the actions of drugs that occur in less than a trillionth of a second. The computer reproduces the action in much slower motion. Researchers can carefully study it. They can stop the process, and focus on the critical moments of the reaction. This may suggest ways of improving the structure and activity of the compound.

Drug candidates never move from the computer screen directly to IND application and clinical trials. Geometrical conformity to target receptors is the area where researchers are most confident about the predictive power of their computerized models. However, scientists are largely unable to account for all the environmental factors that influence the dynamic interactions between potential drugs and human enzymes. For instance, a major problem is that the polarity charges of "ideal" drug compounds tend to change when actually introduced in the live organism, and these changes are often impossible to predict. As a result, drug molecules that seem to work satisfactorily in computers often fail in animal tests (*BTEC*, 1990).

Because of these difficulties, drug designers supply applied chemists with many alternative drug models. Applied chemists synthesize these models, and test them in bioassays and animals. New compounds for clinical tests typically arise from systematic trial and error, and information flows and feedbacks between the design stage and applied laboratory research. Indeed, the most important contribution of computers in drug research is not that they reduce the need for laboratory experiments. Instead, they enhance the efficiency of the interactions between drug design and applied research. They raise the efficiency of the entire process of designing the compound, synthesizing it in the laboratory, and turning back to the design stage to modify it according to information from the experiments.

Abbott's development of a renin inhibitor exemplifies the role of computers in drug discovery. In the search for a new drug, Abbott scientists had already developed an angiotensinogen protein-drug that could bind to the target human protein, renin. They had the amino acid sequence of the protein, but lacked a three-dimensional structure of renin. The three-dimensional structure of renin was important to identify sites where the new drug could bind. Laboratory chemists had already synthesized a number of molecules as potential renin inhibitors. From the computer visualization of the renin structure, computational chemists could discard two-thirds of the molecules synthesized by the applied chemists, as their structural configuration did not fit the renin receptors. Further development could be confined to only one-third of the compounds, with implied time and cost advantages.

Animal tests showed that the molecule could not be given orally. Enzymes in the gut reduced the entity to its inactive form, which was not revealed by computer models. The molecule went back to the computer screen. Scientists realized that chymotrypsin, an enzyme in the gut, was responsible for making the drug inactive. Given the molecular structure and the receptor sites of chymotrypsin, they redesigned the drug compound so that it was no longer affected by the enzyme.

When the redesigned compound was given to pharmacologists to prepare it for administration, the substance proved to be insoluble. The compound returned to the computer. The computational team tried to identify groups of atoms that, on the one hand, could be modified without affecting the activity of the drug, and, on the other, could improve its solubility. They found a residue that was far from the active site of the molecule, and could be eliminated without affecting the therapeutic properties of the drug. The elimination of the residue considerably improved the solubility of the substance. The newly redesigned molecule passed the animal tests, and it was moved to clinical trials (*BTEC*, 1990).

Conclusions: Are we really moving forward?

The present trends in pharmaceutical research present a serious puzzle. Progress in the life sciences and experimentation technologies has not translated into indisputable increases in the number of discoveries and commercializable innovations. A comparison with electronics is striking. In electronics, since the end of the Second World War, advances in basic chemistry and physics, and in the technology of research, have brought about a significant succession of innovations. The miniaturization of chips and the continuous introduction of new generations of computers are only the most apparent examples. In the pharmaceutical industry, there is still a great deal of uncertainty about whether massive and socially very costly developments in theoretical and experimental sciences are producing sizeable economic and social advantages.

This chapter has highlighted the difficulties of drug design. More importantly, the number of new drugs commercialized worldwide between 1987 and 1991 has declined (Figure 2.2). Several reasonable explanations can be advanced. Major developments in biological sciences and experimentation technology have occurred only since the 1980s. Commercializable innovations will come up in the 1990s or even in the new century. Relatedly, the human body is an incredibly complex machine. Enormous efforts in science unravel only tiny portions of this complexity. The "easy" research veins have already been exhausted, so now greater research endeavor is necessary to produce fewer discoveries. Finally, drug development costs and the stringency of regulation are rising. Fewer pharmaceutical companies invest in innovation, which reduces the number of new drugs (Thomas, 1987; Di Masi *et al.*, 1991).

The discussion in this chapter suggests another possible explanation. The present growth in scientific understanding has had a greater impact on our ability to predict failures rather than successful drugs. The discovery of new receptors reveals side-effects. With computerized analyses of drug geometry, researchers can immediately discard compounds that will not bind to target enzymes, and thus will be ineffective. Previously, with limited

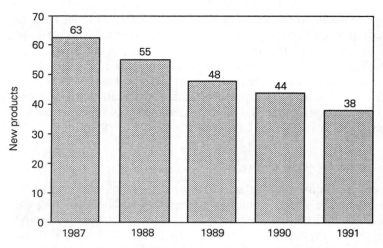

Fig. 2.2. Number of new drugs commercialized worldwide, 1987–91. (*Source:* Prous, 1992.)

ability to predict failures, side-effects or inefficacy would be observed only after long clinical trials and more often only after the drug had been in the market for some years. Thus, more drugs were tested and commercialized only to discover later on that they were ineffective (or worst, toxic). But now many ineffective drugs, or drugs with anticipated side-effects, can be discarded at the outset of the research process, and hence fewer drugs will be tested and commercialized. The desirable facet of this trend is that the fewer drugs that will be tested and sold will have fewer side-effects, and they will be more likely to be really effective drugs.[28]

In effect, attrition rates and the extent of laboratory experimentation do not seem to have diminished. Halliday, Walker, and Lumley (1992) found that in the 1980s only one substance out of 5–6,000 synthesized was marketed. Cox and Styles (1979) obtained similar results using 1970 data. In the 1960s, Vane (1964) obtained an even higher yield (1:3,000). Some of the earlier remarks apply here as well. The benefits of the 1980s' advances will materialize in the 1990s, and scientists approach increasingly complex problems, which require more extensive trial and error.

The idea of a diminishing number of pre-clinical trials rests upon the assumption that the predictive power of science reduces the need for experimentation. Other things being equal, this is true, as the outcome of some experiments can be logically anticipated. As also discussed in chapter 1, in Arora and Gambardella (1994a) it was formally shown that when profit-maximizing agents have greater ability to predict the future pay-offs of innovation projects, they focus on fewer projects with higher expected value. The number of applied research trials shrinks, as less projects are carried out. (However, expected experimentation yields increase, as companies develop only projects with greater expected pay-offs.)

But other factors may work in the opposite direction. As extensively discussed in this chapter, the efficiency of trial and error has risen (because of computers, new laboratory screening techniques, etc.). This encourages companies to perform more hit-and-miss experiments. The efficiency of the interactions between upstream theorizing and downstream experimentation has also increased. Complementarity has become more pronounced, which could be more than offseting the substitution effect. Indeed, the search models discussed in chapter 1 suggest that advances in science enable companies to search for innovations within a set of more productive "techniques." This implies that the optimal number of techniques tested is non-decreasing (Nelson, 1982). Put simply, search theory indicates that, with advances in science, experimentation becomes a more productive input. Hence, rational economic agents will not "buy" less of it.

Moreover, if measured by the *number* of drugs marketed per compound synthesized, as in the studies above, yields will not necessarily increase. The critical contribution of present advances in the life sciences and experimentation technologies lies in the possibility of generating higher quality drugs, i.e. truly effective drugs, and drugs with fewer side-effects. This does not imply more drugs per compound tested. More careful analyses ought to look at the *value* of marketed drugs per compound tested, assuming that the market value of drugs reflects greater quality in the product.

In sum, in comparing the social and economic benefits of the present scientific and technological advances with their massive social costs, the focus should be on whether drug researchers can increasingly eliminate lower quality drugs at the outset of the research process. Benefits will arise if more effective drugs are commercialized, and drugs have fewer side-effects. This analysis, however, is beyond the scope and the possibilities of this book. One would need much finer data, and to wait for a few years for present scientific and technological progress to have a sizeable impact on commercializable products.

Nonetheless, what is important for us, as economists, is that economic agents, viz. pharmaceutical firms, and the scientific community, seem to have good expectations that the current advances will lead somewhere. They are actively investing in molecular biology, genetic engineering, computerized drug design, and new experimentation technologies. Irrespective of whether such things will work, this should be enough to raise the interest of our profession. Expectations are sometimes all that matters in our discipline. Not only can they be self-fulfilling, but more importantly they influence economic behavior. And it is to this that we now turn.

3 Economic implications of greater scientific intensity in drug research

Scientific research in pharmaceutical companies

Growing incentives for scientific research in drug companies

The growing scientific intensity of drug research has increased the incentives for pharmaceutical firms to invest in basic understanding of their compounds. As argued in the previous chapter, the decision of firms to invest in fundamental knowledge is an economic one. When problems are very complex, basic scientific and technological research cannot produce concrete product opportunities in reasonable time and at reasonable cost. Trial and error is economically more advantageous. This is why in the 1950s drug companies engaged in systematic screening of compounds, with limited attempts to understand the action of drugs. But the growth of basic biological and pharmacological knowledge, and the increased efficiency of experimentation, have raised the possibility of comprehending relatively complex problems in economically useful ways. Especially from the 1980s, firms have had greater expectation that knowledge of the properties and action of compounds could be used to disclose new product opportunities.

Advances in the life sciences, instrumentation, and computers have enhanced the efficiency of information flows and feedbacks between theoretical knowledge and experimentation. It is now easier and less costly to perfect and correct theories (and theoretical designs of drugs) using advanced instrumentation techniques. At the same time, knowledge of drugs and the human body supplies valuable frameworks to utilize experimental observations more coherently. As a result, pharmaceutical firms increasingly use theoretical tools and new research technologies to predict the therapeutic effects of their molecules before synthesizing them in the laboratory.

Clearly, greater economic incentives to invest in understanding the properties of drugs are reinforced by the externalities produced by the growth of public knowledge. Firms can focus on problems that have already been clarified, in large part, by public discoveries, and hence that have greater potential for economic returns.

Typically, scientific institutions isolate genes and identify protein structures. Problems in these areas are scientifically the most intriguing, and the pay-off to scientists (reputation, status, etc.) is the greatest. But these areas are remote from tangible product opportunities. Hence, companies are unlikely to specialize in them. However, as our examples of super-aspirins and serotonin in the previous chapter demonstrated, as soon as scientific institutions isolate new genes or identify new receptor structures, pharmaceutical companies rush to exploit the new discoveries. Sometimes they provide supplementary contributions of a fundamental character. They clarify the function of some receptors, they find other functions, or they discover similar receptors. More often, they use knowledge about newly discovered genes or receptors to design new drugs, elucidate their action, etc.

Their reliance upon external knowledge also implies that pharmaceutical companies invest in upstream research as a means of monitoring public scientific advances (Cohen and Levinthal, 1989; Rosenberg, 1990). Many large drug corporations own divisions that perform rather basic research. Apart from studying problems such as the isolation of genes, the determination of protein structures, or improvements thereof, they perform very general studies of drug compounds, or they study pathologies on a very general basis. Such activities can be extremely useful from a commercial point of view. If a company discovers, say, a certain protein structure, it may gain significant first-mover advantages. More importantly, by performing basic research, company scientists remain aware of developments in their own disciplines; by keeping their research skills alive, they have greater ability to utilize new findings and translate them into commercially useful innovations.

Apart from technological opportunities, pharmaceutical research exhibits solid appropriability conditions, which fact augments the incentives of drug companies to invest in understanding the basic properties of their molecules. We saw that the fundamental input of drug discovery is not science *per se*, but a complex blend of scientific knowledge and experimental research. As we shall see in more detail in the next section, both generation of scientific knowledge and mastery in experimental research depend a great deal upon tacit skills, learning, and individual and team-based talents and expertise. More generally, they depend on organization- and team-specific resources, which cannot be easily transferred to other teams, let alone to other organizations.

In addition, unlike many other industries, patents are an effective means of protecting drug innovations (Taylor and Silberston, 1973; Mansfield, Schwartz, and Wagner, 1981; Mansfield, 1986; Levin *et al.*, 1987; Cohen and Levin, 1989).[1] An important reason is that pharmaceutical innovations take well-defined forms, to wit new compounds. Innovations can thus be described, and hence patented, more easily. This also makes it easier to identify the object of patents, which reinforces legal protection.

Because patents are effective, pharmaceutical companies rush to patent their new entities as early as possible. They patent their molecules after pre-clinical research. Thus, not only are patents an effective means of protecting drug innovations, but they are also a means of protecting the output of basic and applied research. This is an important factor in raising the incentives of firms to invest in upstream research. Even though scientific findings diffuse in the external environment, companies can appropriate their economic applications, and hence the principal source of rents produced by investments in fundamental knowledge.

Patents also disclose the content of innovation. Yet, drugs are complex molecules when compared for instance with bulk chemical products. "Inventing around" from information in patents is more difficult than in other branches of the chemical sector. Also, patents are granted a few years after application. This can confer important lead-time advantages. The innovator can start animal and clinical tests as soon as the innovation is generated, i.e. months before the information is disclosed by publication of the patent.[2] If compounds enter clinical trials earlier than competitors, they are more likely to reach the market sooner. First-comer drugs, especially if they are important advances over existing remedies, can secure high customer loyalty (hospitals and doctors), which makes it more difficult for second- or third-comers to gain significant market shares.[3]

Organization of research and scientific creativity

The growing use of scientific knowledge in drug discovery has important implications for the organization of company research. When new compounds resulted primarily from extensive screening of chemical entities, the critical resource for drug discovery was sufficiently large laboratories. Only large laboratories could reach the threshold size of trials that was needed to attain one or a few potential new products. Dynamic economies of scale were also important. Over time, large laboratories could accumulate information about the properties of many families of compounds by testing them under different conditions (e.g., for different pathologies).[4]

Moreover, discovery was more effectively managed by hierarchical organizations. With limited applicability of science, large-scale screening of compounds hinged upon fairly routine tasks. Firms had to employ many "technicians" who had to perform rather conventional experiments to observe and record how different molecules reacted. Typically, hierarchical structures are more efficient for managing large organizations that have to carry out fairly repetitive activities.

With greater need for scientific creativity, the scale of laboratories is no longer the only critical asset for discovery. As argued by many authors, flexible and informal organizations, even relatively small in size, are often conducive to the production of ideas of great originality (e.g., Arrow, 1983; Sylos Labini, 1992). This is especially true of pharmaceutical research (*FT*, 1989b; Shelley, 1991; Ängård, 1991). As a result, pharmaceutical firms have to pay increasing attention to organizing their research so as to stimulate ingenuity. This also intensifies the differences in the character and organization of the research and development stages in this industry. Drug development is still based upon long and routine clinical trials, which are more effectively managed by large hierarchical structures with considerable financial and organizational capabilities. In contrast, the far greater need for creativity implies that in discovery important changes have to take place. (See also Ängård, 1991.)[5]

Successful drug companies will increasingly organize their discovery process around a group of talented scientists. The personality of great individuals has always played an important role in pharmaceutical innovation. Many drugs are associated with the names of the head scientist who managed the project.[6] Sapienza (1987) examines the story of Tagamet, and the roles of Sir James Black and William Duncan, the scientists responsible for its discovery. As she points out, successful completion of the project depended not only on their scientific expertise, but also on their leadership skills, and their ability in creating an atmosphere of great intellectual fervor in the lab.

Moreover, in order to encourage creativity, top managers will have to loosen hierarchical control on company scientists. Top managers have broader vision about the market, the position of their company with respect to its competitors, and the fields in which innovations have greater economic potential. Hence, they should define the key therapeutic areas wherein company researchers have to focus. But within these areas scientists should be accorded great autonomy in choosing specific research lines. They have greater technical competence to pinpoint the best opportunities for technological and even commercial success. In addition, scientists should be granted substantial independence in organizing their research and the activities of their teams.

Of course, some control is necessary. It is then important to devise forms of control that avoid hierarchical pressure, which thwarts creativity. One possibility is to replicate the peer evaluation system in academia. Firms could encourage discussion and periodic revisions of projects, through internal seminars or in other forms, among scientists and researchers working on different company projects. Companies could also encourage discussion with academic scientists. Decisions about whether to abandon a research project or to enlarge its budget should be taken by a council of senior company scientists or by a committee composed of the head scientists of all company projects.

Discussions and seminars could be extended to marketing people and other company managers. They may give important suggestions to make projects closer to commercial opportunities. Conflicts may arise as marketing directors and other managers endorse business-oriented objectives too strongly, whereas scientists want to linger on the more theoretical facets of projects. An important function of top managers will then be to resolve such conflicts by making choices that preserve commercial goals without frustrating research ingenuity.

Research openness in pharmaceutical firms

As they organize research around a group of senior scientists with minimal hierarchical control, firms will also be forced to accept greater openness of their research. This issue was discussed more generally in Arora and Gambardella (1992). Basic research and computerized design of drugs imply that companies will have to employ more people with strong academic backgrounds (Ph.Ds., young researchers, etc.). These people will have internalized to a greater extent the values of the scientific community. Some of them will even remain motivated to do research just for the sake of expanding the stock of knowledge. They will be inclined to publish, participate in conferences, and communicate with their peers.

A related explanation is that qualified scientists and researchers will have individual incentives to enhance public recognition of their human capital. They may want to preserve opportunities of returning to academia, or they may want to maintain visibility for possible employment by other firms, or they may simply want to keep a credible threat of leaving their present companies. While firms could impose restrictions to avoid diffusion of internal information, this would mean applying pressure and control. We have already argued that this may dampen creativity and frustrate motivation for research.[7]

More importantly, there are considerable economic benefits arising from the fact that company scientists publish, participate in conferences, and communicate with their peers. We noted the importance of in-house scientific research as a means of monitoring and absorbing external scientific knowledge. But the ability of company scientists to comprehend and utilize outside knowledge will be greater if they behave like members of the scientific community (which entails publications, participation in conferences, etc.). Again, company scientists will be able to assimilate external scientific knowledge more effectively if they perform similar research themselves (including research of a more academic nature). For instance, they will have greater ability to understand and utilize public discoveries about newly isolated genes or receptor structures to design new drugs. Even though they may not discover the new genes or receptors themselves, research expertise in this field will help in better understanding issues such as the geometrical combination of drugs and receptors and their dynamic interactions.

Moreover, academic scientists will be more inclined to exchange ideas with people that they deem to be part of the same "club" (Arora and Gambardella, 1992). Exchange with academic scientists is important for various reasons. Apart from clues about new research ideas, company scientists may know about discoveries before publication, which often follows discoveries only after a time-lag. Even a few months' lead in knowing about a certain finding can be very important in this industry. Also, publications, or other reports, typically do not convey complete information about a discovery. There is a great deal of useful information that can be transferred between scientists by word of mouth.

The drawback of openness is that firms lose control of internal information. However, the ability to produce – or even to "re-produce" – scientific knowledge depends to a large extent on organizational routines, as well as on talent and skills (including experimental skills) embodied in the human capital of individual researchers (De Solla Price, 1984). Thus, to take advantage of knowledge and information (or even compounds) generated by the research group of the firm, competitors would need to have similar "tacit" capabilities. This also implies that firms will increasingly compete for the services of eminent scientists and qualified researchers. This will be done through pecuniary and non-pecuniary rewards. Among the latter, a fairly important one will be the creation of a stimulating (and "open") research environment – not least because this would enable scientists and researchers to preserve or even enhance public recognition of their human capital, with implied personal advantages discussed earlier.

Moreover, there are learning effects. Company scientists may have accumulated over time great expertise in a specific area. Even if internal information circulated outside the firm, competitors would be unable to exploit it effectively if they had not specialized early enough in the same field. First-mover advantages in promising areas of scientific inquiry, and in new therapeutic and commercial niches, can then become critical. But the ability of firms to move quickly into promising new areas of research will depend, once again, on their proficiency in monitoring the wealth of external information, and in capturing opportunities that are created largely outside of their organization. As the earlier discussion pointed out, this ability will be greater in companies that encourage external linkages and research openness.

In sum, lower control of internal information is an important drawback of openness. However, this is to be weighed against the increasing disadvantages of secrecy. The most important one is that the company is not part of the scientific network, and it cannot trigger effective links with external information. Moreover, as discussed in the earlier subsection, patents are an effective means of appropriating drug innovations. In principle, if the firm patented, earlier than its competitors, the economic output of its scientific ideas, it would not be as compelling to protect the ideas themselves. Paradoxically, stronger patent protection of drug compounds might lead to greater openness of company research. Companies would be able to secure more effectively the ultimate source of their economic rents, and the advantages of openness would outweigh even more strongly its disadvantages.

Relationships between pharmaceutical companies and scientific institutions

Licenses and research collaborations between drug companies and scientific institutions

Collaborations and other relationships between pharmaceutical firms and universities or other research institutions have been common in the drug industry since the early years of this century (NSB, 1982; Swann, 1988; Madison, 1989). The growth of scientific intensity in drug research will strengthen the propensity of companies, and possibly of research institutions, to enter into such relationships (OTA, 1984, 1988 and 1991; Kenney, 1986).

Table 3.1 lists the most important linkages between the largest US pharmaceutical companies and universities or other institutions in the 1980s. As the table shows, such relationships primarily take two forms: licenses to companies arising from independent research conducted by research institutions, and research agreements.

Licensing is a common means of technology transfer from scientific institutions to drug firms. Companies obtain rights (which can be exclusive or non-exclusive) to develop and commercialize an earlier discovery of an academic or government laboratory. The diffusion of university–industry licensing in the pharmaceutical industry is encouraged by the relative ease

Table 3.1. *Agreements and other relationships (in biopharmaceuticals) between large US pharmaceutical firms and universities or other research institutions in the 1980s*

Firms	University or other research center	Products	Type of relation	Year
Abbott Labs.	Nat. Inst. of Health	HIV-1 ELISA diagnostic	Licensing agreement	—
Abbott Labs.	University of Chicago	rDNA lung surfactant	R&D agreement	—
American Cyanamid	Columbia University	Protein chemistry facility	$250,000 for establishment	1985
American Cyanamid (through Lederle)	Columbia University	Polio vaccine program	R&D agreement	1989
American Home Products	Stanford University	Basic cloning procedures	Non-exclusive license	1980
American Home Products	Columbia University	Patented rDNA extraction	Non-exclusive license	1984
American Home Products	National Technical Information Service	Rotavirus vaccine	Limited exclusive license	1987
Bristol-Myers	University of Alabama (with Schering-Plough)	Anti-gp 1200 against HIV	5-year development agreement	1987
Bristol-Myers	Walter and Eliza Hall Inst. of Medical Rsrch. (Melbourne, Australia)	Blood cell growth, patterns for leukemia treatment	Research agreement	1987
Bristol-Myers	MIT (Dr. Susumu Tonegawa)	Genetic operation of immune system	Cancer research study award	1987
Bristol-Myers	National Technical Information Service	Monoclonal antibodies to Chlamydia	Exclusive marketing agreement	1987

Table 3.1. (cont.)

Firms	University or other research center	Products	Type of relation	Year
Bristol-Myers	Max Planck Institute	Antiviral nucleosides	Licensing agreement	1987
Bristol-Myers	Yale University	R&D agreement on anti-cancer medicines	Renewal of 1982 agreement; BM supplies $600,000 per year for 5 years; BM has option on licenses of new products discovered by participating Yale faculty during the period of the agreement	1987
Bristol-Myers	US Dept. of Health and Human Services	DDA, DDI nucleosides for AIDS	BM to develop	1988
Bristol-Myers-Squibb	Institut Pasteur	BMS's US patent for HIV-2 and its components	Licensing agreement	1989
Bristol-Myers-Squibb	Nat. Cancer Institute	Taxol	Joint R&D	1990
Johnson & Johnson	Columbia University	Patented rDNA extraction	Non-exclusive license	—
Johnson & Johnson	MIT	Diagnostics and immunology	Long-run research done at Cambridge research lab located on MIT campus	—
Johnson & Johnson	Scripps Clinic	Pharmaceutical products	$70 million 10-year development agreement	1986
Lilly	Columbia University	Patented rDNA extraction	Non-exclusive license	—
Lilly	Scripps Clinic	Monoclonal antibodies for use in adenocarcinoma	R&D agreement	—

Company	Institution	Subject	Agreement	Year
Lilly	MIT	Polymer-based continuous release drug delivery system	R&D agreement	1986
Merck	Duke University	Beta-adrenergic receptor	Research agreement	—
Merck	Purdue University	Monoclonal-antibodies-based nasal spray for rhinovirus infections	Support R&D of Michael Rossmann	1985
Merck	Mass. Gen. Hospital (with Biogen)	rDNA Mullerian inhibiting substance (MIS)	Development and marketing agreement; M to fund clinicals and marketing	1987
Merck	Istituto Gentili	MK-217 for osteoporosis	Licensing agreement	1989
Merck	Institut Merieux	Vaccine for hepatitis B, diphtheria, tetanus, and polio	R&D agreement	1991
Merck	Instituto National de Biodiversidad (Costa Rica)	Natural sources of new drugs in rain forests of Costa Rica	R&D agreement; M funds res. in exchange for exclusive rights on products	1991
Monsanto	California Institute of Technology	Instrument design	Development agreement	—
Monsanto	Columbia University	Patented rDNA extraction	Non-exclusive license	—
Monsanto	Shemyakin Institute (Moscow)	Biological research	3-year research agreement; M funds research in exchange of rights to market discoveries in the West	1989
Monsanto	Washington University (St. Louis)	Proteins and peptides, virus-resistant plants	4-year research agreement which extends previous 8-year agreement, bringing total funding to nearly $100m; M provides additional $9m per year in 1991–94	1990

Table 3.1. (*cont.*)

Firms	University or other research center	Products	Type of relation	Year
Schering-Plough	Mass. Gen. Hospital	Monoclonal-antibodies-based lytic agents	Research agreement	—
Schering-Plough	Oregon State University	rDNA vaccine for bovines	Funding research	—
Schering-Plough	Pennsylvania State University	rDNA technology	Industrial affiliation program	—
Schering-Plough	Scripps Clinic	rDNA alpha interferon for basal cell carcinoma	Product development and clinical trials	1986
S'kline	Ohio State University	Feline leukemia virus vaccine	Royalty agreement	1980
S'kline	Walter Reed Army Medical Center	Malaria vaccine	Exclusive rights for malaria vaccine to SK	1985
S'kline	Pasteur Vaccines	rDNA surface antigen hepatitis B vaccine	Worldwide licensing agreement	1986
S'kline	National Institute of Health	AIDS therapeutics	R&D grant (to NIH)	1987
S'kline	Stanford University	Processes and products	$7.8 million to construct a building for Center for Molecular and Genetic Medicine; SK has right of first refusal	1987
S'kline	University of Cambridge	Cardiovascular and autoimmune diseases, and virus infections	SK provides $2.25 million to establish a research institute in return for options on patents and commercialization of resulting inventions	1987

Company	Partner	Research area	Agreement	Year
S'kline	Johns Hopkins University	Diagnosis and treatment of allergic and respiratory diseases	SK provides $2.2 million for 5-year research in return for rights of first refusal	1987
S'kline	Washington Research Foundation (with Genentech)	Patented technology for recomb. protein in yeast	License to SK	1988
Squibb	Oxford University	Diagnostic and therapeutic agents for treatment of central nervous system disorders	S provides £20 million for a neuroscience facility and projects in exchange for patent rights on products	1987
Sterling Drugs	Harwell Labs. (UK government)	Macrosorb chromatography system	Licensing agreement	1984
Sterling Drugs	Purdue University	Antiviral agents	Research agreement	1987
Sterling Drugs	Memorial Sloan-Kettering and Columbia University	Polar-planar differentiation agents	Research agreement	1991
Syntex	Stanford University	Molecular genetics	Syntex provides $1.5 million to Stanford's Center for Molecular Genetics and Medicine	1987
Syntex	Hong Kong Insitute of Biotechnology	Drug screening research	Joint venture	1991
Upjohn	California Institute of Technology	Instrument design	Development agreement	—
Upjohn	US Dept. of Commerce	rDNA procedures to turn vaccine virus into live vector	Licensing agreement	—
Upjohn	Battelle Memorial Institute	Human vaccines	Research	1985
Upjohn	University of Kansas	Drug delivery and transport system	Joint collaborative research	1986

Table 3.1. (cont.)

Firms	University or other research center	Products	Type of relation	Year
Upjohn	University of Göteborg (Sweden)	Compounds for treatment of central nervous system disorders	Long-term R&D agreement	1987
Upjohn	Centre Paul de Broca de l'Inserm, University College, London	Compounds for treatment of central nervous system disorders	U has exclusive rights from collaboration	1987
Upjohn	Stanford University	Sleep research	Research	1987
Upjohn	Nat. Cancer Institute	Tetraplatin	Licensing agreement	1989
Warner Lambert	University of Auckland (New Zealand)	Anti-cancer	Joint development of new anti-cancer drug	1983

Note: Table covers relationships found in sources below for all US-based pharmaceutical firms among the first twenty companies in terms of 1986 US drug sales. Pfizer not included because no relationship with research institutions was found in sources below. Monsanto is included because, even though not among the first twenty companies in terms of 1986 US drug sales, it is investing significantly in the pharmaceutical business. Years of some agreements are not given in source.
Source: Bioscan (various years) and *Predicasts Index* (various years).

with which one can transfer the output of basic and applied research in this field. Licensing is a more effective means of technology transfer when the subject of the license can be meaningfully described in blueprints (Mowery, 1988; see also Arora, 1991). University research often leads to the synthesis of new compounds. This can be a deliberate goal of academic projects, or a by-product of more fundamental research. As compounds are well-defined objects, licensing exhibits low transaction costs. For instance, because the object of licensing is well defined, and hence is easily understood by both parties, information transfer displays fewer risks of opportunistic behavior due to asymmetric information or other reasons (Mowery, 1988). Moreover, companies can readily utilize the license, without incurring the costs associated with the transfer of substantial complementary tacit information. As scientific institutions do not normally have resources (and incentives) to carry out long and costly clinical trials (and to commercialize products), they yield the rights on their discoveries to gain funds for future research.

While licensing arises from research conducted independently by scientific institutions, research agreements entail industry funding of university research projects. As shown by table 3.1, they are typically extended arrangements covering 3–5 years or even longer periods. On some occasions, they are pure research contracts wherein companies fund research carried out by university staff. Firms benefit from contractual rights on outcomes, and they can take advantage of easier access to faculty and university outputs (preview of papers, participation in seminars, discussions with faculty, etc.). Agreements can also take the form of genuine research collaborations. Companies fund research jointly conducted by university and corporate researchers.[8]

Firms can gain important benefits from broad research collaborations with academia. For instance, Monsanto's executives declared that the 1982 four-year research agreement with Washington University (St. Louis) proved to be extremely successful in supplying the company with research and product opportunities. This justified the renewal of the agreement in 1986 and in 1990. Moreover, they pointed out that the 1982 agreement justified the 1985 acquisition of Searle, which established Monsanto's entry in the drug business (*BW*, 1986).

Why do pharmaceutical firms finance university research?

The propensity of large pharmaceutical companies to finance academic research can be ascribed, again, to a favorable combination of technological opportunity and appropriability conditions. Opportunities arise because of the "short" distance between scientific research and commercializable applications. We saw that scientific institutions specialize in activities such as isolation of genes and determination of protein structures which can be very useful for drug design and development. Moreover, universities often conduct research down to the discovery of specific compounds, and on many occasions they perform initial development stages (animal tests or even initial tests on human beings). In addition, large pharmaceutical firms can spread the costs and outcomes of "generic" research conducted by their university partner on a fairly wide range of product categories in which they have commercial stakes.

More generally, the scientific community is responsible for most of the present advances in molecular biology and genetic engineering, and it is the repository of most of the knowledge-base in these fields. Thus, apart from specific product opportunities, research collaborations with academia help companies in acquiring familiarity with the "new" science-base of this industry. In view of the short distance between science and commercially useful innovations, prompt acquisition of such capabilities is critical. Relatedly, research collaborations can give rise to privileged relationships with specific institutions. This puts companies in a better position *vis-à-vis* their rivals in exploiting the future discoveries of their partner.[9]

Good appropriability conditions reinforce the incentives of pharmaceutical companies to invest in linkages with academia. In many cases, university–industry contracts involve options or rights on academic discovery (table 3.1). Hence, appropriability can be an inherent feature of such contracts. The effectiveness of patents in protecting pharmaceutical innovations additionally helps in securing the economic outcomes of linkages with universities. In working with academia, companies gain knowledge that can be used for in-house drug discovery. They can then appropriate, through patents, the outcomes of the knowledge acquired from collaborations with research institutions. This encourages investments in academic research, in spite of the fact that part of the knowledge produced by company-sponsored projects (and that represents the basis of some of its innovations) may diffuse in the outside environment.

Appropriability also arises from the fact that companies can establish preferential channels with the institutions with which they collaborate. They can secure research information that is not as easily and promptly available to rivals. Tacit abilities are critical in scientific investigation (De Solla Price, 1984). Through collaborations, companies accumulate experience about methods and other subtleties of the research conducted by their partners, which can be acquired only through systematic, "day-to-day" relationships (e.g., expertise in using instruments such as X-ray crystallography, NMR, or computers for drug design).

The relatively short distance between academic research and commercializable innovations also implies that, with prompt access to findings, companies can pre-empt rivals in developing innovations within specific therapeutic fields. They can start laboratory research, as well as animal and clinical tests, earlier. Because the timing of clinical trials is in large part determined by regulatory conditions, there is little chance that rivals that entered downstream development a few years or even a few months later can reach commercialization before the first innovator. The importance of lead-time advantages in the early stages of pharmaceutical research thus implies that relationships with scientific institutions can bestow a dynamic competitive edge despite the fact that academic findings, including those accomplished through company-sponsored research, eventually become, at least in part, publicly available.

Research collaborations and restrictions to academic freedom

Appropriability of academic research and closer and more intense relationships between pharmaceutical firms and scientific institutions, raise an important issue. Companies may attempt to secure greater appropriability of the university research that they support by imposing greater restrictions on disclosure. Clearly, this problem will intensify as scientific research gains more "economic" value, and it becomes more directly and intimately connected with profitable opportunities.[10] It will become even more intense if public research funds shrink. Academia will have to resort more systematically to firms for research money. Also, with reduced outside opportunities, universities will be in a weaker bargaining position to negotiate restrictions on diffusion with companies.

The extent to which companies seek greater restraints on disclosure in joint research programs with academia is controversial. In discussing the 1987 alliance between Squibb and Oxford University, D. Smith (1991) noted that the major reason that prompted Oxford University to collaborate with Squibb was public budget research cuts in Britain during the mid-1980s. However, he also noted that the agreement posed minimal restrictions on academic freedom, and it has produced net benefits from an academic perspective. For example, Oxford University scientists have been able to produce many valuable publications, and they have patented a few new discoveries. Similarly, Gluck (1987) examined university–industry relationships in biotechnology using data from over 1,200 questionnaires sent to faculty members in forty US schools. In comparing faculty members with and without industry support, he found that the former had better publication records, and spent more time on genuine academic activities (e.g., time with students) (see also Blumenthal *et al.*, 1986).[11]

In contrast, Cohen, Florida, and Goe (1992) examined 500 university–

industry research centers in a number of disciplines in the USA, and found that industry placed restrictions on academic freedom in 57 percent of the cases. Moreover, they found that industry-supported university research tended to shift the focus of academia from basic subjects to more applied research. Also, table 3.1 shows that, among the most important university–industry agreements in the US pharmaceutical industry during the 1980s, there are no consortia, and practically all relationships involve only one firm. It has already been remarked that most linkages are relatively long-term research contracts, and in many of them companies have exclusive rights or first options on discoveries. Direct appropriability of university findings then appears to be an important factor in encouraging pharmaceutical companies to link with academic institutions.

Kenney (1986) discussed at some length whether long-term contracts between large pharmaceutical corporations and universities alter academic freedom and research autonomy. He presented case studies of a number of important university–industry collaborations in biotechnology during the 1970s and the early 1980s. His case studies covered agreements between very large firms and fairly large groups within universities (e.g., entire departments, or substantial parts thereof), which have lasted for a number of years and have involved considerable sums of money (among others, Harvard–Monsanto, Massachusetts General Hospital–Hoechst, Harvard–Du Pont, Washington University–Monsanto).

Kenney expressed concern about restrictions on university findings being made available to the public. In the cases that he examined, corporations tended to direct and control the research agenda of universities. He expressed his concern even though, as he suggested, both the corporations and the universities minimized the extent to which the relationships had compromised academic freedom. His greatest source of concern was the extent to which companies exercised a generalized control on the activities of scientists. In most of his agreements, the companies exerted control on public presentations (e.g., in professional meetings or seminars). Clearly, control was confined to research related to company-sponsored programs. But if corporate funding covers a substantial share of the research time of a certain department, or of individual scientists, this can be a considerable fraction of the overall research work of an institution or scientist. Moreover, with extended corporate funding, and given the natural overlap among the various research projects of scientists or university departments, it can be very difficult to distinguish between non-sponsored research (which can be freely disseminated) and sponsored work.

Companies exerted significant control on other scientists' activities as well. Kenney reported the story of a scientist who joined Massachusetts

General Hospital after the latter had signed a long-term research agreement with Hoechst. The new department member had a previous consulting relationship with Genetics Institute. He was then asked to pass to Hoechst any information acquired while working with Genetics Institute in exchange for similar information gathered in the department and arising from the agreement with Hoechst.[12] More generally, Kenney pointed out that, in such long-term agreements, companies are really buying more than a window on technology. They are buying research assets, in the form of significant shares of university research time.

Thoughtful discussion of the positive implications of, and the policy prescriptions arising from, such a complicated, and still controversial topic is beyond the scope of this book. An obvious positive implication is that greater scientific intensity of drug research will encourage tighter and more systematic interactions with research institutions, and this, in turn, will intensify debate (and controversy) about academic freedom. This will be a particularly hot topic in the pharmaceutical industry, wherein companies enjoy direct innovation opportunities from academic linkages, and hence have greater incentives to control academic knowledge.

My predictions, however, are less ominous than Kenney's (see especially Kenney, 1986, p. 72). In long-term research agreements, and especially if both parties enjoy significant advantages from a successful relationship, breakdown of the relationship can constitute a serious threat for both parties. Both parties will then try to avert the failure of the relationship. They will make serious efforts to comprehend each other's needs and behavioral codes, and they will gradually build up confidence and trust.

More importantly, the discussion earlier in this chapter about the advantages of open communication in company research can be extended to relationships with academia. Companies will recognize that they can derive greater benefits from linkages where scientific creativity is not frustrated by undue restraints on academic freedom, and scientists can take full advantage of open communication with the scientific network to assist their partners more productively. Interestingly enough, it is the ability of large pharmaceutical companies to appropriate the downstream outcomes of scientific research (through patents, lead-time advantages, or development and commercialization assets) that will discourage them from restraining open communication too strongly. If they are confident about their ability to secure part of the downstream outcomes of university research, they will not restrain information exchange too seriously, as they can obtain research inputs of greater value. In this connection, Blumenthal *et al.* (1986) found that small to medium-sized biotech firms seek stronger restrictions from their academic partners than larger firms. They have less ability to protect upstream findings by means of downstream assets, and hence they are more concerned about direct appropriability of scientific results.

Clearly, firms will impose confidentiality on research and information that have critical commercial value. Academia will certainly be more constrained than without industry connection. Yet, this does not necessarily imply that less scientific knowledge will be produced and disclosed. To the extent that companies become less obsessed with secrecy, financial support and other stimuli from industry (e.g., the use of costly instruments, novel research questions, interactions with company scientists) could induce greater production and disclosure of scientific knowledge than if no relationship existed.

Naturally, these remarks are by no means conclusive. Even though companies may become less restrictive about disclosure, there are other unresolved issues. For one, would companies shift the focus of academia from fundamental investigation towards more business-oriented research? A related concern is that, as shown by table 3.1, pharmaceutical companies appear to derive greater benefits from one-to-one relationships with academia than from consortia or other relationships with several partners – and this is clearly connected to the fact that they will encourage open research only if they can appropriate downstream outcomes. A certain company can then monopolize commercial exploitation of the discoveries of its university partner, despite the fact that, from a social point of view, it may not be the most efficient agent to develop them, or at least some of them. An even more serious concern is that a company can prevent other firms from utilizing discoveries that it does not utilize.

Policy prescriptions are even more intriguing. Again, the critical issue here is that, unlike most other industries, pharmaceutical companies have very few incentives to establish connections with university institutions if such linkages also involve some of its rivals. This implies that university policies aimed at preserving academic autonomy from industry cannot be similar across industries and scientific disciplines. Unlike industries wherein the relationships between science and commercializable innovations are less direct, in the pharmaceutical sector university policies that discourage connections with only one industry partner could discourage all university–industry linkages.[13] Financial problems of pharmacology or biology departments could become especially severe if this occurred in periods when public research budgets were undergoing serious cuts. A sensible university policy is probably to avoid interventions that deter linkages with individual industry partners. One would have to rely on the fact that pharmaceutical companies will increasingly recognize that academic freedom and research openness is beneficial from their point of view as well. An even superior policy, at the national level, would be to ensure that university departments enjoy sufficient public research funds, as a form of "outside option," to be in a better bargaining position when negotiating restrictions on disclosure in university–industry collaborations.

Division of labor and the formation of networks in pharmaceutical innovation

The rise of biotechnology firms: from integration to networks of innovators

The market structure of the pharmaceutical industry is undergoing a considerable transformation. For many years, the research-intensive ethical drug segment of the pharmaceutical industry had been composed of large integrated firms, which internalized activities from research to distribution.[14] Between the mid-1970s and the mid-1980s, more than 300 small to medium-sized research-intensive biotechnology firms were founded (Pisano, Shan, and Teece, 1988; OTA, 1988), and quite a number have been formed lately as well (Burrill, 1989; OTA, 1991).[15] The growth of biotech firms has hinged upon the new opportunities opened by molecular biology and genetic engineering. Most biotech companies have specialized in research, and a large fraction of their sales is composed of research contracts for larger companies (Burrill, 1988).

Molecular biology and genetic engineering have displaced traditional "chemical" capabilities for drug discovery. Chemical capabilities were "sunk" in the corporate tradition and "culture" of large pharmaceutical firms. Empirical studies by Henderson and Clark (1990) and Henderson (1993) showed very clearly that "old" technological routines are embedded in the organization of established firms. When radical innovations, or radically new research methods appear, organizational rigidity and inertia hinder the ability of established firms to take advantage of the new opportunities. New entrants, or newly established firms, with no sunk costs and organizational biases towards the old technology, can be far more effective than incumbents in exploiting the new fields.[16]

The rise of biotech firms is consistent with this pattern. However, while molecular biology and genetic engineering have had a notable influence on the discovery process, they have not really changed the type of assets that are needed for drug development and commercialization. The latter still require conspicuous financial, managerial, and organizational resources to conduct long and costly clinical trials, and extended distribution networks to sell the new products. These assets are firmly owned by established corporations, and biotech companies have encountered serious difficulties in acquiring them. A few of the largest biotech companies have discovered important new products, which they have commercialized independently or in collaboration with larger firms (Burrill and Lee, 1991). Yet, in spite of repeated attempts to integrate forward, the vast majority of biotech companies have been unable to obtain the financial resources and marketing assets for independent development and commercialization of their discoveries.

As a result, rather than new entrants ousting incumbent firms from the market, interesting changes have occurred in the organization of the innovation process in this industry. Many new drugs, and especially those that hinge upon the new advances in molecular biology and genetic engineering, no longer result from activities that are integrated within large corporations. They stem from network-like arrangements between biotech companies and large drug manufacturers, based on research collaborations, joint ventures, and the like (see, among others, Pisano, Shan, and Teece, 1988; Burrill and Lee, 1991; OTA, 1991).[17] Biotech companies supply ideas, compounds, therapies, and applied research outcomes. Large companies supply complementary research capabilities (such as those that require lumpy research assets, and hence cannot be borne by smaller firms), as well as resources for large-scale development and marketing. Tables 3.2–3.5 show the complex structures of the external linkages of four representative drug corporations (two American and two European) – Merck, Pfizer, Ciba-Geigy, and Hoffmann La Roche. Networks of similar complexity could be drawn for practically all the largest US and European drug corporations. (See *Bioscan*, 1992.)

Division of labor in innovation

Economists have long debated about the most effective size of innovating firms. The received Schumpeterian view is consistent with the rise of large research-based pharmaceutical corporations since the 1950s: large firms have long-term perspectives for R&D investment plans, and they have adequate resources and organizational capabilities for large-scale R&D. In contrast, Jewkes, Sawers, and Stillerman (1958) argued that most "inventions" arise from individuals or small groups.

Mueller (1962) resolved some aspects of this debate. He presented case studies of Du Pont's twenty-five most important innovations between 1920 and 1950. He showed that the largest fraction of such innovations originated outside Du Pont, from smaller firms or individuals. He thus concluded that "Du Pont has been more successful in making product and process improvements than in discovering new products" (Mueller, 1962, p. 344). Mueller also pointed out that Du Pont's ability to generate major innovations did not rise proportionally with its research expenditures. He

Table 3.2. *Ciba-Geigy's network of agreements*

Name	Products	Content of agreement	Date
Affymax N.V.	Affymax's drug discovery technology to treat diseases such as cancer, arthritis, and autoimmune disorders	R&D agreement – Ciba-Geigy will develop and market any compounds discovered, Affymax will receive milestone payments and royalties on sales	7/91
Agricultural Genetics Co. Ltd.	Microbial insecticides	R&D agreement	6/85
Agricultural Genetics Co. Ltd.	RFLPs	Contract R&D agreement	1/89
Agri-Diagnostics	MAb diagnostic kit to detect fungal disease affecting field crops and horticultural specialties	R&D agreement	3/86
ALZA	Transderm® drug delivery system for scopolamine, and nitroglycerine	Marketing agreement	
ALZA	OTC cough/cold/allergy products based on ALZA's OROS® technology	Marketing agreement through Ciba Consumer Pharmaceuticals	10/88
Aphton Corp.	Aphton's immune system stimulants against parasites in animals	Development agreement	2/92
Applied Microbiology Inc.	AMBICIN antimicrobial peptides to treat bovine mastitis	Worldwide licensing agreement	3/91
Biogen	Ciba-Geigy's yeast promoter system for vaccine production	Licensing agreement	1/86
Biosys	Biopesticides for turf and ornamental pests	Exclusive distribution agreement for the USA	4/91

Table 3.2. (cont.)

Name	Products	Content of agreement	Date
Biosys	Nematode strains as bioinsecticides	R&D and worldwide marketing agreement	4/92
Calgene	Disease resistance in plants	Research agreement	6/86
Chiron	IGF-I and II for osteoporosis and bone and muscle healing (somatomedin)	Development and production agreement, C-G has option for worldwide licensing rights	6/86
Chiron	rDNA vaccines for AIDS, hepatitis A, hepatitis non-A, non-B, CMV, herpes, malaria	50/50 joint venture called The Biocine Co.	10/86
Collaborative Research Inc.	EMIA diagnostic tests, including test for thyroxin levels	Corning holds license to develop, manufacture, and market worldwide through Ciba Corning	2/84
Genencor International Inc.	Enzymes for the pulp and paper industry	Development agreement – Genencor to research, develop, and manufacture, C-G to market the products worldwide	6/92
Genentech	Animal health care products including animal interferons and other lymphokines	$42m. worldwide licensing agreement to develop, manufacture, and market	7/85
ISIS Pharmaceuticals	Antisense technology	Five-year, $30m. co-operative research agreement – C-G to have worldwide exclusive marketing rights	11/90

North Carolina Biotechnology Center, R.J. Reynolds	Plant biotechnology	Funding for Fellowship Program of Consortium for Research and Education in Plant Molecular Biology	
Noven Pharmaceuticals	Noven's transdermal estrogen delivery system	Exclusive licensing agreement for USA and Canada	11/91
Oregon Health Sciences University	Nucleic acid, protein, and peptide chemistry, and molecular biology	$2.5m., five-year co-operative agreement to promote the exchange of information	1987
Panlabs®, International	Natural products discovery	Multiyear research agreement	1991
Plantorgan (Germany)	Eglin, Hirudin	Collaboration and licensing agreement	
Tanox Biosystems	Protective MAbs against HIV	Collaborative development agreement	1989
Tanox Biosystems	MAb products for treating certain allergies	Joint development agreement – C-G to pay Tanox an undisclosed amount of money, with additional payments as product development progresses	5/90

Source: Bioscan (1992).

Table 3.3. *Hoffmann La Roche's network of agreements*

Name	Products	Content of agreement	Date
Ajinomoto Co. Inc., Immunex	IL-2 technology	Exclusive license outside Japan and Asia (royalties from Hoffmann via prior agreement)	11/84
Alpha 1 Biomedicals Inc.	Thymosins	Hoffmann has partial buy-back rights, holds foreign rights	
Alpha 1 Biomedicals Inc.	Thymosin alpha-1	Licensing agreement	1/89
Amgen	Neupogen® G-CSF	Development and marketing agreement for Europe	9/88
Angenics	Screening tests	Licensing and sponsored research agreement	7/86
Biogen N.V.	Hepatitis diagnostic antigen	Supply agreement	
Biogen N.V.	B-cell growth factors	Licensing agreement, Biogen retains co-marketing rights	11/87
Boehringer Ingelheim Vetmedica G.m.b.H.	Antimicrobial substance aditoprim	Joint development agreement, synthesized by Roche, future marketing by Boehringer	11/88
Chiron Corp.	IL-2 patents	Cross-licensing agreement	12/88
Chiron Corp.	Products based on ras oncogene research	Five-year R&D agreement, Hoffmann to share in funding of oncogene research at Chiron in exchange for exclusive marketing rights to the resulting products	1989

Company	Product	Agreement	Date
Chiron Corp.	IL-2 products	Joint development and marketing agreement – both companies to market Proleukin® and Roferon-A® in Switzerland and in all EEC countries except Denmark and Greece	4/90
Cortecs Ltd.	Oral delivery formulation of Roche's genetically engineered alpha-IFN, Roferon-A®	Collaborative R&D agreement – Cortecs to develop drug delivery system	8/90
Dainippon Pharmaceutical Co.	IL-1 alpha	Cross-licensing agreement	2/90
Genentech Inc.	IFN (alpha, beta)	Development and exclusive marketing agreement	
Genentech Inc.	DNase to treat cystic fibrosis and chronic bronchitis	Ten-year development and marketing agreement	3/92
Genica Pharmaceuticals Corp.	PCR DNA analysis	Development agreement	
Genzyme	HA as drug delivery vehicle	Research agreement, Genzyme provides therapeutic grade HA	1987
Harvard Univ. Medical School, Institute for Chemistry	Treatments for immunological diseases	Five-year $10m. research agreement, Roche to receive rights to license patents	11/89
Immunex, Ajinomoto	IL-2	Collaboration agreement to research, develop (Immunex), and market (Hoffmann) – originally signed (1/84), extended	8/86
Immunomedics	Radiolabeled MAbs for CEA for cancer diagnostics	Licensing agreement	6/86
Interferon Sciences Inc.	Alferon® N alpha-IFN for treatment of genital warts	Marketing agreement	3/88

Table 3.3. (cont.)

Name	Products	Content of agreement	Date
Interferon Sciences Inc.	Alferon® N Injection	Licensing agreement	3/91
Marion Merrell Dow	Ro-40-5967 third-generation calcium channel blocker	Joint development and marketing agreement	4/91
MetPath Inc.	DNA probe assays for cancer, infectious diseases, and genetic disorders using PCR technology	Development agreement	7/91
Protein Design Labs.	PDL anti-Tac MAb to prevent organ rejection	Licensing agreement	1989
SangStat Medical Corp.	Pregnancy test kits to detect the presence of human chorionic gonadotrophin	Supply agreement through Produits Roche	12/90
Schering-Plough Corp.	Alpha-IFN	Cross-licensing agreement (Biogen holds European patent, Hoffmann holds US, developed through Genentech), Europe not included in agreement	5/85
Scios Inc.	Nazdel® delivery system with Hoffmann's anti-obesity and growth hormone products	Scios to conduct pre-clinical investigation	6/86
Summa Medical Corp.	MAb for imaging blood clots	Licensing agreement	10/87
Syntex Corp.	Toradol IM (ketorolac tromethamine) injectable analgesic	Joint development and marketing agreement – Syntex to manufacture and distribute, Roche to co-ordinate marketing	4/90

Xenova	Novel biochemical assay for immunosuppressant screening	Roche granted exclusive worldwide rights to develop and market active compounds arising from earlier research collaboration	4/92
XOMA Corp	MAb cell lines for STD diagnostics	Licensed to Hoffmann	1985

Source: Bioscan (1992).

Table 3.4. *Merck's network of agreements*

Name	Products	Content of agreement	Date
AB Astra	Tonocard to treat cardiac arrhythmia	Marketing agreement	1982
AB Astra	Losec for ulcers	Marketing agreement for USA	1986
AB Astra	Plendil® entry for blocker hypertension	Marketing agreement for USA	
ALZA Corp.	Oral controlled-release form of diltiazem	Licensing agreement – Merck to market drug worldwide under a royalty-bearing license, ALZA retains some rights to market in USA	3/90
ALZA Corp.	Sustained-release bolus delivery system for ivermectin, a bovine antiparasitic	R&D agreement	1985
Behringwerke	Vaccines	Marketing rights in Germany	
Biogen N.V., Mass. General Hospital	rDNA Mullerian inhibiting substance (MIS)	Development and marketing agreement – Merck to fund clinicals and market worldwide, Biogen to manufacture	2/87
Celltech Group p.l.c.	Oral arthritis therapeutic based on enzyme research	R&D agreement	1989
Chiron	Recombivax® HB yeast-based hepatitis **B** vaccine	Exclusive worldwide licensing agreement giving Merck right to produce and market	10/84
Duke Univ.	Beta-adrenergic receptor	Research agreement	
E.I. Du Pont	Angiotensin II (AII) receptor antagonists for treating high blood pressure and heart disease	Collaborative research and marketing agreement – Du Pont to have exclusive marketing rights in North America to two of Merck's products (Sinemet and Vaseretic®)	9/89

Hoechst A.G.	Hepatitis B vaccine	Distribution agreement through Behringwerke	1986
ImmuLogic Pharmaceutical Corp.	Vaccines to prevent autoimmune diseases, and AIDS vaccine program	Collaborative development agreement (10/89), extended for two additional years	4/92
Immunetech Pharmaceuticals	Certain future products, excluding pentigetide	Option to market in Germany, Austria, Switzerland, and Benelux countries	2/84
Imperial Cancer Research Technology	MAb M340	Licensing agreement	
Imperial Chemical Industries (ICI)	Prodiax® for diabetes	Licensing agreement	10/86
Imperial Chemical Industries (ICI)	Lisinopril (Prinivil®)	Licensing agreement	1986
Institut Mérieux	Combined vaccine for hepatitis B, diphtheria, tetanus, and polio	R&D agreement	6/91
Instituto Nacional de Biodiversidad (INBio) (Costa Rica)	Natural sources of new therapeutics from the rain forests of Costa Rica	R&D agreement – Merck will fund research in exchange for exclusive rights to any products developed	9/91
Istituto Gentili	MK-217 for treating osteoporosis	Licensing agreement	11/89
Johnson & Johnson	OTC medicines	50/50 joint venture called Johnson & Johnson Merck Consumer Pharmaceuticals Co.	3/89
MedImmune, Inc.	Technology to produce cellular immunity	Acquired licensing rights to technology	1/91
MedImmune, Inc.	HIV MAbs	Development and marketing agreement	12/91
Panlabs®, International	Fermentation strain improvement	Five-year research agreement	1989

Table 3.4. (cont.)

Name	Products	Content of agreement	Date
People's Republic of China	Hepatitis B vaccine	Licensing agreement for vaccine production using Merck's genetically engineered materials	11/89
Purdue Univ.	MAb-based nasal spray for treating rhinovirus infections	Support R&D of Michael Rossmann	late 1985
Repligen Corp.	AIDS polypeptide subunit vaccines	R&D and marketing agreement – Merck has worldwide rights to vaccine technology, Repligen to receive royalties and manufacturing rights	5/87
Shionogi & Co. Ltd.	Recombivax® HB hepatitis B vaccine (developed by Chiron)	Joint development agreement for clinical trials and marketing in Japan	1984
Singapore Biotechnology	Heptavax-B® conventional hepatitis B vaccine	Six-year agreement to produce	
Singapore Biotechnology	rDNA hepatitis B vaccine	Distribution agreement	7/86
SmithKline Beecham Biologicals S.A.	Hepatitis B surface antigens	Worldwide sublicensing agreement covering the manufacture and sale of recombinant hepatitis B vaccines	4/90
Syva	Polyclonal and MAb diagnostics	Formed Syva–Merck joint venture to market	1982
Vical Inc.	Gene-based vaccines for infectious disease	R&D and licensing agreement	6/91

Source: Bioscan (1992).

Table 3.5. *Pfizer's network of agreements*

Name	Products	Content of agreement	Date
Advanced Polymer Systems Inc.	APS microsponge technology	Marketing agreement	4/90
ALZA	OROS® Procardia® nifedipine delivery system	Joint development agreement	1985
Bayer A.G.	Nifedipine GITS	Exclusive marketing rights for Bayer overseas	7/88
Celltech	Celltech's patented rDNA chymosin	Licensing agreement	1988
Collaborative Research, Dow Chemical Co.	Rennin for making cheese by genetic manipulation of yeast	Research, licensing, and worldwide marketing agreement – Dow assigned marketing rights to Pfizer	1/88
Ecogen Inc.	Bt-based biopesticides	Manufacturing agreement	1/92
Genzyme	Orthopedic products using hyaluronic acid technology	R&D agreement through Howmedica	2/87
Ligand Pharmaceuticals Inc.	Therapeutics for osteoporosis and other bone diseases	Five-year joint discovery program	5/91
The Liposome Co.	TLC D-99	Licensing agreement – Pfizer to have worldwide marketing rights	11/90
Microvascular Systems, MPS (IGI)	Liposome formulations for injectable animal vaccines	Development agreement	9/87
Moleculon	Poroplastic® controlled-release disc used in Paratect® antiparasitic bolus system	Manufacturing agreement	

Table 3.5. (*cont.*)

Name	Products	Content of agreement	Date
Natural Product Sciences Inc.	Central nervous system agent with excitatory amino acid antagonists	Three-year agreement and licensing agreement with $2.75m. Pfizer investment (1987), original agreement extended for two years	10/90
Neurogen Corp.	Drugs to treat anxiety	Five-year R&D collaboration – Pfizer to fund Neurogen's R&D program in exchange for worldwide manufacturing and marketing rights to one anxiolytic drug developed through the collaboration	2/92
Oncogene Science	Anti-oncogenes (tumor suppressor genes), oncogenes, TIF, TGIs (tumor growth inhibitors) as cancer therapeutics	Five-year, $12m. collaborative R&D agreement, licensing options, Pfizer to fund construction of lab and to have exclusive worldwide rights to all resulting products (7/86) – agreement extended to add five years, $16m. in research support to Oncogene for a new project based on tumor suppressor genes	12/90
Petroferm	Petroferm's Emulsan®	Manufacturing and marketing agreement	1984
Scios Inc.	Products to treat diabetes and obesity	Five-year, $30m. joint development agreement through Metabolic Biosystems Inc. (unit formed by Scios for venture) – Pfizer and the new unit will share manufacturing and marketing	1988

Wellcome Group	Pfizer's beta thymidine for Wellcome's Retrovir®	rights for certain therapeutics in the USA and Canada, Pfizer will hold exclusive manufacturing and marketing rights for the rest of the world	
		Long-term supply agreement	
XOMA	Xomen E5® MAb-based therapeutic for septic shock	Development and marketing agreement	6/87

Source: Bioscan (1992).

speculated that Du Pont's research expenditures during the period 1920–50 would be more highly correlated with its less spectacular, incremental improvements:

Although ... [large industrial firms] ... may be perfect vehicles of applied research and innovation, they may not have adequate economic incentives for sponsoring the ideal environment for conducting the basic research leading to the inventions underlying important innovations, or they may not be able to create that environment. (Mueller, 1962, pp. 345–6.)[18]

Many authors have now recognized that large firms have comparative advantages in large-scale development and commercialization of innovations, whereas smaller groups are better suited for upstream research (e.g., Arrow, 1983; Holmstrom, 1989; Scherer and Ross, 1990; Sylos Labini, 1992). Big firms have large organizations, which are critical for systematic product and process development, and they have extended commercialization assets. They also face lower capital costs. A reason for this is that they can resort more extensively to internal funds. Small firms cannot finance large-scale development projects internally, and they have to borrow. In innovation, moral hazard is severe, and capital markets command a premium. Moreover, large firms face a lower cost of external capital, as they can spread uncertainty over a larger number of activities (and innovation projects), and more generally their solvency is less at risk.

But the flexible and informal organizations of small groups facilitate invention and the production of ideas. Arrow (1983) suggested that the organizational "distance" between inventors and the people responsible for internal financing of innovation is greater in large firms than in small ones. This generates greater information loss in internal communication. Larger firms thus face more intense problems of asymmetric information, and therefore smaller firms make closer to optimal investments in more novel and riskier innovation projects (provided that they can finance them). (See also Holmstrom, 1989.)

This suggests that a division of labor in innovation can be socially efficient, as it allows different agents (small and large firms) to focus on the tasks in which they have comparative advantages (Arora and Gambardella, 1993b). Arrow (1983) also argued that large and small firms will recognize their "natural" abilities, and they will specialize accordingly. Large firms will recognize that they can save budgets by resorting to small innovative firms for ideas and risky innovation projects.[19] Small firms will then invest in research even though they know that they will be unable to develop and commercialize their inventions, as they expect to sell their research outcomes to larger firms. Patents and intellectual property rights will be critical to prevent opportunistic behavior in information exchange. But with adequate intellectual property laws, a market for research outcomes arises:

The existence of markets for research outcomes ... alters the incentives for research within large firms ... For now the firm has an alternative supply of research outcomes on which to base its development of innovations. The constraints on its development expenditures imply that anticipated availability of research outcomes on the market will reduce the incentives to use only internally generated research outcomes.

There are limits to relying on the market for research inputs into the development process. For example, internal research capability ... is needed to evaluate ... [externally purchased research outcomes] ... and to synthesize them with other research outcomes, whether internal or external. But clearly some substitution takes place.

If this analysis is meaningful, it suggests a division of labor according to firm size. Smaller firms will tend to specialize more in the research phase and in smaller development processes; larger firms will devote a much smaller proportion of their research and development budget to the research phase. They will specialize in larger developments and will buy a considerable fraction of the research basis for their subsequent development of innovations. (Arrow, 1983, pp. 26–7.)

But if this argument is correct, why did we not see a division of labor in innovation in the pharmaceutical industry for many years? Why do we see it only now? After all, patents have been a forceful instrument for protecting drug innovations at least since the end of World War II.

In Arora and Gambardella (1993b and 1994b), we addressed these questions on a general basis. We argued that in many industries there has been a "technical" constraint upon what we called the "division of innovative labor." With limited understanding of the general and abstract laws of phenomena, highly experimental research produced information that was very context-specific. Research outcomes depended upon the local conditions in which experiments were conducted, and they could be used only for the specific purposes for which they were generated. Because it was difficult to extend technological information to other situations, the market for research outcomes was "thin", which reduced economic incentives to specialize in research in order to sell its findings. Moreover, the production of research outcomes depended primarily on learning, experience, and tacit capabilities. It was therefore difficult to articulate technological information in forms that could be usefully (and cheaply) transferred and used by other agents. Relatedly, it was difficult to describe it in forms that could be effectively patented or protected by intellectual property rights. Hence, research outcomes had to be used, for development and commercialization purposes, by the same agent that produced them, with the implied absence of a division of innovative labor.

This also implied that large firms, which had established development, production, and commercialization assets, were then at an advantage, and they had greater incentives to invest in R&D. Smaller firms, with limited downstream assets, could not utilize their research outcomes themselves, and they had fewer incentives to invest in research.[20]

With the growth of scientific knowledge and computational capabilities (especially over the last ten or twenty years), information for innovation, including information arising from experimental observations, can be increasingly related to different objects and contexts; hence, it can be used for different purposes, and it can be used by agents other than those who produced it. The market for research outcomes becomes "thicker". This enhances the economic advantages of specializing in research to sell technological information or other research outcomes (provided that intellectual property rights adapt). Also, as information for innovation can be related to more general frameworks, it can be articulated in forms that are more immediately intelligible to other parties. Not only can it be transferred at lower costs, but, because it can be articulated in more meaningful ways, it can also be protected more forcefully. A division of innovative labor between large firms and small innovative companies, along the lines suggested by Arrow, can then arise.

Division of labor in drug research and innovation

The pharmaceutical industry is a natural application of the framework discussed above. As argued earlier in this chapter, when drug discovery depended primarily upon extensive screening of molecules, and scientists had little knowledge about the human body and the action of drugs, the key assets for innovation were static and dynamic economies of scale. But scale and learning are indivisible assets. They can be created and utilized only in lumpy forms. Also, they can only be exchanged in lumpy forms (i.e., by selling the entire laboratory). Moreover, pharmaceutical companies had to have sales capabilities to generate the necessary cash flow to maintain large in-house research facilities, and to invest in extensive applied research screening. Thus, with established commercialization assets and financial resources, it was natural that they developed and marketed their own discoveries.[21]

With the recent advances in molecular biology and genetic engineering, drug innovations increasingly depend upon knowledge and information that are "generic" in nature, and that can be transferred at low cost among different agents. For instance, information about receptor structures can be comprehended by agents different from the ones who discovered them (provided that the "buyer" is knowledgeable in the field). Similarly, the properties of certain compounds, the action of drugs, or newly discovered activities of the human body can be expressed in fairly universal categories, and they can be transferred and used by other parties.[22]

More generally, unlike scale and experience, the knowledge-base for drug discovery has become more "divisible." With suitable contracts and intellectual property rights, relevant "fragments" of knowledge can be exchanged among specialized agents. A certain company or scientific institution can establish the structure of a family of receptors in the human body. Another party can clarify their biological activity. A third agent can determine the molecular action of a family of compounds that fit the receptor sites and counteract the undesired behaviour of cells. The entire set of information can be brought to a fourth party who controls resources to carry out long and costly clinical trials, and market the product.

A division of labor in pharmaceutical innovation then becomes "technically" possible. (See also Arora and Gambardella, 1993c.) Large firms recognize that they can take advantage of knowledge, information, and product opportunities created by small innovative firms. Moreover, they can take advantage of the fact that, by resorting to an external market for ideas, they can "buy" only research outcomes that have shown some success. They save costs of unsuccessful projects, and they can shift at least part of the risk of initial research stages onto the small innovative firms. The latter, which have natural comparative advantages in producing ideas, realize that, with "divisibility" of science, they can invest in discovery, and sell their research outputs to larger firms. Patents and intellectual property rights will be very important to sustain the incentives of smaller firms to invest in upstream research.[23] The rise of biotech companies is also encouraged by the general applicability of their knowledge-base. Knowledge about the properties of certain drugs, and the way they act inside human receptors, can be employed for different purposes (e.g., different uses of the same family of drugs). Markets for knowledge are thicker, and small firms can supply their services to many clients.[24]

Moreover, a knowledge-based division of labor cannot be mediated by arm's-length market transactions (Arora and Gambardella, 1993b). The transfer of knowledge and other relevant information for drug research and innovation requires longer-term contracts and tighter interactions, like joint ventures, research contracts, and similar arrangements. The transfer of knowledge requires mutual learning and the exchange of complementary tacit information (Arora, 1991). It also requires mutual trust. Furthermore, fruitful relationships often depend on the ability of joining resources and knowledge-bases to carry out specific projects, rather than on the mere delivery of an idea, or compound, from a biotech firm, or a university, to a large firm.

Finally, tighter relationships between large pharmaceutical manufacturers and smaller biotech companies may be necessary to relieve the latter of part of the risk of initial research stages. Through collaborative agreements, small capital investments in innovative firms, or other relationships, larger companies would provide financial and organizational support. Small innovative companies might be unable to bear the entire risk of their research efforts, and thus they might not engage in research in the first place. Although large companies would now bear some of the risk of starting research (with respect to pure arm's-length market transactions), they would nonetheless bear lower risks than with full internalization of these projects, and they could take advantage of the greater abilities of the smaller companies in earlier research stages.

The changing attitude of large pharmaceutical companies towards a division of labor in innovation

The formation of many small–medium research-intensive biotech companies in the 1980s might suggest that present network relationships in the pharmaceutical industry are driven by an increased supply of specialized research skills. In fact, established pharmaceutical companies display increasing demand for such collaborations. This is important, as it is sometimes argued that the present wave of network arrangements in the drug sector is a transitory phenomenon, prompted by a change in the technological paradigm. But as large firms realize the advantages of a division of labor in innovation, the new trend may become a more persistent feature of this industry. As the previous discussion suggested, if a market for technological ideas arises, the large firms themselves will find it advantageous to use this market instead of relying entirely on their internal research.[25]

Large firms show strategic and organizational inertia (Henderson and Clark, 1990; Pavitt, 1992; Henderson, 1993), and pharmaceutical corporations are no exception (Sharp, 1991b). Sapienza (1989a) argued that established drug companies exhibit "bureaucratic stolidity," which brings about managerial risk aversion rather than innovation. But some pharmaceutical multinationals are modifying their innovation strategies, and they are recognizing the benefits of a division of innovative labor.

One could easily list the vast number and the heterogeneous forms of agreements of major pharmaceutical corporations worldwide. Tables 3.2–3.5 reported the external linkages of four representative companies. As suggested earlier, many large US and European (and even Japanese) drug corporations have established linkages of similar breadth and intricacy. Moreover, chapter 7 will present careful statistical analysis of the propensity of large companies to develop external relationships in this industry. Here we look instead at the recent position of some large pharmaceutical firms. Although they provide somewhat scattered evidence, these examples elucidate the important changes in the views of drug corporations about innovation strategies and knowledge-sharing with partners. (See also *FT*, 1989a.)

Some pharmaceutical multinationals have recognized their "bureaucratic stolidity," and have undertaken profound reorganizations to encourage creativity and risky innovations. Alex Kramer, the Chairman of Ciba-Geigy, has declared that his company "should no longer navigate as a supertanker, but as a flotilla with independent captains on every ship" (*Scrip*, 1991b, p. 15).[26] More importantly, large companies are changing their attitude towards external partnering. William Parfet, President of Upjohn, declared that the only way pharmaceutical firms can afford the increased R&D costs is to form strategic alliances with academia, technology start-up firms, and even with competitors with complementary R&D strengths and strategies (*MKTLTR*, 1992). Similarly, as we shall see in more detail in the next chapter, Eli Lilly recognized its narrow vision about full internalization of resources for innovation. It is now hiring high-profile scientists from research institutions, it is trying to combat its "not invented here" syndrome, and it is encouraging systematic partnerships with research-intensive companies (*BW*, 1992b). Finally, Sandoz set up a 150 million dollar program, called Innovascan, which sponsors promising new lines of research suggested by internal divisions or in collaboration with external parties. The program plans to support the various projects, including collaborations, from research to the marketplace (*Scrip*, 1991a). An official declaration of Max Link, the CEO of Sandoz Pharma Ltd., epitomizes the changing attitude of pharmaceutical multinationals: "We believe that the stronger a multinational is in a particular field, the higher the probability that a co-operation will yield positive results" (*Scrip*, 1991a, p. 7).

The new philosophy of pharmaceutical corporations is also exemplified by some recent remarks of Jurgen Drews, Director of Corporate Research at Hoffmann La Roche (*MKTLTR*, 1991). He emphasized that even large multinationals have to abandon the idea of covering an exhaustive range of research areas. The key for success is to specialize in selected fields, and to rely on partners for complementary research and specialized technical expertise. He also argued that individual competitiveness will be replaced by competition among networks of firms based on trust, credibility, and openness of research.

More recently, Drews discussed the transformation of the market structure of the international drug sector (Drews, 1992). He predicted that the industry will polarize around two fundamental agents: giant multinational corporations with considerable abilities to manage large and complex organizations, and small–medium firms with sophisticated scientific expertise in selected areas, which will act as "suppliers of ideas, product opportunities and new technologies" (Drews, 1992, p. 138).

4   In-house scientific research and innovation: case studies of large US pharmaceutical companies

Introduction

As argued in the previous chapters, there are important differences in the ability of firms to utilize scientific knowledge. As scientific knowledge influences the most creative stages of drug development, this can translate into notable differences in the innovation and market performance of drug companies. Moreover, these differential abilities can be magnified by the growing scientific intensity of pharmaceutical research:

The scientific ferment ... is separating the drug companies in terms of capability much more than they used to be. Some are going into much more imaginative processes to look for new drugs, others are still conducting things the way they used to. The sky is indeed bluer, but only for some. (Dr. Peter Goldman, Professor of Pharmacology, Harvard University, quoted in *BW*, 1979, p. 137.)

Pharmaceuticals are changing ... from a business in which everyone succeeds to one in which success is more selective ... [T]here will be a greater divergence in individual performances. (Eugene L. Step of Eli Lilly, quoted in *BW*, 1979, p. 145.)

This chapter examines whether, in spite of the public nature of science, large US pharmaceutical firms differ in their ability to exploit scientific knowledge, and whether this implies differences in their innovation and market performance. The analysis is based upon case studies of some major US drug manufacturers. The case studies show that the most successful US pharmaceutical firms during the 1980s were those that invested systematically in scientific research. This enabled them to generate scientific knowledge internally, and to exploit external knowledge more successfully. The case studies also show that better capabilities of exploiting science, and hence better innovation and market performance, are associated with firms that organized, at least in part, their internal research in ways that encouraged a scientifically creative atmosphere through open research and linkages with the scientific community.

The case studies also highlight the self-reinforcing properties of the science–innovation spiral in the pharmaceutical industry. Firms with better scientific capabilities have been able to produce a systematic flow of new drugs. They have accumulated internal funds that were reinvested in science, thereby strengthening their competitive position. Firms with limited in-house scientific expertise have faced serious difficulties in becoming major innovators in this industry.

The case studies cover the following firms: Merck, Eli Lilly, Bristol-Myers, Squibb, Smithkline, Syntex, American Home Products, and Rorer. It can be seen from table 4.1 that they include the first four firms in terms of 1986 US pharmaceutical sales, and five out of the first six. Overall, the eight firms above cover 36 percent of the 1986 US pharmaceutical sales of the top fifty companies in this market (*MAN*, 1987).

The case studies provide a representative sample of the different strategies of the largest US pharmaceutical companies. Merck and Eli Lilly are highly research-intensive firms with strong in-house scientific capabilities. Bristol-Myers has strong marketing assets and a strong competitive position in non R&D-intensive products; it invested heavily in research during the 1980s to enter the market for patented drugs. Squibb, Smithkline and Syntex have good in-house research; their marketing position, however, relied upon the sales of one major product ("one-drug companies"). American Home Products is another marketing giant with a strong position in non R&D-intensive products. Rorer is a medium-sized firm with modest in-house research; during the 1980s, it attempted to expand its research operations to break into the market for R&D drugs.

By and large, these stories cover all the interesting cases for our purposes. One could add cases of other major US pharmaceutical companies (e.g., Pfizer, Upjohn, Warner-Lambert). However, they would only reiterate the points developed for the firms that have been investigated. The following sections present each case study in turn. There is also a concluding section presenting the lessons from the case studies.

Merck

Merck was the most successful pharmaceutical firm during the 1980s. It introduced a host of new drugs. It also has a number of compounds in late clinical trials, which suggests that its competitive position is likely to be reinforced in the near future (see table 4.2; see also *CMR*, 1987b, and *UST*, 1987).

Merck's high performance rested upon superior in-house research expertise. This, in turn, is associated with an organization of internal research that stimulates scientific creativity, and that resembles that of

Table 4.1. *1986 pharmaceutical sales and 1983–88 average R&D/sales ratio of the eight firms in the case studies*

Company	Rank of company in 1986 US pharm. sales	1986 US pharm. sales (million $)	1986 world pharm. sales (million $)	Average R&D/sales ratio (percent)
American Home Prods.	1	2,053.0	2,933.3	4.4
Merck	2	1,749.0	3,441.0	11.3
Smithkline-Beckman	3	1,626.3	2,502.2	9.8
Bristol-Myers	4	1,592.5	3,598.0	5.9
Eli Lilly	6	1,493.8	2,120.0	11.8
Squibb	11	1,016.9	1,529.6	10.8
Syntex	19	537.5	803.2	14.7
Rorer	23	471.0	845.0	7.1

Source: 1986 sales data and company ranking from *MAN* (1987); average R&D/sales ratio from R&D and sales data in *Moody's Industrial Manual* (various years).

Table 4.2. *Merck: major new drugs in the market or in the pipeline, late 1980s*

Drug	Category	Year of market approval/status	Notes
Primaxin	Antibiotic	1985	—
Pepcid	H2 antagonist	1985	—
Vasotec	ACE-inhibitor (anti-hypertensive)	1986	Second ACE-inhibitor drug in the market after Squibb's Capoten
Mevacor	Anti-cholesterol	1987	First anti-cholesterol drug; spectacular sales growth in first two years of marketing
Prinvil	ACE-inhibitor	1988	Second-generation Vasotec; marketed with ICI
Losec	Anti-ulcer	1990(?)	Expects approval also for therapies other than ulcer (Zollinger–Ellison syndrome and gastro-esophageal reflux disease)
Proscar	Benign prostate tumor	1992	Expected to become Merck's third one-billion-dollar drug by 1994
MK 538/Prodiac	Aldose reductase inhibitor	In late clinical trials	

Source: BS&C (1989d), and other trade magazine sources.

academic departments.[1] Merck's laboratories are very informal, and scientists can easily be in touch with one another, which is explicitly meant to attract top-ranking scientists from university, and make them feel comfortable in an academic-like environment. Moreover, Merck's scientists enjoy unusual freedom. They often take autonomous decisions about research lines to pursue, and on many occasions they investigate topics of personal interest (*BW*, 1987).

Research at Merck is divided into therapeutic areas, which are organized into projects. Projects typically correspond to compounds that have shown some promise in early experimental stages. Each project, including apparently successful ones, has no budget granted by authority. This is an interesting feature of Merck's research organization. If the head scientist of a particular project believes that her work needs additional resources, she has to convince researchers in other fields or projects to commit part of their budgets and time to her program. Resources are thus allocated according to the scientists' evaluation of different research lines (*BW*, 1987; *UST*, 1987).

This model bears interesting similarities with peer-group evaluation in the scientific community. Moreover, within the scientific community, when early breakthroughs open new research opportunities, many scientists rush into the new areas. They are lured by the pecuniary and non-pecuniary rewards that may derive from research in relatively unexplored directions, which exhibit higher potential for discovery. Thus, the allocation of scientists' time and resources is chosen by the scientists themselves, who are the best "judges" of the scientific potential of different research programs. Similarly, company scientists at Merck enjoy some discretion (albeit probably not full) to move across projects, and therefore to contribute to projects that they regard to be of some value. Their incentives to move into potentially successful projects are, of course, the pecuniary and non-pecuniary rewards that may arise from being part of a fruitful research endeavor.

Merck's research organization also fosters systematic relations with the scientific community. Merck's library has a reputation comparable to the best academic centers. The company regularly organizes internal seminars of the world's top academic scientists.[2] In addition, Merck's scientists are encouraged to establish autonomous linkages with academic institutions, even for projects not officially approved by top managers.[3]

The story of Mevacor, the anti-cholesterol drug marketed in 1987, illustrates Merck's scientific skills in drug discovery, and the effectiveness of a research organization that draws in many ways from the model of academia. As discussed in chapter 2, Mevacor is a major example of discovery by design. Merck scientists first studied how cholesterol is formed within the human body. They then searched for a "weak" link in the peptide chain that produces cholesterol. They found an enzyme that, if inhibited, could block the production of cholesterol. Finally, they searched for a compound with suitable characteristics that could inhibit the action of the enzyme.

Mevacor's story also highlights Merck's ability to build upon publicly available science. Although mevalonic acid, a chemical link in the cholesterol chain, was first isolated by Merck's scientists in 1956, research on anti-cholesterol drugs was spurred by later findings. Between 1972 and 1974, Michael S. Brown and Joseph L. Goldstein of the University of Texas identified the key steps in the production of cholesterol, work for which they were awarded the Nobel Prize in 1985. Brown and Goldstein's findings motivated Merck's scientists to launch research on cell culture assays for cholesterol inhibitors as early as 1975. In 1978, Merck isolated lovastatin, the Mevacor compound, from a micro-organism of the soil. Mevacor's NDA was approved for marketing in August 1987. The product reached $260 million sales in 1988, the first full year of marketing, and it reached $1 billion sales in 1991 (*BW*, 1987; FDA, 1988; *BS&C*, 1989d; *FT*, 1992a).

As soon as their discovery had been made, Brown and Goldstein's achievements became publicly available. Yet, Merck was the only company that effectively exploited their findings. Other firms had interests in the anti-cholesterol business. Bristol-Myers, for instance, already had an anti-cholesterol product, Questar. As we shall see later, in the early 1980s Bristol-Myers did not have significant in-house scientific expertise. Unlike Merck, it was unable to use the new (publicly available) discovery to improve Questar, and it has not yet come up with a major new anti-cholesterol product.[4]

Mevacor's success also depended upon strict ties between research and marketing. In 1979, soon after the synthesis of lovastatin, Merck's scientists gathered with marketing managers to assess the commercial potential of an anti-cholesterol product. They wanted to know the market opportunities of a new anti-cholesterol drug before committing large fractions of the company's research time and expenditure to the project. Marketing managers suggested that the market for anti-cholesterol drugs was wide open. Moreover, early contacts with marketing managers helped in perfecting some characteristics of the drug. The marketing staff informed the scientists that Bristol-Myers' Questar, the major product in the market, was unpleasant to swallow. Merck's scientists then directed part of their research to make the new drug more palatable. Although not a key feature of the product, this proved to be a non-trivial factor in promoting its market diffusion (*BW*, 1987).

Apart from Mevacor, in 1985 the FDA approved Vasotec, the second ACE-inhibitor anti-hypertensive drug after Squibb's Capoten. By 1988,

Vasotec had already captured 46.6 percent of the hypertensive market against Capoten's 49.3 percent. Merck has also launched Pepcid, an anti-ulcer drug which is competing against the "old" anti-ulcer compounds Tagamet of Smithkline and Zantac of Glaxo, as well as with the newcomer Axid of Eli Lilly. In 1992 it launched Proscar against benign enlarged prostate in men. Proscar rationally inhibits an enzyme that is responsible for enlargement of the prostate, a condition that affects millions of men. Proscar has very good commercial expectations. It is expected to become Merck's third one-billion-dollar drug after Mevacor and Vasotec.[5]

Merck has also capitalized on its previous research successes. At present, it is developing Zocor, the second-generation Mevacor, and it is launching (jointly with ICI Chemicals of the UK) Prinvil, the second-generation Vasotec. It is also launching Losec (with the Swedish company Astra), a new anti-ulcer drug. Losec, which exploits previously accumulated knowledge of anti-ulcer drugs (which led to the introduction of Pepcid), is also believed to be effective in treating the Zollinger-Ellison syndrome (a hypersecretory disease) and a gastro-esophageal reflux disease. Although Proscar is pioneering an entirely new market for Merck, its development relied on Merck's expertise in designing enzyme inhibitor drugs (BS&C, 1989d; NYT, 1992a and 1992b).

Finally, Merck's high-quality research and its experience in drug development have enhanced its reputation with the FDA. Mevacor was approved by the FDA in the record time of ten months (BW, 1987; FDA, 1988). Similarly, Prinvil was approved in twenty months, about 10 months less than the average waiting time (BW, 1988d). Development of many new drugs has helped Merck in acquiring good expertise about how the FDA wants the clinical trials to be conducted, and how to properly file an NDA. Moreover, Merck has a staff of 120 people to organize information from laboratory and clinical trials and to prepare NDA reports (BW, 1987). The company pays a great deal of attention to the structure, format, and composition of NDA reports, which is of great help in speeding up the revision process.

Eli Lilly

Eli Lilly is another research-intensive firm, with a long-standing tradition of drug research and innovative performance, especially in antibiotics. It was one of the first corporations worldwide to undertake biotechnology research, as early as the mid-1970s (OTA, 1984; Pisano, Shan, and Teece, 1988). This translated into a successful early entry into biotechnology. By 1985 Eli Lilly had already commercialized two biotechnology-based human therapeutics, human insulin (the first biotech drug to reach the

Table 4.3. *Eli Lilly's drugs with 1989 sales of at least $100 million*

Drug	Category	1989 sales (million $)
Ceclor	Oral antibiotic	715
Prozac	Anti-depressant	350
Humulin	Human insulin	300
Keflex–Keftab	Oral antibiotics	190
Animal insulin		165
Dobutrex	Heart failure drug	150
Tylan		145
Vancocin	Injectable antibiotic	130
Darvon		125
Axid	Anti-ulcer	100
Nebcin	Injectable antibiotic	100

Source: NYT (1990g).

market, which was developed and commercialized jointly with Genentech) and the human growth hormone.[6] Eli Lilly also ranked second among all institutions, and first among companies (including large firms and biotech companies), in terms of US patents in genetic engineering granted by December 1987 (twenty-seven patents) (OTAF, 1987).[7]

Eli Lilly is investing in computer-based molecular modeling, and by the end of the 1980s it had already planned to install a supercomputer to design complex molecular structures (*CW*, 1989e). In 1988, it signed an agreement with Agouron Pharmaceuticals, a small biotechnology firm specializing in three-dimensional computerized design of drugs. The agreement involves joint development of new compounds using three-dimensional computer techniques. Lilly is "learning" the new technique from the specialized concern, and it has first manufacturing and marketing rights on new products in exchange for multi-year funding of Agouron research (*Bioscan*, 1988; *CW*, 1988a).

Table 4.3 summarizes Eli Lilly's market performance in the 1980s. In 1989 it had eleven drugs with sales greater than $100 million. Among them, Prozac and Axid, an anti-ulcer drug approved in 1988, are expected to be its major products in the 1990s.

As discussed in chapter 2, Prozac, an anti-depressant approved in December 1987, is an important example of discovery by design. Its development hinged upon vast research efforts, mostly in the public domain, especially since the mid-1970s. Such research efforts were prompted by a new basic understanding of protein receptors, and particularly of the chemistry and action of serotonin. In the 1980s, many companies invested in serotonin drugs. However, Prozac was the first major breakthrough in this field. Eli Lilly's scientists effectively exploited the public information that depression is triggered by quick absorption of serotonin by nerve cells. In-house research expertise was critical for the careful design and development of a drug that attenuated depression by slowing the absorption of serotonin. It was also critical for monitoring and utilizing public knowledge. Lilly's scientists did not develop a new map of the structure of brain receptors, nor did they produce original knowledge about new receptor sites or other characteristics of serotonin receptors. But they utilized this knowledge effectively to make an important discovery.[8]

Moreover, serotonin appears to have numerous potential effects, and Eli Lilly is trying to capitalize on its early entry in this area. Apart from careful monitoring of public research (which is revealing new effects of serotonin, and new serotonin receptors), Lilly's scientists have noted that Prozac spurs weight loss, and they are studying its action against obesity. Paradoxically, they have also observed that, with suitable modifications, Prozac could treat the opposite problem, anorexia (BW, 1988a). Lilly has also signed a $12 million contract with Synaptic Pharmaceutical, a small company specializing in serotonin research. Synaptic has cloned a number of receptors, and it is helping the company in developing serotonin drugs for anxiety, depression, etc. The agreement has already produced four candidate serotonin drugs, which are now in animal tests (BW, 1992a).[9]

In spite of its solid knowledge-bases and research successes, Eli Lilly's competitive prospects for the 1990s have shown some signs of weakness. Prozac is facing increasing competition, and in 1992 its sales did not grow as expected (BW, 1992b). Also, a number of firms with sound in-house scientific bases are entering the field of serotonin drugs (among others, Merck, Smithkline, Glaxo, Janssen Pharmaceutica; see BW, 1992a; see also chapter 2). Moreover, in December 1992 Eli Lilly's patent on its antibiotic Ceclor, one of its key products, expired. Generic manufacturers have already applied to the FDA for competitive products. More importantly, in 1992 Eli Lilly's profits declined considerably (BW, 1992b).

Eli Lilly is reacting through a profound reworking of its strategy (BW, 1992b). Lilly's action appears to match rather closely the discussion in chapter 3. Vaughn Bryson, the new CEO, is making significant steps to transform Eli Lilly's rigid, bureaucratic organization into a far more decentralized decision-making structure.[10] Bryson is also hiring scientists from outside the company. Eli Lilly has now hired high-profile researchers from institutions such as the National Institute of Health and the Center for Disease Control. Executives hope to gather a significant group of talented scientists to revamp Lilly's research. More generally, they are taking serious steps to make both managers and researchers more receptive to outside ideas.

Table 4.4. *Eli Lilly's research alliances in the early 1990s*

Company	Project	Lilly's investment (million $)
Centocor	Developing a drug to combat massive bacterial infections	100.0
Repligen	Hoping to produce drugs to treat trauma shocks and respiratory distress	14.0
Synaptic Pharmaceut.	Research on serotonin-based drugs	12.0
Oclassen Pharmaceut.	Developing an oral drug to treat hepatitis B	7.5
Shaman Pharmaceut.	Working on drugs to treat respiratory virus and herpes	4.0
Sibia	Developing drugs to treat nervous-system diseases such as Alzheimer's	4.0
Bioject	Developing a system to inject medication through the skin without a needle	4.0

Source: BW (1992a and 1992b).

Lilly also recognized that its previous successes produced an excessive "not-invented-here" syndrome. The company has changed dramatically its attitude towards external partnering. Since 1991 it has signed agreements with a number of small companies, and acquired minority stakes and marketing rights for products in development (table 4.4). Such alliances are an obvious recognition of the advantages of the division of innovative labor with smaller research firms: "Bryson is ... expanding an ambitious plan to forge strategic alliances with young research companies that he hopes will pump new products in Lilly's pipeline" (*BW*, 1992b, p. 72).

Of particular importance is the agreement signed in 1991 with Centocor to revamp development of Centocor's compound Centoxin, which treats bacterial infection. Although grounded on a solid research basis, Centoxin's NDA was rejected by the FDA, which cited poor test results. This was an important setback for Centocor, which hoped that Centoxin's commercialization would have helped it in becoming a fully integrated pharmaceutical manufacturer. Eli Lilly offered its greater expertise in drug development to properly meet FDA requirements. Lilly also offered financial resources to enable Centocor to perform additional research that would prove Centoxin's worthiness to the regulator. Finally, Lilly will supply its extended commercialization network for Centoxin sales. In short, while Centocor had considerable research capabilities, Lilly offered better downstream resources. More importantly, both companies have recognized each other's specialization, and they are taking advantage of division of labor instead of seeking forward or backward integration (*BW*, 1992b).

Bristol-Myers/Squibb

In 1989, Bristol-Myers and Squibb merged to form a new giant corporation. During the 1980s, the two firms had fairly diverse, but "partially" successful stories. The merger suggests that neither's strategy was sufficiently effective to cope with the rising competitive pressures of the US pharmaceutical market in the 1990s.

Before the 1980s, Bristol-Myers was specializing in health care and consumer products. It had strong marketing capabilities, but a modest research base. In the 1980s, it took major steps to become a research-oriented group. It started an extensive program to reorganize internal research. In 1986, it concentrated its research laboratories, previously scattered in three separate US locations, in one new research center in Connecticut. The location was chosen because of its proximity to Yale – with which it had signed a broad research agreement in 1982 (see below) – and other universities of New England. This was explicitly meant to facilitate informal contacts between academic and industry scientists (*CMR*, 1986; *WSJ*, 1988a). During the 1980s, Bristol-Myers also made important in-house research investments in genetic engineering and molecular biology (*WSJ*, 1988a).

Moreover, Bristol-Myers entered into research collaborations with various academic institutions.[11] Particularly, in 1982, it signed a comprehensive agreement with Yale University on anti-cancer research. The agreement, which was renewed in 1986, covered a broad number of scientific disciplines, and established that Bristol-Myers financed research at Yale in exchange for a first option on licenses. (See table 3.1; see also *JC*, 1988.) The company also acquired research capabilities in biotechnology via acquisitions. In 1985 and 1986, it acquired Genetic Systems and Oncogen, two important medium-sized firms specializing in biotechnology research (*Bioscan*, 1988; *WSJ*, 1988a).

The new strategy produced some results. Bristol-Myers now performs frontier research in a number of fields, including sophisticated basic research in the area of nerve and brain cell chemistry, and in biotechnology (*WSJ*, 1988a). However, in spite of this successful shift towards research, its market performance did not improve considerably during the 1980s. The company was unable to market a fundamentally new drug, nor were radically new compounds in the pipeline. The sales of its major product, Buspar, a tranquillizer, were not as successful as expected. Moreover, Bristol-Myers was unable to capitalize on its experience in anti-cholesterol drugs. Bristol-Myers pioneered the field with Questar. Yet, Merck's Mevacor has now taken the lead.

Bristol-Myers' story suggests that rapid catch-up strategies are not sufficient to become a leading innovator in this industry. Apart from enormous research costs, clinical trials may well take a decade before new drugs can be marketed. The ten-year time span since Bristol-Myers reorganized its internal research is probably only a fraction of the time actually needed for this strategy to pay off. Moreover, scientific expertise has to be paired with experience in drug development. We saw that Merck's scientific reputation and its expertise in drug development have favored a climate of mutual trust with the FDA, which has often streamlined Merck's drug approvals. In contrast, Buspar's NDA was blocked by the FDA for more than one year. The FDA claimed that the company had not properly conducted two important clinical studies during pre-marketing trials on patients (*WSJ*, 1988a).

Squibb's story during the 1980s is different from Bristol-Myers'. The company had a good research-base. Squibb's success during that decade rested upon the discovery, development and marketing of the first angiotensin-converting-enzyme (ACE) inhibitor anti-hypertensive drug, Capoten.

The origins of Capoten were in the 1960s, and involved two different lines of research (*WSJ*, 1987b). The first line of research was concerned with the genesis of hypertension. Researchers working on hypertension realized that renin, a chemical released by the kidneys, causes blood to produce another chemical, angiotensin I, which in turn produces angiotensin II. Angiotensin II is the ultimate regulator of blood pressure. Overproduction of angiotensin II is a major cause of hypertension as it sharply increases blood pressure. Scientists then realized that they had to find a drug that blocked the action of the enzyme responsible for releasing angiotensin II.

The second line of research was related to the cause of death from the venom of the Brazilian viper. Researchers found that the victim dies because the venom contains an extract that lowers blood pressure by inhibiting the production of angiotensin II. Thus, understanding the chemical structure of the venom offered the opportunity of re-producing a compound for treating hypertension.

John Vane, a British pharmacologist, brought these findings to Squibb. The company was working on heart medicines. Building upon previous knowledge about the causes of hypertension and the action of the viper's venom, Squibb's scientists constructed a molecule that mimicked the function of the viper's compound. Captopril, the chemical compound of Capoten, effectively blocked the enzymes responsible for the conversion of angiotensin. Capoten was first approved for marketing in 1981 to treat severe hypertension, and then in 1985 to treat milder forms.

Once again, the discovery was spurred by publicly available scientific knowledge. Knowledge about angiotensin conversion, the properties of the chemicals that influence blood pressure, as well as the properties of the viper's venom were public information. Squibb had adequate in-house research capabilities to take advantage of the information. First, it was performing scientific research in related domains. This gave it a lead in monitoring external research and in recognizing the potential of the new advances. Second, Squibb's skills in drug design enabled it to use the external knowledge to generate a compound with unique therapeutic properties.

Squibb tried to capitalize on its expertise gained with Capoten's research. It started rational investigation of new uses of Capoten, which led to its approval as a treatment for congestive heart failure, a problem afflicting some 3 million Americans and therefore likely to give additional impetus to the drug's sales. In addition, Squibb has begun studying Capoten as a means of preventing heart attack, which could considerably boost its market performance. In the late 1980s, Squibb also had other drugs in the pipeline. Apart from three new ACE inhibitors and an anti-inflammatory drug, it had high expectations about a new anti-cholesterol drug, Pravachol (*BW*, 1988d).

Despite these actual and potential opportunities, Squibb's market position in the 1980s was not completely secure. Squibb was a "one-drug company." Capoten accounted for about 40 percent of its sales (*BW*, 1988d). The risks for one-drug companies are apparent. As competitors erode the market shares of their main product, a substantial fraction of their profits can be affected. In effect, Capoten faced increasing competition from Merck's Vasotec and Prinvil. This posed no immediate threat to the company. The market for anti-hypertensive drugs was large enough to sustain three products. However, Squibb clearly needed to escape its one-drug-company status. This was necessary to gain greater financial stability, and to plan long-run research.

The 1989 merger integrated two important complementary assets. Apart from the cash flow generated by Capoten, Squibb brought major research capabilities. Bristol-Myers brought marketing skills and an extended marketing network. Bristol-Myers' marketing assets will be particularly valuable to support Capoten's sales. They will also be critical in promoting the commercialization of Squibb's new drug Pravachol.[12] Moreover, Bristol-Myers' financial resources, which stem primarily from its health care and consumer product business, will help Squibb escape the problems typically associated with one-drug companies. They will supply the necessary stability for further research, thereby diminishing the risks of relying only upon the financial flows generated by Capoten. Particularly, Bristol-Myers' financial resources have enabled the new company to invest in research on brain-related disorders, a field that Squibb was planning to investigate but lacked adequate funds. Bristol-Myers also supplied a good research-base in anti-cancer, where Squibb had only just started new research programs (*WSJ*, 1989d).

Smithkline

Smithkline's story during the 1980s is largely associated with Tagamet, the first H2–antagonist anti-ulcer drug, which it introduced to the market in 1977. The company enjoyed a virtual monopoly in the anti-ulcer market between 1978 and 1983. In 1983, Glaxo, a British company with a modest presence in the USA at the time, introduced a competing product, Zantac. Zantac had a few advantages over Tagamet, such as a twice-daily dose against the four times of Tagamet, and less severe side-effects. Moreover, Glaxo undertook an aggressive marketing strategy. In a few years Zantac overtook Tagamet to become the leading anti-ulcer drug (*ECON*, 1986; *BW*, 1988c).

Smithkline reacted by attempting to improve Tagamet. It successfully reduced its dosage to twice per day. Moreover, Smithkline sought to develop various "sons" of Tagamet to diminish its side-effects. These attempts proved to be unsuccessful, and the company has not been able to produce a significantly improved version of the drug (*BW*, 1988c; *WSJ*, 1988b and 1989a).

In 1988, Tagamet's sales fell by 16 percent. Smithkline was another one-drug company. Tagamet accounted for about 25 percent of its sales and 40 percent of its profits. The drop in Tagamet's sales had a major impact on Smithkline's financial performance. Moreover, in 1987, its patent of Dyazide, a blood pressure drug, expired. Dyazide sales dropped by 51 percent because of competition from manufacturers of generic products. In 1988, Smithkline's net income fell to $229.2 million from $570.1 million in 1987 (*BW*, 1988b; *Moody's Industrial Manual*, 1989; *WSJ*, 1989a).

In addition, Smithkline's future prospects were uncertain. In the late 1980s, it had twenty-eight drugs under development, compared with a handful in the early years of the decade. Moreover, in the 1980s it marketed a genetically engineered vaccine against hepatitis B. Yet, its most important

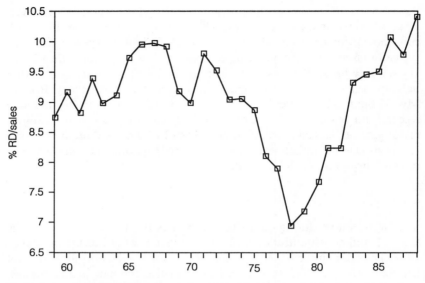

Fig. 4.1. Smithkline's R&D/sales ratio, 1959–88. (*Source:* R&D and sales data for 1959–85 from NBER–Compustat files [Hall *et al.*, 1988]; for 1986–88 from *Moody's Industrial Manual* [various years].)

new drugs had not performed as expected. The sales of its new antibiotic, Monocid, were modest. Its new anti-arthritic drug, Ridaura, showed non-trivial side-effects in clinical tests, which dampened its potential for sale (*Bioscan*, 1988; *BW*, 1988b; *WSJ*, 1989a).

Some industry analysts suggested that Smithkline's low performance depended on its inability to establish major in-house research capabilities during the 1980s (*BW*, 1988b and 1988c; *WSJ*, 1989a). Figure 4.1 reports the ratio of Smithkline's R&D expenditures to sales between 1959 and 1988. The ratio peaked during the late 1960s and the early 1970s. These were the years of Tagamet's research, and a period of strong scientific and intellectual ferment at the Welwyn (UK) research laboratory, where Tagamet was discovered (Sapienza, 1987). The ratio declined immediately after 1974. Tagamet was under regulatory revision for marketing approval, and the bulk of research on the product had ended.[13] The ratio, however, started rising again in 1979, when Tagamet's sales increased sharply, and it rose all the way to 1988. The company appears to have reinvested its profits in research, which suggests that Smithkline's problems did not really arise from its inaction in translating Tagamet's surplus into new research.

In fact, Smithkline's poor research performance can be ascribed to the type of research investments it carried out in the 1980s. Particularly,

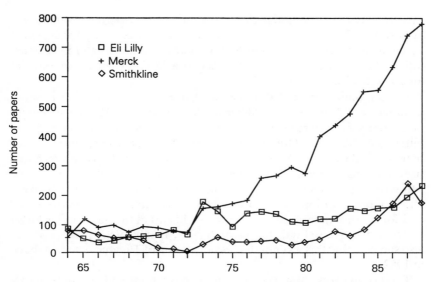

Fig. 4.2. Scientific papers published by company scientists: Smithkline, Eli Lilly, and Merck, 1964–88 (number of papers from a constant 1981 journal set of *Science Citation Index*). (*Source:* CHI Research/Computer Horizons and *Science Citation Index* [various years]. See appendix to chapter 5 for further detail on sources and construction of data.)

Smithkline did not reinvest any substantial portion of its profits in upstream research. Figure 4.2 shows the 1964–88 trend in the number of scientific papers published by Smithkline's scientists, and compares it with Merck's and Eli Lilly's. Although publications are only an approximate measure of in-house scientific capabilities, they can be taken as evidence of the extent to which company scientists are plugged into the scientific network. Between 1975 and 1985 Smithkline had systematically fewer papers than Merck and Eli Lilly. Merck showed a significant upward trend. Eli Lilly had about 100–120 papers per year (in a constant 1981 journal set). Smithkline scientists published about 50 papers per year up to 1981, and only in 1985–88 do we observe a major upswing from below 100 to about 150–200 papers.

Apart from papers, the two scientists responsible for Tagamet's success, James Black and William Duncan, left the company immediately after Tagamet's research ended. Black left in 1973, Duncan in 1979. Black and Duncan were quite valuable assets. Not only did they lead the Tagamet project, but they also helped in creating an environment especially congenial to scientific research. When Black and Duncan resigned, the company did not strive to hire other leading scientists that could replace not only their research skills, but also their capabilities in furthering a stimulating atmosphere. Tagamet's profits were used, for instance, to acquire Beckman Instruments in 1982. Beckman had a good research basis in instrumentation. The acquisition, however, was to a large extent an investment alternative to scientific research.

In sum, Smithkline failed to use the proceeds and the market position acquired with Tagamet to establish as early as the mid-1970s a strong in-house scientific research basis, or at least to continue the research tradition initiated by Black and Duncan. As suggested by the rise in scientific papers between 1985 and 1988, Smithkline did attempt to boost its in-house scientific capabilities after Tagamet had been on the market for some years. Moreover, the 1988 drop in profits prompted executives to undertake a major reorganization of research. They concentrated various research divisions in one major facility. They also sold part of the stakes in Beckman Instruments to raise funds for research (*BW*, 1988b; *WSJ*, 1989a) – which also suggests that this was not the best allocation of Tagamet's surplus back in 1982.

These initiatives, however, appear to have been spurred by external events. The rise in scientific papers during 1985–88 corresponds to the first threats from Glaxo's Zantac. The reorganization of research followed evident needs for restructuring after the drop in performance. In a sector like drugs, where scientific research pays off after a decade or so, these moves were unlikely to yield immediate commercial results. Tagamet had a virtual monopoly in the anti-ulcer market for five years. Smithkline could have established strong in-house scientific research capabilities before Glaxo entered the market. It did not find such stimuli internally, and waited until competitive pressures rendered it necessary to accomplish a profound reorganization of research.

Paradoxically, Smithkline's story corroborates the view that market success in the research-intensive ethical drug business is a self-reinforcing process. Previous successes bring about resources to afford long-run investments in scientific research, which sets the ground for future successes. Smithkline failed in one link of this chain. It did not exploit past successes to build a solid in-house scientific research basis, and this undermined its capabilities for enjoying cumulative advantages. In 1989, Smithkline merged with the British pharmaceutical company Beecham. The new company is another giant corporation in the drug business, with significant research and marketing capabilities. Among other things, Beecham has supplied the necessary financial stability after Smithkline's decline in performance following its difficulties in building on its early success with Tagamet.

Syntex

Syntex is another one-drug company. It produces Naprosyn, a non-steroidal anti-inflammatory drug based on the compound naproxen. Naprosyn, which was first marketed in 1976, is one of the world's top-selling drugs. At the end of the 1980s, it had yearly sales of around $700–800 million. [14]

As with all one-drug companies, Syntex's major concern is that its overall performance depends on one product. Naprosyn is experiencing a serious competitive challenge from Ciba-Geigy's Voltaren, which was introduced in the USA in late 1988, and which is gaining market share against Naprosyn. In 1989, Upjohn introduced another non-steroidal anti-inflammatory drug, Ansaid, which poses additional competitive threats (*BS&C*, 1988 and 1989f). Syntex also faces potential competitive threats from generic products that may flood the market after the expiry of Naprosyn's patent in 1993.

Syntex is reacting to Naprosyn's patent expiration. It is developing new production technologies to manufacture Naprosyn at competitive prices after 1993. It hopes to meet competition from generic products by cutting Naprosyn's price. It now produces Naprosyn in five plants which use batch processes. Syntex is developing and testing three continuous processes which make extensive use of cost-saving automated technologies, and hopes to concentrate all Naprosyn's production in one large efficient plant. Although this is an important strategy, Syntex will probably be unable to cut Naprosyn's price substantially. Because of the relatively small size of the market for pharmaceutical products, drug manufacturers cannot usually exploit economies of scale as extensively as in the commodity chemical business (*CW*, 1988c).

Syntex is also patenting a number of different ways to fabricate Naprosyn. For instance, only one of the three processes under development uses Naprosyn's base compound, naproxen, as raw material. The company also claims it can manufacture Naprosyn using different feedstocks and processes. By patenting various Naprosyn processes, Syntex can make it harder for generics producers to manufacture the product after its patent expires (*CW*, 1988c).

Moreover, Syntex is trying to improve Naprosyn. It has already introduced important enhancements, like a new controlled-release version and different formulations. Further, in 1988 it signed a deal with Procter & Gamble to market an OTC version of Naprosyn. Procter & Gamble has an extensive marketing network, which can be of great help for large-scale distribution, and can be an effective barrier against competitive products.

Finally, Syntex is offering to supply generics manufacturers with the basic chemical ingredients of Naprosyn so that they can formulate their own version of the drug. This is unlikely to prevent a fall of Naprosyn's sales after its patent expires. However, Syntex hopes to recover part of the forgone revenue by selling the bulk chemical products (*CW*, 1988c; *BW*, 1988e).

These attempts to protect Naprosyn's position after 1993 are dictated more by the need to curb Naprosyn's decline than by aggressive competitive goals, like increasing Naprosyn's market share or, more generally, reinforcing Syntex's overall competitive position. Syntex is also trying to develop new drugs. In the late 1980s, it had a number of compounds waiting for FDA approval, e.g., Cardene, an anti-hypertensive, which is produced under license from Yamanouchi Pharmaceuticals; Ticlid, a stroke-prevention drug; Toradol, a non-narcotic analgesic for pain relief; Ketorac, eyedrops to relieve post-surgery eye inflammation; Gardrin, an anti-ulcer drug; and Cytovene, an orphan drug to combat a virus that can cause blindness in AIDS patients. Yet, these are not major new drugs which could boost Syntex's sales as much as Naprosyn did in the mid-1970s (*CW*, 1988c; *BW*, 1988e; *BS&C*, 1988).

Syntex is implementing an aggressive strategy for in-house research. Its R&D to sales ratio has increased from 12.7 percent in 1983 to 17.1 percent in 1988, and it has been around 17.5 percent between 1989 and 1991 (*Moody's International Manual*, various years). The company appears to reinvest Naprosyn's profit in research, and it is trying to exploit its patented position to build up future competitiveness. Further, Syntex is setting the basis for sound in-house basic research. Among other things, it is building a new center for cancer research in Palo Alto, which will host advanced research equipment and qualified personnel for scientific work in this field (*CW*, 1988c).

Syntex's story illustrates how a one-drug company is attempting to depart from its reliance on one major product. On the one hand, it is aggressively protecting its compound against competition from generic products after its patent expires. On the other hand, it is investing heavily in research to develop major new prescription drugs. Will this strategy succeed? This is still an open question. Syntex is clearly relying on research. But good in-house research capabilities do not necessarily translate into profitable outcomes. For one reason, even with sound research skills, pharmaceutical innovations still depend a great deal upon serendipity. More generally, the high costs, length, and uncertainty of drug research imply that Syntex faces high risks, and it is unclear whether it will be able to come up with an important new product.

Syntex exhibits an important peculiarity with respect to the other drug companies examined in this chapter. It is really on the boundary between being a "pure" research company and a "true" drug manufacturer with significant development and distribution assets. Syntex is the smallest among the "large" US drug companies (see table 4.1), and it is more renowned for its research (especially in contraceptives) than for its development and distribution assets.

This suggests that a sensible strategy might be to reinforce its research capabilities, and aim at alliances for development and distribution. Clearly, this is not to say that Syntex should become a "research boutique," like many small to medium-sized biotechnology companies. But Syntex could make important choices about specialization. It could encourage even more strongly in-house research in the fields wherein it already has relatively greater strength. It could then take advantage of the emerging opportunities for a division of labor in drug innovation. In the end, Syntex might even benefit from acquisition of part of its equity capital by larger pharmaceutical groups, if it could maintain sufficient organizational and strategic autonomy, gain the necessary financial stability for research, and obtain access to extended complementary resources for development and commercialization.

American Home Products

American Home Products (AHP) is one of the largest pharmaceutical firms in the US market. Yet, it is not a major competitor in the research-based segment of this industry; nor does it have major in-house research capabilities. AHP has important presences in oral contraceptives and infant nutritionals. It has an extended line of OTC products, and it is active in the food and household business. Its performance in these markets is considerable. AHP's case shows that not all large pharmaceutical corporations base their strategy on solid in-house research bases, and some of them found their competitiveness on marketing capabilities and related assets in non-research-intensive businesses.

In the late 1980s, AHP had some new drugs in the pipeline. Ultradol, a new anti-arthritic agent, was awaiting FDA approval. In the early 1990s, AHP expects to file an NDA for Tolrestat, a drug to treat the debilitating effects of diabetes. Tolrestat is already marketed in Italy and Ireland (*BS&C*, 1989e).

In 1988, AHP acquired Robins, a pharmaceutical company for which chapter 11 of the Bankruptcy Act was filed because of lawsuits against its Dalkon Shield contraceptive, which had been responsible for infertility in women. Again, the acquisition of another large pharmaceutical company was a major step in meeting the rising competitive pressures of the drug market. However, the mergers between Bristol-Myers and Squibb, and

Smithkline and Beecham, sought to join significant research and marketing skills and assets, to form giant companies with considerable capabilities in the ethical drug business. Robins had a strong OTC product line, and it was not a research-based company. In spite of its financial difficulties arising from large legal compensation payments to women harmed by the Dalkon Shield, Robins still had good in-house capabilities in many of its product lines. AHP's acquisition was then not used to enter into the prescription drug market. It reinforced AHP's traditional businesses. More generally, AHP does not seem to be taking any significant steps to enter the highly competitive research-based ethical pharmaceutical market.

Rorer

In the mid-1980s, Rorer had a modest research base. Its major operations were cosmetics and OTC medicines. It had an important OTC drug in the market, Maalox, the leading consumer antacid product in the USA. But it had practically no prescription drug line.

In 1986, Rorer embarked on an aggressive strategy to enter into the market for R&D-based drugs. It acquired the ethical pharmaceutical business of Revlon, which raised its sales from 313.7 and 338.1 million dollars in 1984 and 1985 to 844.6, 928.8, and 1041.6 million dollars in 1986, 1987, and 1988. Its R&D expenditures increased by almost four times, from 16.3 and 17.9 million dollars in 1984 and 1985 to 69.7, 81.8 and 102.8 million dollars in 1986, 1987, and 1988, i.e., a rise in the R&D to sales ratio from slightly more than 5 percent in 1983 and 1984 to above 8 percent in 1986 and 1987 and to almost 10 percent in 1988 (*Moody's Industrial Manual*, various years). Rorer also embarked on a program to focus on its most promising research lines. It concentrated research in five areas (cardiology, gastroenterology, hypersensitivity, bone metabolism, and hematology) (*WSJ*, 1987a).

Rorer's strategy, although a courageous one, was also risky. Rorer needed to achieve a quick breakthrough. The cash flow from Maalox did provide the necessary funds to carry out Rorer's research restructuring. But Maalox, an OTC drug, did not generate a cash flow comparable to that of a major prescription drug. An important success was necessary to break into the spiral of self-reinforcing advantages, namely the obtaining of a major boost in sales and profits to support further research on a long-term basis.

Rorer was unable to produce a major new discovery in a relatively short time. In 1990, it was acquired by Rhone-Poulenc. The French company had undertaken a program of internal reorganization similar to Rorer. It had abandoned various business lines, including some of its traditional concerns like textiles and fertilizers, to concentrate on research-based pharmaceutical products. Like Rorer, it had acquired various companies to expand its remaining operations (*BW*, 1990a). The merger with Rorer integrated various complementary assets, and it was explicitly aimed at reinforcing both firms in the research-intensive segment of the drug business. Rorer brings to the new company some of its internal research capabilities. Moreover, apart from its US sales force, which will help in selling Rhone-Poulenc's products in this market, it carries Maalox profits to sustain joint research. Rorer's research assets will pool with Rhone-Poulenc's research organization, built around its major research center, Institut Merieux, and the recently acquired Connaught Biosciences, a small biotechnology company specializing in vaccines (*Bioscan*, 1988; *BW*, 1990a).

Conclusions: Lessons from the case studies

We can draw three main conclusions from the case studies. First, although a public good, science is not a "free" good. Internal scientific capabilities are critical for taking advantage of the public good. Firms like Merck and Eli Lilly paid systematic attention to scientific research and they run research laboratories almost like academic departments. They have been more effective than their rivals in taking advantage of new scientific ideas, and in the 1980s they showed notable innovation and market performance. Squibb, Syntex, and Smithkline had good internal research operations, and they produced important innovations. However, their one-drug company status put considerable pressures on their performance. Bristol-Myers and Rorer had no long-standing research tradition. They reorganized their internal operations to gain research capabilities. However, although intensive and to some extent successful, these efforts were insufficient to sustain the competitive pressures of an industry in which solid intra-mural research expertise cannot be acquired even within a decade. American Home Products had no research tradition, nor did it attempt to establish one. It reinforced its non-R&D businesses, and it is not investing in the patented drug market.

Second, the case studies showed that in this industry innovation and market performance are cumulative, and they can be a source of persistent heterogeneity across firms. The commercialization of important new drugs generates the cash flow that is necessary to sustain further, expensive long-term research.[15] Merck and Eli Lilly used their proceeds from past breakthroughs to invest in new research. In the 1980s they developed a steady flow of new drugs. The importance of a sound financial basis from previous successes is epitomized by Smithkline's story. Despite Tagamet's success, Smithkline did not reinvest its resources in scientific research. It forwent the opportunity of exploiting cumulative advantages, and faced poor innovation performance. As Rorer's case suggests, it is extremely difficult to build an extensive research basis from scratch, and Rorer was unable to break into the market of R&D-intensive drugs.

Finally, the case studies hinted at some new trends in the market structure of this industry. Rising R&D costs imply that only giant corporations with formidable R&D, marketing, and financial capabilities will be able to afford extensive new drug developments and commercialization. In the 1980s we observed important consolidations: Bristol-Myers and Squibb merged; Smithkline merged with Beecham; American Home Products acquired Robins; Rorer merged with Rhone-Poulenc. Moreover, Sterling Drug, a major drug manufacturer, was acquired by Eastman Kodak in 1988; Merrell Dow and Marion Laboratories merged in 1989; in 1990 Hoffmann La Roche acquired 60 percent of Genentech, one of the few biotechnology companies that succeeded in becoming an integrated pharmaceutical manufacturer. Merck itself set important marketing and research deals with Johnson & Johnson and Du Pont, two other giants in the medical and chemical business.[16]

Does consolidation, and the formation of giant corporations, imply the demise of a division of innovative labor in the drug sector? The formation of giant companies is necessary to accumulate significant development and marketing capabilities to sustain increasing innovation costs. Very large firms can also accumulate considerable financial and organizational resources to perform, among other things, upstream research based on lumpy assets. Yet, this does not imply that they will forgo the opportunity of taking advantage of smaller specialist suppliers of research and ideas, especially if the latter have greater comparative ability in "invention."

In fact, the very tendency towards establishing huge development and commercialization assets can be thought of as an attempt to strengthen downstream capabilities, and hence downstream specialization. This implies greater marginal benefits from relationships with agents endowed with complementary assets, and particularly with those that possess complementary abilities in upstream generation of research ideas. As Eli Lilly's story suggests, large drug companies are increasingly recognizing these opportunities, and they are taking advantage of external linkages in research. Moreover, a very important factor that will encourage large companies to exploit the benefits of a division of labor in innovation is that, as argued in the previous chapter, they can pick only promising research outcomes in the market, thereby moving the risks of early research stages onto their suppliers. If the new trend is really less bright for some, it will probably be so for the medium-sized (or even large) drug companies that will be "caught in the middle." They may be unable to acquire (or build) solid assets for very large-scale development and marketing, or to specialize in research and produce ideas that can be matched with the complementary downstream resources of larger companies.

5 Scientific research and drug discovery: an econometric investigation

Introduction

It should now be clear, even to the reader with little knowledge of the pharmaceutical industry, that drug innovation can be broken down into two distinct stages: drug discovery, and development and commercialization. Discovery is the more creative step, but it is very far from sales. Although less ingenious, development commands considerable outlays of resources, and it takes place over a fairly long span of time. As they can be distinguished so clearly, we shall examine these two stages separately. This chapter focuses on the economics of drug discovery, whilst the next chapter looks at development and commercialization.

As the previous chapters suggested, drug discovery depends on two factors. The greater the number of molecules tested, i.e. the greater the scale of applied laboratory research, the greater the expectation of finding a given number of compounds for clinical trials. Drug discovery also depends on the scientific capital of firms. The latter helps in discerning areas wherein researchers are more likely to find candidate drugs, thereby increasing the probability of discovery.

This chapter presents a model of drug discovery in pharmaceutical companies. Discovery is assumed to stem from expenditures on two inputs. Each year firms invest in testing a number of molecules in their laboratories. This is the variable input, which can be thought of as applied research. They also invest in accumulating knowledge capital, which is the stock input, and it is proxied by the past scientific publications of firms. The number of discoveries is proxied by the number of company patent applications.

The number of patents will be greater the greater the number of molecules tested. But a greater number of patents can also arise because firms search for new drugs among more prolific families of compounds. As discussed in previous chapters, this is precisely what is provided by scientific capital. Whether because it enables firms to produce scientific information internally, or to utilize external knowledge more effectively, scientific capital enhances the ability of firms to test compounds in areas with better yields.

The model assumes that firms maximize the expected discounted stream of the benefits that they derive from their yearly patents, net of expenditures on testing molecules, and of the costs of investing in knowledge capital. Using a standard result in the literature, knowledge capital times its shadow price is proportional to market value. The model produces a patent equation and an equation for scientific papers, which are jointly estimated.

In the patent equation, patents depend upon past scientific papers, and variables that proxy for the unit cost of testing molecules in the laboratory. The coefficient of the unit cost variable is related to the productivity of laboratory research, whereas the coefficients of past papers measure the productivity of knowledge. The second equation relates the annual flow of company scientific publications to market value and past knowledge capital.

The model is estimated using data for the fourteen largest US pharmaceutical companies during 1968–91. (The firms are listed in the appendix to this chapter.) Other studies have estimated the relationships between drug company patents and their scientific papers. (See Koenig, 1983; Halperin and Chakrabarti, 1987; Narin, Noma, and Perry, 1987.) They all found positive correlations. This chapter, however, develops an economic model to interpret such correlations. Moreover, it relates the accumulation of knowledge capital to the expected future profitability of drug companies, as proxied by market value. Finally, it estimates the patent and paper equations in two sample periods, 1968–79 and 1980–91. We can thus assess whether there have been structural changes in the productivity of either laboratory research or knowledge capital, or both.

The next two sections present the model and discuss the empirical results, respectively. The final section summarizes the chapter. An appendix describes the data.

A model of drug discovery

Search models typify the basic features of drug discovery.[1] Laboratory research is like the sampling of balls from urns which contain black and red balls in different ratios. Urns are families of compounds. "Black" balls are inactive compounds; "red" balls are active compounds, which can be submitted for clinical trials. Applied chemists draw balls from the urns. Scientific knowledge provides information about the ratio of black to red balls in the different urns. It helps scientists in making more informed choices about the urns from which they can make their draws.

Define N to be the number of draws of a given firm in a certain year, i.e., N is the number of molecules tested in the laboratory. Define K to be the knowledge capital of a firm, and P the number of patent applications of a given firm in a certain year. Patent applications are a good proxy for discoveries in pre-clinical research. Because patents are an effective means of appropriating drug innovations, pharmaceutical companies patent their compounds as early as possible. Typically, they apply for patents concurrently with application for an Investigational New Drug Exemption (IND) to obtain permission for clinical trials. Patent applications are thus a better measure of pre-clinical discoveries than new drugs sold.

Patent applications P increase with the number of molecules tested, N. They also vary with K, as greater K implies greater ability to search urns with better (expected) ratios of red to black balls. Using a multiplicative specification, the production function of patents can be written as

$$P = A(t)N^{\alpha}K^{\beta}e^{\epsilon} \tag{1}$$

where all variables have subscripts i and t for firms and time, which have been suppressed for notational convenience; α and β are the elasticities of N and K. The function $A(t)$ is a time trend that influences discovery. Grabowski, Vernon, and Thomas (1978) found that, other things being held constant, in the 1960s and the 1970s time had a negative effect on the number of discoveries. They attributed this result to depletion of research opportunities. The term ϵ is a stochastic factor. Serendipity plays an important role in drug research (see, among others, Schwartzman, 1976). It is assumed that $\epsilon = \rho\epsilon_{-1} + \mu$, where μ is a stochastic term with finite mean and variance and uncorrelated over time, and $\rho \in [0,1]$ measures the persistence of serendipity over time, i.e., the extent to which "news" in previous years (e.g. unexpected discoveries of prolific families of compounds) influences present discoveries.

It is also assumed that the accumulation of knowledge capital takes the following form

$$K = X^{\theta}K_{-1}^{1-\theta} \tag{2}$$

where X is the number of scientific papers published by the ith firm in year t, and $\theta \in [0,1]$ is the percentage increase in knowledge capital produced by a unit percentage increase in the flow of papers. Papers are not an infallible measure of knowledge capital. The number of papers does not account for quality differences in publications. In addition, a large fraction of papers published by pharmaceutical industry scientists are in clinical research (about 45 percent of all papers published by this group; see Narin and Rozek, 1988). Clinical papers are typically statistical analyses of the effects of drugs in patients. They are likely to be more strongly correlated with the extent of clinical trials than with basic knowledge. (See, for instance, Spangenberg *et al.*, 1990.)[2]

Publications, however, are a common means by which scientific knowledge circulates. Thus, even though the number of papers may not provide a completely satisfactory measure of pre-clinical knowledge capital, it is correlated with the intensity of linkages of company scientists with the scientific community. As also discussed in chapter 3, pharmaceutical companies allow their scientists to publish to encourage solid ties with the scientific network, which provides advantages such as easier and more effective communication with academic scholars. Papers would then be a fairly appropriate measure of the type of scientific capabilities that one is trying to measure here. After all, what is really meant by internal scientific capital of firms in this discussion is the extent to which they are plugged into the outside scientific network.

Relatedly, Halperin and Chakrabarti (1987) found a high correlation between the number of papers of pharmaceutical companies and the number of "elite" scientists that they employ. Elite scientists are people with a good reputation within the scientific community. The number of papers is thus correlated with an important measure of the breadth of linkages of company scientists with the scientific network.[3]

Pharmaceutical firms choose N, X, and K to maximize the present value of the expected discounted stream of utilities that they derive from their patents, net of variable costs in molecular testing, and the costs of accumulating knowledge capital, i.e.

$$\max_{(N,X,K)_{\tau=1}^{\infty}} V_0 \equiv E_0 \sum_{\tau=1}^{\infty} [U(P) - CN - \Phi(X,K) - \lambda(K - X^\theta K_{-1}^{1-\theta})]r$$

subject to (1) and (2). In this expression:

- subscripts i for firms and τ for time have been suppressed for notational convenience. (From now on, I shall use subscripts -1 and 1 to denote previous and next period.)
- V_0 is the market value of the firm at the beginning of the period, and E_0 is the expectation operator given all information at the beginning of the period.
- $U(\cdot)$ is the utility of each year's discoveries. One can think of $U(\cdot)$ as the present value of profits that firms expect to obtain from future sales of innovations. I assume that $U(\cdot)$ is homogeneous of degree 1 in N and K, i.e. $U(\cdot)$ is proportional to $P^{\frac{1}{\alpha+\beta}}$.
- C is the cost of testing one molecule in the laboratory.
- $\Phi(X,K)$ is the adjustment cost of knowledge capital, defined to be $\Phi \equiv QX^\phi K^{1-\phi}$, with $\phi > 1$; Q is a proportionality factor.

- λ is the Lagrange multiplier associated with the capital accumulation constraint.
- r is a discount factor.

The first-order conditions with respect to N, K, and X are

$$U_N - C = 0 \tag{3}$$

$$U_K - \Phi_K - \lambda + \lambda_1 r_1 (1 - \theta) X_1^\theta K^{-\theta} = 0 \tag{4}$$

$$-\Phi^X + \lambda \theta X^{\theta-1} K_{-1}^{1-\theta} = 0 \tag{5}$$

where subscripts N, K and X denote first derivatives. Following standard analysis in the literature (see Hayashi, 1982, and Wildasin, 1984), multiply (3), (4), and (5) by, respectively, N, K, and X. Sum these expressions together and over $\tau = 1, 2, 3, \ldots, \infty$. All terms involving future λ's cancel out. Linear homogeneity of U and Φ implies that $U_N N + U_K K = U$, and $\Phi_X X + \Phi_K K = \Phi$. Eventually, one obtains $V_0 - \lambda(1 - \theta)K = 0$, or

$$\lambda = \frac{1}{1-\theta} \frac{V_0}{K}.$$

We can now derive the equation for scientific papers to be estimated. Substitute the expression above for λ in (5), and solve for X. Using the fact that $X^\theta K_{-1}^{1-\theta} = K$, one obtains

$$x = \text{const.} + \frac{\phi-1}{\phi} k + \frac{1}{\phi}(v_0 - q) + \psi(t) + \omega$$

where lower-case letters denote logs. $\psi(t)$ was added to account for time factors, and ω as a stochastic term. Time factors would represent, for instance, effects that influence adjustment costs – e.g. the growth of public scientific knowledge may reduce the cost of investing in knowledge capital (or, equivalently, it may reduce the unit cost of producing a paper, as company researchers can build upon additional public knowledge).

Expression (2) can be written as $\quad k = \dfrac{\theta}{1-(1-\theta)L} x \quad$ or

$$k = \theta x + \frac{\theta(1-\theta)}{1-(1-\theta)L} x_{-1} \tag{6}$$

where L is the lag operator. This can be substituted in the expression for x above. Solving for x, one obtains

$$x = \text{const.} + \delta \frac{\theta}{1-(1-\theta)L} x_{-1} + \gamma(v_{-1} - q) + \phi_1 t + \psi_2 t^2 + \omega \tag{7}$$

where $\delta \equiv \dfrac{(\phi-1)(1-\theta)}{\phi-(\phi-1)\theta}$, $\quad \gamma \equiv \dfrac{1}{\phi-(\phi-1)\theta}$, $\quad \psi(t)$ is a function of a time trend and a squared time trend, i.e. $\psi(t) \equiv \psi_1 t + \psi_2 t^2$, and ψ_1, ψ_2, and ω have been normalized with respect to $\dfrac{\phi}{\phi - (\phi - 1)\theta}$.[4] Notice that given $\phi > 1$, and $0 < \theta < 1$, then $0 < \gamma < 1$, and $0 < \delta < 1$. Moreover, while γ increases with θ, δ decreases with increasing θ.[5] The factor that normalizes ψ_1, ψ_2, and ω also increases with θ. Expression (7) is the scientific paper equation to be estimated.

To derive the patent equation, first derive the expression for N. From first-order condition (3), given (1), and given the fact that $U(\cdot)$ is proportional to $P^{1/(\alpha+\beta)}$, one obtains, after some algebra,

$$n = \text{const.} - \frac{\alpha+\beta}{\beta}c + k + \frac{1}{\beta}[a(t) + \epsilon]$$

where again lower-case letters denote logs. As $p = \text{const.} + \alpha n + \beta k + a(t) + \epsilon$, then, after replacing n from above, one obtains

$$p = \text{const.} - \frac{\alpha}{\beta}(\alpha+\beta)c + (\alpha+\beta)k + \left(1 + \frac{\alpha}{\beta}\right)[a(t) + \epsilon]$$

Replace k with (6), ϵ with $\rho\epsilon_{-1} + \mu$, and substitute ϵ_{-1} with the one-period lagged expression for p above. Eventually, one obtains

$$p = \text{const.} + \left(1 + \frac{\alpha}{\beta}\right)\rho p_{-1} - \frac{\alpha}{\beta}(\alpha+\beta)(c - \rho c_{-1}) + (\alpha+\beta)\theta(x - \rho x_{-1})$$
$$+ (\alpha+\beta)\theta\frac{(1-\theta)}{1-(1-\theta)L}(x_{-1} - \rho x_{-2}) + \left(1 + \frac{\alpha}{\beta}\right)\eta(1-\rho)t + \mu \quad (8)$$

which is the patent equation to be jointly estimated with (7). In (8), $a(t)$ has been replaced by a parameter η multiplied by a time trend.[6]

Non-linear estimation of (7) and (8) enables us to estimate a number of the structural parameters. First, we can estimate the productivities α and β of laboratory research, N, and knowledge capital, K. Notice that, from (2), β is the percentage increase in patents (discoveries) at time t given a unit percentage increase in papers at time t and in all previous periods. It is thus a measure of the long-run productivity of knowledge capital. Second, we can estimate θ, i.e. the fraction of long-run productivity β accounted for by current papers. Third, we can estimate ρ, which measures the importance of serendipity in drug discovery. The closer ρ is to 1, the more present discoveries depend upon the persistence of stochastic factors that influenced discovery in previous periods. Finally, the sign of η would indicate whether there has been depletion or revamping of research opportunities.

Empirical results

Equations (7) and (8) (in log–log form) were estimated using data for the fourteen largest US pharmaceutical companies during 1968–91. The variables p and p_{-1} are logs of the number of US patent applications in the current period and the previous period, respectively; x and its lagged equivalents are (logs of) the numbers of company papers published in corresponding years. In estimation four lags for x were used. (The lag operator L in (7) and (8) took the values $L = 0$, 1, 2, and 3.) A greater number of lags was tried, but the empirical results did not change. Patent applications reflect discoveries in the same year or one year earlier. Published papers report research that took place about two to three years earlier because of the natural delays between submission of papers and their publication.

The term $(v_{-1} - q)$ was measured by the log of market value deflated by the US price index for non-residential investment goods.[7] The unit cost of laboratory research, C, was measured by the ratio of company sales (in nominal terms) to R&D expenditures (in real terms), lagged one period. (The sales to R&D ratio is lagged two periods for C_{-1}.) This is justified by the fact that, with a Cobb–Douglas technology, profit maximization implies that the price of a given input is proportional to the ratio between nominal sales and real expenditures on that input. The sales to R&D ratio is lagged one period to avoid endogeneity with current variables in (8). As indicated in the previous section, t and t^2 are a time trend and a squared time trend.

Data up to 1985 are from the NBER–Compustat file. The Compustat data were updated to 1991 using consistent sources (see the appendix to this chapter). Compustat reports data on all variables in (7) and (8) (including patents) with the exception of scientific papers. The 1973–86 numbers of scientific papers were obtained from CHI Research/Computer Horizons Inc. The 1964–72 and 1987–91 numbers of papers are from *Science Citation Index* (various years). See the appendix for more details on data construction, sources, and definitions, and tables 5.1 and 5.2 for descriptive statistics.

Company averages were subtracted from all variables in (7) and (8) to control for firm-specific effects. Also the variables x and x_{-1} that appear in the fourth term of the right-hand side of (8) were replaced by the expressions for x and x_{-1} in equation (7) and in (7) lagged one period. The system (7)–(8) was estimated by generalized least squares.[8]

Equations (7) and (8) were also estimated after allowing for the parameters α, β, θ, ρ, and η to differ in the two sample periods, 1968–79 and 1980–91. Significant advances in the technology of experimentation and in

Table 5.1. *Descriptive statistics: levels*

Variable	Mean	Std. dev.	Min.	Max.	BVAR (%)	WVAR (%)
Number of patents	87.9	45.7	11.0 (46.0)	316.0 (192.0)	91.9	53.1
Number of scientific papers	132.7	142.6	6.0 (23.0)	850.0 (289.0)	65.3	56.9
Sales/R&D	17.4	8.2	5.5 (11.2)	42.2 (41.0)	76.9	26.1
Market value (const. 1982 $m.)	5,703.6	4,805.9	622.1 (883.7)	36,383.3 (7,013.1)	62.5	60.3

Notes: Fourteen firms, 1968–91. Number of observations = 303. Because of missing values, descriptive statistics are computed using only observations in the estimated sample (see table 5.3). The sales/R&D ratio and market value are lagged one year (1967–90). In parentheses min. and max. for central year, 1979 (1978 for sales/R&D and market value) (fourteen observations). BVAR is the ratio of the between-group variance to total variance, i.e. $BVAR = \sum_{it}(y_{it} - y_t^*)^2 / \sum_{it}(y_{it} - y^*)^2$, where y_t^* is y_{it} averaged over firms, and y^* is the overall average. WVAR is the ratio of the within-group variance to total variance, i.e. $WVAR = \sum_{it}(y_{it} - y_i^*)^2 / \sum_{it}(y_{it} - y^*)^2$, where y_i^* is y_{it} averaged over time.

Table 5.2. *Descriptive statistics: logs*

Variable	Mean	Std. dev.	Min.	Max.	BVAR (%)	WVAR (%)
Number of patents	4.34	0.54	2.40 (3.83)	5.76 (5.26)	91.9	53.8
Number of scientific papers	4.50	0.85	1.79 (3.14)	6.75 (5.67)	51.9	54.8
Sales/R&D	2.75	0.46	1.70 (2.41)	3.74 (3.71)	71.4	26.5
Market value (const. 1982 $m.)	8.38	0.74	6.43 (6.76)	10.50 (8.89)	69.1	49.0

Notes: Fourteen firms, 1968–91. Number of observations = 303. Descriptive statistics computed using only observations in the estimated sample (see table 3.3). The sales/R&D ratio and market value are lagged one year (1967–90). In parentheses min. and max. for central year, 1979 (1978 for sales/R&D and market value) (fourteen observations). BVAR and WVAR are the ratios of the between-group and within-group variances to total variance, and they are computed as described in table 5.1.

scientific knowledge produced important changes in pharmaceutical research during the 1980s. One can thus test for changes in the productivities of laboratory research and knowledge capital. Relatedly, one can evaluate whether the lag structure of papers has changed. One reason for this is that, with greater scientific intensity in drug research, drug company papers may have become more "basic." This would mean longer lags before publication in the 1980s, and hence lower θ.[9]

The very same fact that drug discovery has become more "scientific" would suggest lower ρ as well. With greater confidence in their ability to understand phenomena in "rational" terms, companies would be less inclined to pursue projects arising from unexpected and probably transient opportunities, and that are not grounded on solid knowledge. This was also discussed at some length in chapter 2 when suggesting that companies had less incentive to pursue different uses of molecules when information about other applications arose unexpectedly from clinical trials or from the market. In contrast, they may have greater stimuli today as they can rationally pursue different therapeutic applications of given compounds. Finally, by distinguishing between η in the 1970s and the 1980s, one can test whether greater scientific knowledge and better experimentation technology have curbed exhaustion of innovation possibilities.

The structure of the model also entails that differences in θ in the two periods imply differences in γ, δ, ψ_1, and ψ_2, as the latter are functions of θ. (See the previous section.) Particularly, γ, ψ_1, and ψ_2 increase with θ, whereas δ decreases with θ. Hence, in allowing for the possibility that a, β, θ, ρ, and η may be different, one must also allow for the possibility that all other parameters in (7) and (8) may be different. Estimation is accomplished by multiplying each term in (7) and (8) by a dummy variable which takes the value one for 1968–79 and zero otherwise, and by adding these expressions to similar expressions multiplied by a dummy equal to one for 1980–91 and zero otherwise.

The results are given in tables 5.3 and 5.4. Table 5.3 reports the results for the constrained model. Table 5.4 presents results for the model with different parameters in the two sample periods. (In table 5.4, parameters have subscripts "70" and "80" to denote estimates for the 1970s and the 1980s, respectively) Table 5.4 also reports results from estimating the system (7)–(8) separately for the two subsamples 1968–79 and 1980–91.[10]

From table 5.3, a and β are positive and statistically significant. However, their combined effect is not large. A 1 percent increase in both the number of molecules tested and knowledge capital implies only a 0.30 percent increase in the number of patents. As expected, companies need to test a large number of molecules, and they need to develop their knowledge capital a great deal in order to make just a few discoveries. The parameter η is negative, which suggests depletion of research opportunities.

Table 5.3. *Estimated parameters,
equations (7)–(8)*

Parameters	Estimates
α	0.146 (0.036)
β	0.146 (0.064)
ρ	0.399 (0.085)
η	−0.020 (0.007)
θ	0.861 (0.123)
γ	0.181 (0.050)
δ	0.542 (0.071)
ψ_1	0.058 (0.013)
ψ_2	−0.001 (0.0005)

Notes: Fourteen firms, 1968–91.
Number of observations = 303.
Number of observations smaller
than 336 (= 14 × 24) because of
missing values. Log likelihood
function = − 38.23. Heteroskedastic
consistent standard errors in
parentheses.

An interesting result in table 5.3 is the high value of θ. About 90 percent of the knowledge capital of firms in a given year depends on papers published in the same year. In other words, about 90 percent of the effect of the long-run elasticity β is explained by present papers, i.e. by scientific research performed two to three years earlier. Scientific research and drug discovery appear to be intimately connected. Many papers and patents probably deal with the same subject. While patents describe the molecules, papers elucidate the method with which they were discovered and other scientific details.

The results in table 5.4 are even more intriguing. While α increases by

Table 5.4. *Estimated parameters, equations (7)–(8) with structural differences in parameters, 1968–79 and 1980–91*

Parameters	Estimates		
	(1)	(2)	(3)
α_{70}	0.060 (0.091)	0.022 (0.097)	—
β_{70}	0.238 (0.115)	0.262 (0.132)	—
ρ_{70}	0.597 (0.219)	0.689 (0.277)	—
η_{70}	−0.031 (0.016)	−0.036 (0.030)	—
θ_{70}	0.902 (0.180)	0.895 (0.180)	—
γ_{70}	0.230 (0.076)	0.231 (0.076)	—
δ_{70}	0.488 (0.108)	0.489 (0.108)	—
$\psi_{1;70}$	0.066 (0.021)	0.066 (0.021)	—
$\psi_{2;70}$	−0.001 (0.001)	−0.001 (0.001)	—
α_{80}	0.192 (0.050)	—	0.191 (0.050)
β_{80}	0.150 (0.094)	—	0.149 (0.094)
ρ_{80}	0.360 (0.118)	—	0.359 (0.118)
η_{80}	−0.021 (0.010)	—	−0.021 (0.010)
θ_{80}	0.687 (0.151)	—	0.684 (0.153)
γ_{80}	0.087 (0.051)	—	0.093 (0.050)
δ_{80}	0.716 (0.086)	—	0.717 (0.087)
$\psi_{1;80}$	0.044 (0.018)	—	0.045 (0.017)

Table 5.4. (*cont.*)

Parameters	Estimates		
	(1)	(2)	(3)
$\psi_{2;80}$	-0.001	—	-0.001
	(0.001)		(0.001)

Notes: Heteroskedastic consistent standard errors in parentheses. Subscript 70 denotes parameter estimates for 1968–79. Subscript 80 denotes parameter estimates for 1980–91.

(1) Fourteen firms, 1968–91. Number of observations = 303. Number of observations smaller than 336 (= 14 × 24) because of missing values. Log likelihood function = − 32.58.

(2) Fourteen firms, 1968–79. Number of observations = 154. Number of observations smaller than 168 (= 14 × 12) because of missing values. Log likelihood function = − 34.80.

(3) Fourteen firms, 1980–91. Number of observations = 149. Number of observations smaller than 168 (= 14 × 12) because of missing values. Log likelihood function = 13.09.

more than three times between the 1970s and the 1980s, β, ρ, η, and θ decrease (in absolute value). The model exhibits internal consistency. The parameters γ, ψ_1 and ψ_2 ought to decline with θ, while δ ought to increase with θ. Although no parametric restrictions were imposed, the estimated values of γ, δ, ψ_1, and ψ_2 vary consistently with the decline in θ. As reported in table 5.5, the statistical significance of inter-period differences in α, β, ρ, η, and θ is only marginal. Also, from table 5.5, using the likelihood ratio test, one cannot confidently reject the null hypothesis that the models with and without structural changes are statistically equivalent. However, the discussion in the previous chapters suggests that the point estimates do capture some important changes in the evolution of drug industry research.

The notable increase in α stems from two complementary effects. First, greater scientific knowledge implies that each draw from an urn is more likely to be a draw of a "red" ball: scientific knowledge provides industry researchers with information about more prolific urns, and they sample from those urns. Second, the technology of molecular testing has improved dramatically. Compounds can be tested via computer simulation and other sophisticated instruments, which has augmented the productivity of laboratory research. This implies that it is less costly to test compounds in the laboratory, and the unit cost of assaying one molecule (C in our model) has declined. In other words, with similar (real) expenditures in applied

Table 5.5. *Hypothesis testing*

Testing of the estimated parameters, first column of
table 5.4; $s(\cdot)$ = estimated standard error of parameter
difference.

Null hypothesis	Test statistics (Student's t)
$H_0: a_{70} - a_{80} = 0$	$\dfrac{a_{70} - a_{80}}{s(a_{70} - a_{80})} = \dfrac{-0.132}{0.104} = -1.269$
$H_0: \beta_{70} - \beta_{80} = 0$	$\dfrac{\beta_{70} - \beta_{80}}{s(\beta_{70} - \beta_{80})} = \dfrac{0.088}{0.148} = 0.595$
$H_0: \rho_{70} - \rho_{80} = 0$	$\dfrac{\rho_{70} - \rho_{80}}{s(\rho_{70} - \rho_{80})} = \dfrac{0.237}{0.249} = 0.952$
$H_0: \eta_{70} - \eta_{80} = 0$	$\dfrac{\eta_{70} - \eta_{80}}{s(\eta_{70} - \eta_{80})} = \dfrac{-0.010}{0.019} = -0.526$
$H_0: \theta_{70} - \theta_{80} = 0$	$\dfrac{\theta_{70} - \theta_{80}}{s(\theta_{70} - \theta_{80})} = \dfrac{0.215}{0.235} = 0.915$

Notes: Likelihood ratio test for difference in
"aggregate" and "disaggregate" models. Unrestricted
model = first column of table 5.4. Restricted
model = model in table 5.3. Number of
restrictions = 12. Twice difference in likelihood
functions = $11.3 < 21.03 \equiv$ theoretical chi-squared at 5
percent significance and with 12 degrees of freedom.

research, companies can test a far greater number of molecules, which has a
positive effect on the number of discoveries.

The increase in α is an important result. It suggests that an important
implication of advances in scientific knowledge and experimental technologies in drug research is not, in reality, a greater ability to "deduce" new
compounds from "pure" *a priori* principles, thereby reducing the extent of
experimentation. Rather, the more important effects probably arise from
the possibility of conducting experiments in a far more efficient way, which
ensues from a complex blend of scientific knowledge and advances in
experimentation technologies. The former gives researchers the opportunity of sampling from better urns, whilst the latter enables them to test
molecules (and theories) more rapidly and more efficiently. Both factors
make experimentation a more productive input. Hence, we expect an
increase in the propensity of economic agents to conduct experiments, and
a corresponding increase in the extent of experimentation.

The decline in β may seem contradictory. In fact, it is consistent with our characterization of the effects of fundamental knowledge in drug research. Chapter 2 emphasized that the major contribution of the greater scientific understanding of drugs and the human body is not the ability to predict successes, but rather to foresee failures. In many cases, *a priori* knowledge or computerized simulation of compounds reveals areas that are unlikely to generate useful results. Hence, molecules in these areas are not tested.[11] In the past, many such molecules were tested. A number of them would become candidate new drugs for clinical trials. They would be claimed to be new discoveries (thereby increasing the number of patents), only to be rejected later on in clinical trials. Some of them, especially if safe, would have even been marketed, simply because there was no clear indication that they were ineffective.

But now scientific knowledge provides logical, *a priori* evidence that certain molecules are unsafe or ineffective. Many compounds that would have been asserted to be new discoveries will be rejected at the outset of the research process. This reduces the number of "claimed" discoveries, which is precisely what was suggested by the estimation.

This result is also consistent with what was conjectured in Arora and Gambardella (1994a). There it was argued that scientific knowledge enhances the ability of firms to evaluate innovation projects, in the sense of greater ability to predict their pay-offs. The model there suggested that ability to evaluate implies that firms engage in fewer innovation projects, but with greater expected returns.

A very similar effect is at work here. Pharmaceutical companies can predict more precisely the outcomes of projects seeking new compounds. They thus focus on fewer projects, and produce fewer asserted discoveries. However, such fewer discoveries will be of greater quality and potential pay-off, as they are more likely to be truly safe and effective drugs. This result also offers statistical support to the conclusions of chapter 2. There it was predicted that we shall observe fewer discoveries in the future. While many authors and industry analysts see this as a serious downturn of drug research, it is submitted here that this is precisely what we have to expect from advances in scientific knowledge. The fewer discoveries, however, will be safer and more effective compounds.

This also suggests that it makes an important difference whether the dependent variable in a drug patent equation like (8) is the number of patents or some quality-adjusted measure of patents. While "better" knowledge implies a smaller increase in the number of patents with a unit increase in knowledge capital, it will also imply a greater increase in the quality of innovations, with quality measured by some correlate of their expected economic pay-off. In effect, Narin, Noma, and Perry (1987) found notable variations in the quality of patents among pharmaceutical firms, with quality measured by patent citations. They also found that while the number of patents is not correlated with the financial performance of pharmaceutical firms, the mean number of citations per patent is highly correlated with it. Unfortunately, no data on the "value" of patents were available to this study, and it was not possible to test whether knowledge capital in the 1980s exhibited greater impact on the expected pay-off of patents.

Table 5.4 also shows that θ declined between the 1970s and the 1980s. As suggested earlier, drug company papers may have become more basic. This would ensue from a number of factors, as discussed in chapter 3. With greater scientific intensity of pharmaceutical research, companies will be naturally more involved in basic studies of drugs and pathologies, and they may also allow their scientists to perform more fundamental research to take advantage of the rise of public scientific knowledge. Moreover, drug manufacturers will hire more scientists and researchers with solid scientific backgrounds, who will have greater incentives to perform basic research.

As drug company papers become more basic, there will be more extended lags on discoveries. In the 1970s most papers were probably just scientific reports about new discoveries. In the 1980s drug company papers might also have dealt with issues such as the analysis of protein structures and related topics. The latter may point to areas for new discoveries, but they are more distant from the actual finding of new drug candidates.

The parameter ρ declined between the 1970s and the 1980s. It has already been argued that, with greater confidence in "rationally" controlled research, companies would be less inclined to pursue transient opportunities. Intuitively, firms face a choice between pursuing "rational" and "occasional" innovation opportunities. With resource constraints, greater confidence in rational capabilities suggests that they will allocate relatively more resources to the former type of projects: the relative marginal value of serendipity declines, and companies "buy" less of it.

Finally, the 1980's time trend parameter η is smaller in absolute value. Depletion of research opportunities seems to have become less severe. However, η_{80} is still negative. Hence, other things being constant, even during the 1980s there was a decay of innovation possibilities in the drug industry.

Conclusions

This chapter presented a model of the drug discovery process using 1968–91 data for the largest fourteen US pharmaceutical corporations. Two equations were estimated. The first equation relates company patents to a lag structure of company scientific publications (as a proxy for knowledge capital), the sales to R&D ratio (as a proxy for the cost of applied laboratory research), and time. The second equation explains scientific papers as a function of past knowledge capital, the market value of the firm (as a measure of expected future profitability), and time.

The empirical results corroborate some claims made in the previous chapters. First, in the 1980s the productivity of applied research increased, which is related to significant advances in scientific knowledge and in the technology of experimentation (e.g., computerized drug design). Second, in the 1980s the elasticity of papers on the number of patents has declined. This is consistent with the conjecture that the present rise of scientific knowledge in drug research provides greater ability to predict failures rather than successes. Many drugs that in the past would have been tested and maybe commercialized can now be rejected at the beginning of research, as researchers can rationally anticipate that they are unsafe or ineffective. We have fewer discoveries, but they are of greater quality and expected economic pay-off.

The estimation also indicated that the lag structure of papers on patents has lengthened. One possible interpretation is that in the 1980s papers became more basic, with implied lengthening of the period before their impact on patents. Also, serendipity appears to be less important. Companies seem to pursue fewer projects arising from occasional findings. Finally, a time trend exhibited a negative impact on discovery. In the 1980s drug companies still faced an exogenous decay of research opportunities.

Appendix: Description of data

The fourteen firms in the sample are Abbott Laboratories, American Home Products, Bristol-Myers, Johnson & Johnson, Eli Lilly, Merck, Pfizer, Schering-Plough, Squibb, Smithkline, Sterling Drug, Syntex, Upjohn, and Warner-Lambert. They are the top US-based pharmaceutical firms in terms of 1986 US pharmaceutical sales; if one includes foreign multinationals, they are fourteen out of the first nineteen firms in 1986 US pharmaceutical sales (*MAN*, 1987).

Data on sales, R&D, market value, and US patent applications from the October 1988 update of the NBER–Compustat file were used. This update provides data from 1959 to 1985. (See Hall *et al.*, 1988.)

Data for 1986–91 on sales and R&D were obtained from *Moody's Industrial Manual* (various years). In overlapping years sales and R&D data in Moody's and Compustat were practically identical, which ensured consistency of the entire series. Real R&D expenditures were obtained by deflating nominal expenditures with a price index for R&D goods in industry from the Battelle Research Institute (1992).

Data on market value in 1986–91 were again from Moody's. In using Moody's data, an attempt was made to replicate the Compustat definition of market value, which is reported in the appendix to the next chapter. In short, market value is the sum of various items representing short-term debt, long-term debt, and equity capital.

In overlapping years (1984–85), market value from Moody's data did not coincide with Compustat's. This is because Compustat uses an age adjustment structure for long-term debt which I could not replicate. However, differences were small. The 1986 growth rate from Moody's data was applied to the 1985 Compustat variable, and then Moody's 1987–91 growth rates were applied to market value in the preceding years. Market value was deflated by the US fixed non-residential investment deflator.

In the October 1988 Compustat file the number of US patent applications is available only from 1965 to 1979.[12] Compustat patent data in 1965–66 seemed to contain serious measurement errors. The empirical analysis thus starts with 1968 (1967 patents are also used, as equation (8) includes patents lagged one year). The numbers of US patent application in 1980–86 were obtained from on-line search of Dialog files 224 and 225 ("US Patents Files"), and the 1987–91 patent data from on-line search of World Patent Index.

In extending Compustat's patent applications to 1991, the following problem arose. Compustat collects the number of patent applications that are ultimately granted. This ensures that patent applications reflect "genuine" innovations. But then in order to obtain the number of patent applications in a certain year one must conduct the search for at least five or six years after that year (patent review takes on average two to three years), so that by then a sufficiently large fraction of applications will have been examined (and are either granted or rejected).

Dialog search was conducted in 1992. One can thus be confident that most patent applications up to 1986 had been considered by the Patent Office. From Dialog 1976–86 data were retrieved. The years overlapping with Compustat were necessary to compare the series. Comparison indicated a practically perfect match for the 1976–79 patent applications of twelve out of fourteen firms. For two firms (Bristol-Myers and Eli Lilly), Compustat data were systematically higher. The differences however were small (in the order of 5 percent for Bristol-Myers, and 20 percent for Eli Lilly). To obtain a consistent sequence, Dialog's 1980–86 data for these two firms was multiplied by the 1976–79 average proportional difference between patents in the two series.

Problems are more serious for the 1987–91 patent applications as, in 1992, decisions about many of these applications had not yet been reached.

Data on 1983–91 patents granted were collected from World Patent Index. The choice of World Patent Index is justified by the fact that it distinguishes between "basic" and total patents. Basic patents are the first patents granted for a certain discovery in one country. (Total patents include extensions of the same patent to other countries.) This makes the year in which patents were granted as close as possible to the application year, as we record patents in the very first country where they were granted (and we count them only once, for the first country).

The overlapping years were used to compute for each firm the 1983–86 average of the ratio between the Compustat–Dialog patent applications and the World Patent Index series. This firm average was used as a constant factor to multiply the 1987–91 World Patent Index data. In practice, it was assumed that, for each firm, the 1987–91 patent applications were proportional to the World Patent Index data.[13]

The 1973–86 data on the number of company publications were obtained from CHI Research/ Computer Horizon, Inc. The 1973–1980 data are from a constant 1973 journal set of *Science Citation Index*. The 1981–86 data are from a constant 1981 journal set.[14] The 1964–72 and 1987–91 company publications were collected directly from the *Science Citation Index* volumes (various years).[15]

The entire 1964–91 series was adjusted to conform to a 1981 constant journal set. First, the 1973–80 CHI series was multiplied by the ratio of the total numbers of papers surveyed by *Science Citation Index* in 1981 and 1973. Then, a similar adjustment was performed for the 1964–72 and 1987–91 papers. The number of company papers in each year was multiplied by the ratio of the total number of papers surveyed by *Science Citation Index* in 1981 and the particular year.

6 A model of the innovation cycle in the pharmaceutical industry

Introduction

This chapter estimates a model of the drug innovation cycle. It employs the 1968–91 sample of the fourteen largest US-based pharmaceutical companies used in the previous chapter.

There has been a fair number of empirical studies of innovation in the drug sector. Some studies have analyzed the determinants of product innovation. They have regressed the number of new chemical entities or the sales of new products on past R&D, company characteristics (e.g. size) or measures of the stringency of regulation (Comanor, 1965; Baily, 1972; Schnee, 1972; Vernon and Gusen, 1974; Schwartzman, 1976; Grabowski, Vernon, and Thomas, 1978; Wiggins, 1981; Jensen, 1987; Thomas, 1987; for a survey, see Comanor, 1986). A second group of studies has examined the determinants of R&D. They regressed R&D on firm characteristics or the extent of regulation (Grabowski, 1968; Vernon and Gusen, 1974; Schwartzman, 1976; Grabowski and Vernon, 1981; Wiggins, 1983; Thomas, 1987; Jensen, 1988; for a survey, again see Comanor, 1986).

Most works have thus focused on a subset of the relations among R&D, innovation, and characteristics of the firm or of the environment. The model presented in this chapter jointly estimates four equations: a sales equation, an R&D equation, an equation for the capital stock of firms, and a market value equation, where market value measures expected future profitability. The model purports to offer a more comprehensive view of the determinants of sales, R&D, physical capital, and profitability of the largest US drug companies, and proposes a structural interpretation of the interdependence among these variables. The analysis is based on a longer time series than other empirical studies of the drug sector. Not only is this more consistent with the long cycles of drug innovation, but it offers the opportunity to evaluate whether there have been structural changes between the 1970s and 1980s.

The next section discusses the issues addressed by the model, and examines related works in the literature. The model and the equations to be estimated are presented in the subsequent section, and this is followed by a discussion of the empirical results. A concluding section summarizes the findings. The data are described in an appendix.

The issues addressed by the model

Length and risks of drug development

The development of new drugs, from applied research to distribution, is a long process. Pre-clinical research takes on average two years, clinical trials take about five or six years, and the final NDA review by the FDA takes about two years.[1] Baily (1972), Grabowski, Vernon, and Thomas (1978), and Wiggins (1981) found that R&D influences the number of new chemical entities introduced in the USA three to five years later. The second and third stages of clinical trials, which occur three to five years before commercialization (see figure 2.1), account for 60–80 percent of total R&D costs in the pharmaceutical industry (see table 2.1). These studies thus found that expenditures on the latest stages of clinical trials are good predictors of innovation a few years later.

The model in this chapter estimates a specific form of the lag structure of R&D on sales. Some studies suggested that in recent years regulatory requirements have become more stringent, and that they have lengthened drug development times; particularly, the NDA review process has become longer.[2] The model presented here tests whether there were changes in the lag structure of R&D between the 1970s and 1980s. The model also estimates the long-run productivity of drug R&D, and tests whether in the 1980s it increased or decreased with respect to the previous decade.

Drug R&D is risky. Only very few compounds discovered during applied research pass the subsequent clinical tests, and are eventually approved for marketing by the FDA (see chapter 2). Clymer (1969) estimated that in the early 1960s only one out of nine chemical entities that entered clinical trials reached the market. Lasagna and Wardell (1975) used data from a questionnaire survey of fifteen large research-based pharmaceutical firms. They found that only 7.1 percent of all new chemical entities for which an IND was submitted between 1963 and 1967 had become approved new drugs by 1974. Hansen (1979) used data on the new chemical entities developed by fourteen pharmaceutical companies between 1963 and 1975. He regressed $(N_t/N_0) = \exp(-\delta t) + \mu$, where N_0 is the number of new chemical entities that enter clinical testing at time zero, N_t is the number of new chemical entities that survive t years later, δ is the attrition rate to be estimated, t is a time trend, and μ is an error term. He estimated $\delta = 0.44$, which implies that only 64 percent ($\equiv \exp(-0.44)$) of the compounds existing at time $t-1$ survive one year later.

The model in this chapter assumes that each year pharmaceutical firms launch a number of innovation projects. R&D expenditures are assumed to be a function of the number of projects that are still in process every year. The model estimates the fraction of R&D expenditures at time t that is explained by R&D in the previous year. It interprets this coefficient to be a measure of the percentage of projects in any year which are expected to survive one year later. The attrition rate thus obtained can be compared with those estimated by previous works, and particularly with Hansen's.

Competition

The model does not offer a structural analysis of competition. However, it examines a few "facts" about competition in this industry. The drug sector is composed of two distinct markets: R&D-based drugs and non R&D-intensive products (generic and OTC medicines) (Thomas, 1988; ADL, 1988). Although the market of R&D-based drugs is dominated by large firms (see Thomas, 1988), not all large US drug companies are very R&D-intensive producers. Some of them are more active in the markets for non R&D-based drugs or other non-R&D products.

The rise of new scientific and technological opportunities in the 1980s has intensified the importance of innovation-based competition in the drug industry. Yet, as also discussed in chapter 4, not only are innovation capabilities unevenly distributed among drug companies, but also less research-intensive firms have had difficulties in acquiring such capabilities in relatively little time.

The fourteen firms in the sample were put in three groups: high, medium, and low R&D-intensive firms. The model then estimated the impact, on the sales of each firm, of variables capturing the performance of competitors in each group. New drugs drive old, less effective products out of the market, especially if they are a more effective cure for certain pathologies, or they cure pathologies for which there was no previous remedy. High and, in part, medium R&D-intensive firms produce a steady flow of new drugs. As a result, their market performance ought to exert important negative effects on the sales of competitors. In contrast, the performance of companies in the low group ought to exert a less important effect on the sales of their rivals.

This can also be cast in the form of a test of some of the implications of the case studies of chapter 4. There we saw that leading innovators accumulate profits, which can be reinvested in research, thereby stimulating new innovations. Less R&D-intensive firms can have serious difficulties in breaking into this "virtuous" spiral. The high, medium, and low R&D-intensive firms were distinguished according to their average R&D–sales ratio for 1966–91. Thus, being in the high, medium or low group reflects long-run characteristics of the firms. If we observed that low firms have important competitive impacts on rivals, this would suggest that they have been able to produce competitive products, typically new drugs, and hence they have been able to break into the market for R&D-based goods.

Hypotheses from the error structure of the model

The model assumes that drug manufacturers face three types of shock: a shock to sales, a technological opportunity shock, and a shock idiosyncratic to the capital stock.

Grabowski (1968), Grabowski and Vernon (1981), and Jensen (1988) found that internal funds have a positive and significant effect on the R&D expenditures of firms. In the drug industry, product innovations elicit high growth of sales and profits. Sales shocks then ought to have a positive effect on R&D. The model tests this hypothesis. It also proposes a structural interpretation of this phenomenon. It suggests that unexpected increases in profits (typically from innovation) are used to finance new innovation projects, i.e. they are an important determinant of expenditures in pre-clinical research. The model also tests whether the sales shock affects physical capital. As firms vary their capital stock in response to unexpected increases or decreases in demand (and in internal financial resources), the sales shock ought to exhibit positive correlation with physical capital.[3]

The technological opportunity shock is interpreted to be unexpected successes or failures during the innovation process. However, because of the length and risks of drug development, signals from pre-clinical and clinical research are likely to be volatile. Companies would be cautious about varying their capital stock in response to news during experimentation stages. Thus, technological opportunity shocks are unlikely to have significant effects on physical capital.

Finally, the model evaluates the effects of the sales shock, the technological opportunity shock and the shock idiosyncratic to capital on the market value of firms. The literature on the returns from new drugs is voluminous. Most studies attempted to improve accounting measures of rates of return by taking into consideration the stock nature of research or by adjusting for taxes and inflation. Friedman and Associates (1973) used data for six major pharmaceutical companies for the period 1967–72. They estimated that the rate of return from capital R&D expenditure at constant prices is 13.7 percent. Similarly, Ayanian (1975) estimated a rate of return of about 14 percent for six major drug companies in 1973. Schwartzman (1975 and 1976) used industry data, and found that the rate of return in 1973 was between 3.3 percent and 7.5 percent. Stauffer (1975) used data for two firms during 1963–72. He found rates of return of 15 percent and 16.4 percent. Clarkson (1977 and 1979) used data about one large pharmaceutical company for 1965–74, and found a rate of return of 11.1 percent. Virts and Weston (1980) used data on 119 new chemical entities introduced between 1967 and 1976. They estimated that the return to R&D per new chemical entity is less than 8 percent. Grabowski and Vernon (1990) used data on 100 new chemical entities between 1970 and 1979. They obtained returns from new product introductions of about 9 percent. Chien and Upson (1980) is the only study on the returns from drug industry stocks. They found that during 1947–75 the rate of return of drug industry shares was about 11.5 percent.

The returns estimated by these studies vary considerably. This is because the estimated returns are likely to be sensitive to assumptions about capital depreciation rates and the discount factors that are used to construct the stocks. More importantly, different estimates may arise because of the heterogeneity of the samples employed. Chien and Upson used drug industry stocks, Virts and Weston and Grabowski and Vernon used data on new chemical entities, Schwartzman used industry data. Friedman and Associates, Ayanian, Stauffer, and Clarkson used firm data. However, they considered only a few firms – one, two or at most six. An important claim of this work is that rates of return in the pharmaceutical industry are likely to differ across firms. Thus, when comparing studies that employ hetero-geneous data, or data regarding few and different companies, rates of return are likely to vary.

The model of this chapter studies the sources of inter-firm differences in profitability. It estimates whether the sales and technological opportunity shocks determine inter-firm differences in the growth of market value. It also estimates whether the capital shock influences market value. The shock idiosyncratic to capital is interpreted to be news about demand for non R&D-based products. One can then test whether innovation is the critical source of profitability in the pharmaceutical industry. If so, the capital shock ought to have a negligible effect on market value.

A model of the innovation process in the pharmaceutical industry

The model

At each stage of drug development (applied research, animal tests, IND revision, clinical stages I, II and III, and NDA review – see Figure 2.1), various properties of compounds are tested. Only a fraction of the compounds that enter a certain stage are considered viable, and they are moved to the next stage. This suggests a particular model of the innovation cycle. Assume that every year pharmaceutical companies undertake a certain number of innovation projects. Define P_{it} to be the number of innovation projects of the ith firm at time t; P_{it} is equal to the sum of the projects started $t - v$ years earlier ($v = 0, 1, 2, \ldots$) that still survive at time t, i.e. $P_{it} = {}_tP_{it} + {}_{t-1}P_{it} + {}_{t-2}P_{it} + {}_{t-3}P_{it} + \ldots$, where subscripts before variables denote the starting date of projects.[4]

Assume that the number of projects started at $t - v$ that survive at time t is equal to a fraction γ of the projects started at $t - v$ that survived at $t - 1$, plus a random component ${}_{t-v}\theta_{it}$, i.e. ${}_{t-v}P_{it} = \gamma({}_{t-v}P_{it-1}) + {}_{t-v}\theta_{it}$. Hence,

$$P_{it} = {}_tP_{it} + \gamma P_{it-1} + \theta_{it} \tag{1}$$

where $\theta_{it} \equiv \sum_{v=1}^{\infty} {}_{t-v}\theta_{it}$. The parameter γ is thus a measure of the expected yearly survival rate of innovation projects. The technological opportunity shock θ_{it} is a factor that, in any particular year, makes the number of new drugs moving to the next stages higher or lower than the expected yearly survival measure γ.

Pharmaceutical companies maximize the expected sum of discounted future earnings by choosing capital stock and variable factors at time t and future periods. They also choose the number of projects started at t and later years, i.e. ${}_\tau P_{i\tau}$, $\tau \geq t$. Annual profits are equal to variable profits minus capital cost and the total cost of the projects $P_{i\tau}$, with $\tau \geq t$.

If the firm has already optimized over the variable factors, the optimization problem can be written as

$$\max_{(K_{i\tau}; P_{i\tau})_{\tau=t}^{\infty}} E_t \sum_{\tau=t}^{\infty} \{\pi_{i\tau}[n_{i\tau}(P_{i\tau-h}^*, \epsilon_{1i\tau}), K_{i\tau-1}, Z_{ij\tau}, \epsilon_{2i\tau}] - a_{i\tau}K_{i\tau} - C_i(P_{i\tau})\}\rho^{\tau-t}$$

subject to (1). In the problem above, E_t is the expectation operator given all information at time t, $\pi_{i\tau}(\cdot)$ is the variable profit function, $C_i(\cdot)$ is the cost function (assumed to be different between firms) of undertaking the projects $P_{i\tau}$, K is a measure of the capital stock in real terms, and ρ is a discount factor. The user cost of capital $a_{i\tau}$ is assumed to be equal to the sum of firm- and time-specific components. It is also assumed that pharmaceutical companies take the behavior of rivals as given; $\pi_{i\tau}[\cdot]$ depends upon $Z_{ij\tau}$, where $Z_{ij\tau}$ is a vector of variables correlated with the performance of i's competitors j, $j \neq i$.

Apart from variable factor prices and the capital stock K_{it-1} (assume a one-period gestation lag of capital), the variable profits $\pi_{i\tau}[\cdot]$ depend upon the number of new drugs introduced by the firm, $n_{i\tau}(\cdot)$. The latter depends upon $P^*_{i\tau-h}$, defined to be the total number of projects at the end of clinical testing $\tau-h$ years earlier, where h measures the years of NDA revision by the FDA.

The variable profits also depend upon two shocks, ϵ_1 and ϵ_2. The number of new drugs $n_{i\tau}(\cdot)$ may deviate from its expected level, given the number of projects at the end of clinical testing h periods earlier, because the FDA may approve a higher or lower number of NDAs than expected, or it may take more or less time than expected to approve them. This is captured by ϵ_1. The shock ϵ_2 captures additional information about the quality of new drugs that have already been on the market for some years. Market diffusion of a new medicine may reveal side-effects and adverse reactions which were not anticipated during clinical trials.[5] The market may also provide evidence that the new medicine is more effective than expected, and sometimes it indicates that the new drug can be used for therapeutic needs other than those for which it was developed.[6]

The estimated equations

From the optimization problem, three equations were derived. The first is the sales equation. It is obtained by imposing a functional specification on the technology of the firm. R&D is the dependent variable of the second equation. The latter is derived from (1) after imposing a structure on the optimal path of $_tP_{it}$. Capital stock is the dependent variable of the third equation. The capital stock equation follows from the first-order conditions of the optimization problem.

In order to derive the sales equation, assume that the technology is Cobb–Douglas. Then, the variable profit function is Cobb–Douglas, and sales are proportional to variable profits. Define S and R to be real sales and real R&D. Using lower-case letters for logs, one can write

$$s_{it} = c_{sit} + ak_{it-1} + \sum_{\tau=2}^{\infty} \beta_\tau r_{it-\tau} + f(\mathbf{Z}_{ijt}) + \epsilon_{it} \qquad (2)$$

where past R&D expenditures proxy for P^*_{it-h}, a and the β_τ's are parameters, c_{sit} is a constant equal to the sum of firm- and time-specific components, $f(\mathbf{Z}_{ijt})$ is a function of the vector of variables $\mathbf{Z}$ correlated with the performance of i's competitors, j, and ϵ is an error which combines ϵ_1 and ϵ_2. The variable factor prices are assumed to be common to all firms, and they are captured by the time-specific component of c_{sit}. Also, the average NDA period is two years (see figure 2.1). During this period, the firm does not play any significant role, and it has to wait for the final decision of the FDA. Hence, R&D lags start with $t-2$.

To derive the full specification of the sales equation to be estimated, we have to impose a specific form for the lag structure of R&D and for $f(\mathbf{Z}_{ijt})$ in (2).

Assume that the lag structure of R&D takes the following form

$$\beta \cdot \sum_{\tau=2}^{\infty} \exp(-\lambda) \cdot [\lambda^{\tau-2}/(\tau-2)!] r_{it-\tau}$$

where β and λ are parameters to be estimated. This is a useful specification for a number of reasons. First, because of the Poisson-like structure of the "weights" $\exp(-\lambda) \cdot [\lambda^{\tau-2}/(\tau-2)!]$, the parameter β has a straightforward interpretation. It is the total variation in sales given unit variations in all R&D lags. It is thus a synthetic measure of long-run research productivity.[7]

Second, this specification is flexible enough to allow for the possibility that the impact of past R&D expenditures on sales either declines monotonically over time, or increases and then decreases. The latter possibility is especially useful for our purpose. As stages II and III of clinical testing account for 60 to 80 percent of total R&D expenditures of pharmaceutical firms, the estimated impacts of R&D on sales will capture primarily the effects of R&D spending in the development stages immediately preceding the NDA review. If the NDA review takes more than two years, the greatest impact of R&D will take place three or more years before sales. On the other hand, if the NDA review takes two years or less, the impact of R&D lags will decrease monotonically over time, with R&D at $t-2$ showing the largest effect on sales.

Moreover, the lag structure of R&D in the "1970s" was distinguished from that in the "1980s". The lag structure of R&D in the sales equation (2) can thus be written as

$$\beta_{70} D70_t \sum_{\tau=2}^{\infty} \exp(-\lambda_{70}) \cdot [\lambda_{70}^{\tau-2}/(\tau-2)!] \cdot r_{it-\tau} +$$

$$\beta_{80} D80_t \sum_{\tau=2}^{\infty} \exp(-\lambda_{80}) \cdot [\lambda_{80}^{\tau-2}/(\tau-2)!] \cdot r_{it-\tau}$$

where β_{70}, β_{80}, λ_{70}, and λ_{80} are parameters to be estimated, and D70 and D80 are dummy variables that take, respectively, the value 1 for 1968–79 and 0 otherwise, and the value 1 for 1980–91 and 0 otherwise. By looking at the estimated parameters β_{70} and β_{80}, one can test for changes in the research productivity of pharmaceutical companies between the 1970s and the 1980s. The parameters λ_{70} and λ_{80} control for differences in the forms of the lag structures in the two periods.

As far as expression $f(\mathbf{Z}_{ijt})$ is concerned, the firms in the sample were divided into three groups: high (H), medium (M), and low (L) R&D-

intensive firms. Firms were allocated to each group according to their average R&D–sales ratio during 1966–91. (See the appendix, which also lists the firms in the H, M, and L groups.) After-tax net income (NY) is used as a proxy for the performance of i's rivals (to avoid endogeneity, net income is lagged one year). Define $z_{iGt-1} \equiv (1/N_{iG}) \sum_j \log(NY_{jt-1})$, $G = H, M,$

L, where the summation runs over all $j \in G$ provided that if $i \in G$, then $j \neq i$; N_{iG} is the number of terms in the summation. Hence, z_{iGt-1} is the net income of the "average" G-type competitor of i.[8] Then, $f(\mathbf{Z}_{ijt-1}) \equiv \sum_G \phi_G z_{iGt-1}$,

$G = H, M, L$, where the ϕ_G's are parameters to be estimated. They account for the impact of lagged average profits of the firms in group G on the sales of the ith firm, for $G = H, M, L$. One can then test for differences in the intensity of competition from the H, M, or L firms by looking at the estimated parameters ϕ_H, ϕ_M, and ϕ_L.

Ultimately, the estimated sales equation becomes

$$s_{it} = c_{sit} + ak_{it-1} + \beta_{70}D70_t \sum_{\tau=2}^{8} \exp(-\lambda_{70}) \cdot [\lambda_{70}^{\tau-2}/(\tau-2)!] \cdot r_{it-\tau} +$$

$$\beta_{80}D80_t \sum_{\tau=2}^{8} \exp(-\lambda_{80}) \cdot [\lambda_{80}^{\tau-2}/(\tau-2)!] \cdot r_{it-\tau} +$$

$$\phi_H z_{iHt-1} + \phi_M z_{iMt-1} + \phi_L z_{iLt-1} + \epsilon_{it} \qquad (3)$$

where eight R&D lags have been used to estimate the β's and the λ's.[9]

The second equation is the R&D equation. Assume that the (real) cost of innovation projects is an exponential function of P_{it}. R&D in real terms is the cost of undertaking such projects in a certain year. Then, $R_{it} = m_{0i} \cdot \exp(mP_{it})$, with m_{0i} and $m > 0$. Solve this expression for P_{it}, substitute P_{it} in (1), and solve (1) for r_{it} (recall $r_{it} \equiv \log R_{it}$). One obtains

$$r_{it} = \text{const}_i + m_t P_{it} + \gamma r_{it-1} + \theta_{it} \qquad (4)$$

where θ_{it} has been normalized with respect to m.

To derive the R&D equation to be estimated, an expression was specified for the optimal path of $_tP_{it}$, i.e. the number of innovation projects initiated by the firm at time t. Pharmaceutical companies allocate funds to basic and applied research according to their financial capabilities, which depend upon present and past market performance. Assume that the optimal path of $_tP_{it}$ depends upon log-sales in previous years, which capture the effect of past market performance, and the shock ϵ_{it} to sales and variable profits, which captures the effect of present factors on the decision to start innovation projects. The optimal path of $_tP_{it}$ also depends upon firm-specific characteristics (e.g., different managerial attitudes towards research). Assuming linearity, one can write

$$r_{it} = c_{ri} + \gamma r_{it-1} + \xi_1 s_{it-1} + \xi_2 s_{it-2} + \xi_3 s_{it-3} + \xi_4 s_{it-4} + x_\epsilon \epsilon_{it} + \theta_{it} \qquad (5)$$

where four sales lags are used to account for the effect of past market performance (ξ_1, ξ_2, ξ_3, and ξ_4 are parameters); c_{ri} is a firm-specific (deterministic) component, and x_ϵ is a parameter that measures the impact of present sales shocks on the decision to start new innovation projects. The estimated values of x_ϵ and the ξ's will test whether, as suggested by Grabowski (1968), Grabowski and Vernon (1981), and Jensen (1988), internal funds are correlated with R&D in the pharmaceutical industry. The proposed structure of the model suggests that internal funds influence the number of innovation projects $_t P_{it}$ started at time t, i.e. they are an important determinant of expenditures in pre-clinical research.

The third equation is the capital stock equation. It follows from the first-order conditions of the optimization problem. The first-order condition with respect to capital stock at time t is $E_t \, \rho(d\pi_{it+1}/dK_{it}) = a_{it}$. With Cobb–Douglas technology, variable profits are proportional to sales. If a is the elasticity of capital, one can write $E_t \rho \cdot a \cdot \text{const} \cdot (S_{it+1}/K_{it}) = a_{it}$. Take logs of both sides. Substitute $E_t s_{it+1}$ from the one-period lead of (3). Assume that $E_t \epsilon_{it+1}$ depends only on ϵ_{it}, and not on $\epsilon_{it-1}, \epsilon_{it-2}, \ldots$. Moreover, assume that $E_t f(\mathbf{Z}_{ijt}) = \phi_0 \cdot f(\mathbf{Z}_{ijt-1})$, i.e. the performance of competitors at time t is predicted by their performance at $t-1$ (ϕ_0 is a parameter). Solve for k_{it} ($\equiv \log K_{it}$), and obtain

$$k_{it} = c_{kit} + [\beta_{70}/(1-a)]\text{D70}_t \sum_{\tau=2}^{8} \exp(-\lambda_{70}) \cdot [\lambda_{70}^{\tau-2}/(\tau-2)!] \cdot r_{it-\tau+1} +$$
$$[\beta_{80}/(1-a)]\text{D80}_t \sum_{\tau=2}^{8} \exp(-\lambda_{80}) \cdot [\lambda_{80}^{\tau-2}/(\tau-2)!] \cdot r_{it-\tau+1} +$$
$$[\phi_0/(1-a)](\phi_H \cdot z_{Ht} + \phi_M \cdot z_{Mt} + \phi_L \cdot z_{Lt}) + y_\epsilon \cdot \epsilon_{it} + y_\theta \cdot \theta_{it} + \delta_{it} \qquad (6)$$

where c_{kit} is the sum of firm and time components. The parameters y_ϵ and y_θ measure the impact of the shocks ϵ and θ on capital stock; δ_{it} is an error idiosyncratic to capital, which is interpreted to be a demand shock for non R&D-based products.[10]

The error components of (6) can be justified as follows.[11] Sales shocks ϵ affect investment in physical capital. News of sales raises the incentives of firms to expand their capital stock to satisfy the increased demand. ("Bad" news would work in the opposite way.) Technological shocks θ may also influence the capital stock. Unexpected advances or failures during the innovation process may alter the propensity of firms to build new capital in anticipation of possible future sales expansions or contractions. Yet, given the length and risks of drug development, technological shocks are likely to be too distant from commercialization, and they can be very volatile.

Hence, companies could be very conservative in responding to signals during clinical trials. Drug firms would expand physical capital only when new products were almost ready to be marketed, presumably during NDA revision. This hypothesis can be tested. If drug companies change their capital stock only during NDA revision, the shock ϵ will have a substantial impact on capital, whereas θ will explain only a modest fraction of the variance of k.

Empirical results

Four equations were estimated. The first three equations were the sales equation (3), the R&D equation (5), and the capital stock equation (6).

The fourth equation was a market value equation. Following Pakes (1985), under the assumption of stock market efficiency, deviations of market value V_{it} from its expected level, given all information at $t-1$, depend only on news at t, i.e. $[(V_{it} - \mathrm{E}_{t-1}V_{it})/V_{it}] = w_\epsilon \epsilon_{it} + w_\theta \theta_{it} + w_\delta \delta_{it} + \psi_{it}$, where ψ_{it} is a measurement error and the w's are parameters.[12] If $(V_{it} - \mathrm{E}_{t-1}V_{it})$ is small with respect to V_{it}, then $[(V_{it} - \mathrm{E}_{t-1}V_{it})/V_{it}] \approx \log(V_{it}/\mathrm{E}_{t-1}V_{it})$. Assume that the value of the firm is expected to grow at a rate q_t common to all firms but different over time. Then, $\mathrm{E}_{t-1}V_{it} = V_{it-1}\exp(q_t)$, and one can write

$$\log\frac{V_t}{V_{t-1}} = q_t + w_\epsilon \epsilon_{it} + w_\theta \theta_{it} + w_\delta \delta_{it} + \psi_{it} \tag{7}$$

which is the value equation to be estimated.

The sales equation (3), the R&D equation (5), the capital stock equation (6), and the value equation (7) were estimated using data on total sales (in real terms), real R&D expenditures, and a measure of the value of the capital stock in real terms, for the largest fourteen US pharmaceutical companies between 1968 and 1991. The market value of the firm is debt plus equity. Net income is equal to net sales plus other incomes minus costs of products sold, other expenditures, and taxes. Tables 6.1 and 6.2 report descriptive statistics. The appendix to this chapter describes the data.

First differences were used in the sales equation (3), the R&D equation (5), and the capital stock equation (6), to eliminate firm-specific effects in c_{sit}, c_{ri}, and c_{kit}.[13] As their constant terms also have time-components, the dependent variables and the regressors in the sales and capital stock equations are differences from time means. Similarly, in the value equation, the dependent variable $\log(V_{it}/V_{it-1})$ is measured in terms of differences from time means, and it is regressed against a constant.[14] The system (3)–(5)–(6)–(7) was estimated by maximum likelihood, and the results are given in table 6.3.

Table 6.1. *Descriptive statistics: levels*

Variable	Mean	Std. dev.	Min.	Max.	BVAR (%)	WVAR (%)
Sales	2,672.3	1,534.8	195.6 (598.7)	9,174.3 (5,358.2)	67.3	29.0
R&D	194.5	136.1	20.9 (53.7)	742.3 (246.0)	39.6	64.4
Net value of capital stock	2,289.4	1,433.8	155.1 (618.0)	7,432.3 (3,327.7)	50.0	58.2
After-tax net income	368.3	299.6	9.9 (81.9)	2,078.1 (509.0)	49.6	62.7
Market value	6,411.3	6,414.9	622.1 (883.7)	56,954.1 (7,013.1)	54.8	68.4

Notes: Fourteen firms, 1968–91. Number of observations = 277. Because of missing values, descriptive statistics are computed using only observations in the estimated sample (see table 6.3 below). Values in constant 1982 million dollars. In parentheses min. and max. for central year, 1979 (fourteen observations). BVAR is the ratio of the between-group variance to total variance, i.e. BVAR $=\sum_{it}(y_{it}-y_t^*)^2/\sum_{it}(y_{it}-y^*)^2$, where y_t^* is y_{it} averaged over firms, and y^* is the overall average. WVAR is the ratio of the within-group variance to total variance, i.e. WVAR $=\sum_{it}(y_{it}-y_i^*)^2/\sum_{it}(y_{it}-y^*)^2$, where y_i^* is y_{it} averaged over time.

Table 6.2. *Descriptive statistics: growth rates – log (y_{it}/y_{it-1})*

Variable	Mean	Std. dev.	Min.	Max.	BVAR (%)	WVAR (%)
Sales	0.052	0.073	−0.187	0.550	75.4	87.7
R&D	0.081	0.060	−0.077	0.330	71.9	93.5
Net value of capital stock	0.074	0.085	−0.264	0.530	74.1	87.8
After-tax net income	0.067	0.357	−3.135	2.877	90.0	98.0
Market value	0.068	0.234	−0.608	0.777	55.1	98.0

Notes: Fourteen firms, 1968–91. Number of observations = 277. Descriptive statistics are computed using only the observations in the estimated sample (see table 6.3 below). Growth rates computed from variables in constant 1982 dollars. BVAR and WVAR are the ratios of the between-group and within-group variances to total variance, and they are computed as described in table 6.1.

Table 6.3. *Estimated parameters, equations (3), (5), (6), and (7)*

Parameters	Estimates	Parameters	Estimates
α	0.064	ϕ_M	-0.489
	(0.039)		(0.278)
β_{70}	0.111	ϕ_L	-0.079
	(0.064)		(0.154)
λ_{70}	0.664	γ	0.638
	(0.722)		(0.053)
β_{80}	0.459	ξ_1	-0.040
	(0.152)		(0.068)
λ_{80}	2.816	ξ_2	0.041
	(0.903)		(0.052)
ϕ_0	1.399	ξ_3	0.119
	(0.506)		(0.043)
ϕ_H	-0.755	ξ_4	0.095
	(0.364)		(0.051)

$$\text{VCOV} = \begin{bmatrix} 0.00368 & & & \\ 0.00135 & 0.00442 & & \\ 0.00228 & 0.00081 & 0.00496 & \\ 0.00313 & 0.00217 & 0.00211 & 0.02999 \end{bmatrix}$$

Notes: Fourteen firms, 1968–91. Number of observations $= 277$. Number of observations smaller than 336 ($= 14 \times 24$) because of missing values. Log likelihood function $= 1,252.8$. Heteroskedastic consistent standard errors in parentheses. VCOV $=$ Estimated variance–covariance matrix of the residuals (equations (3), (5), (6), and (7)).

The estimated value of α is small. With constant R&D, variations in capital stock have a small impact on sales (and variable profits). This provides additional evidence that, in the pharmaceutical industry, sales growth is determined primarily by product innovations. Variations in the capital stock that occur irrespective of research and innovation, i.e. which depend essentially on market opportunities for non R&D-based products, have unimportant effects on sales and profitability.

The estimation offers interesting evidence about the lag structure of R&D. In the first place, R&D productivity in the drug industry appears to have increased in the 1980s. The estimated value of β_{80} is more than three times greater than the estimated value of β_{70}. The rise of new scientific and technological opportunities in the past decade has augmented considerably the marginal product of research. The lag structure of R&D has also

Table 6.4. *Estimated lag structure of R&D*

"1970s"		"1980s"	
Parameters	Estimates	Parameters	Estimates
$\beta_{70;2}$	0.0569	$\beta_{80;2}$	0.0275
$\beta_{70;3}$	0.0378	$\beta_{80;3}$	0.0774
$\beta_{70;4}$	0.0126	$\beta_{80;4}$	0.1090
$\beta_{70;5}$	0.0028	$\beta_{80;5}$	0.1023
$\beta_{70;6}$	0.0005	$\beta_{80;6}$	0.0720
$\beta_{70;7}$	0.0000	$\beta_{80;7}$	0.0406
$\beta_{70;8}$	0.0000	$\beta_{80;8}$	0.0190
$\beta_{70;9}$	0.0000	$\beta_{80;9}$	0.0076
$\beta_{70;10}$	0.0000	$\beta_{80;10}$	0.0027
$\beta_{70;11}$	0.0000	$\beta_{80;11}$	0.0008
$\beta_{70;12}$	0.0000	$\beta_{80;12}$	0.0002
$\beta_{70;13}$	0.0000	$\beta_{80;13}$	0.0001

Notes:

$\beta_{70;\tau} = \beta_{70} \cdot \exp(-\lambda_{70}) \cdot [\lambda_{70}^{\tau-2}/(\tau-2)!]$, for $\tau = 2,3,4,\ldots$

$\beta_{80;\tau} = \beta_{80} \cdot \exp(-\lambda_{80}) \cdot [\lambda_{80}^{\tau-2}/(\tau-2)!]$, for $\tau = 2,3,4,\ldots$

β_{70}, β_{80}, λ_{70}, and λ_{80} are the estimated parameters in table 6.3.

changed. Using the estimated parameters λ_{70} and λ_{80}, table 6.4 reports the estimated values of the β_τ's, for $\tau = 2,3,4,\ldots$, i.e., the impact of the R&D growth rate at time $t - \tau$ on present sales. (See also figure 6.1.) From table 6.4, in the 1970s the impact of past R&D declines monotonically after two years. In the 1980s, the highest effect of R&D lags is after four to five years. This suggests that, in the 1970s, NDA review was shorter than two years. Increases in R&D growth (typically because of increased expenditures in stages II and III) had a prompt effect on sales growth. In contrast, in the 1980s, variations in expenditures on the latest stages of clinical trials influence sales with four or five lags, thereby suggesting that NDA review has lengthened.

The expected survival rate of innovation projects, γ, is 0.64. This suggests a high mortality rate of innovation projects during clinical trials. As the latter last about five to six years (Hansen, 1979; Wardell, May, and Trimble, 1982; Kaitin, Richard, and Lasagna, 1987), a yearly attrition rate of 0.64 implies that 7–10 percent of the compounds that entered the clinical trials survive at the end of the clinical trials themselves. The estimated survival rate γ is identical to the one estimated by Hansen (1979) using 1963–75 data on the actual number of new chemical entities that survive during the

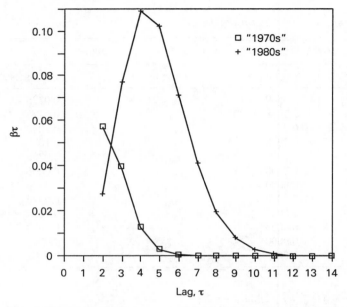

Fig. 6.1. Estimated lag structure of R&D (impact of lagged R&D growth on present sales growth).

various stages of drug development. If one compares the present result with Hansen's, the risks of drug development do not seem to have changed in recent years.

The sum of the estimated parameters ξ_1, ξ_2, ξ_3, and ξ_4 is positive. With constant growth rate of sales, past sales growth has a positive impact on R&D growth.[15] As discussed in the previous section, this suggests that past market performance influences the decision of firms to start new innovation projects.

The estimated parameters ϕ_H, ϕ_M, and ϕ_L highlight the different competitive potential of firms in the H, M, and L groups. All three parameters are negative (and the statistical significance of ϕ_H is especially high). But the estimated value of ϕ_H is greater (in absolute value) than that of ϕ_M which in turn is greater than ϕ_L. A unit increase in the growth rate of profits of the "average" H competitor produces a 0.75 decline in the growth of sales of a given firm; a unit increase in the growth rate of profits of the "average" M competitor reduces the growth rate of sales by about 0.50, whereas the "average" L competitor reduces the growth rate of sales by only 0.08. Competitive threats in this industry come primarily from high (and medium) research-intensive firms, and hence they are most likely to be

Table 6.5. *Estimates of the shock parameters and shock variances*

(a) *Shock parameters[a]*

Parameters	Estimates
x_ϵ	0.366
y_ϵ	0.619
y_θ	-0.006
w_ϵ	0.852
w_θ	0.260
w_δ	0.049

(b) *Shock variances*

$\sigma_\epsilon^2 = 0.00368$
$\sigma_\theta^2 = 0.00392$
$\sigma_\delta^2 = 0.00355$
$\sigma_\psi^2 = 0.02705$

Note: [a] Computed from the variance–covariance matrix in table 6.3.

associated with the commercialization of new drugs. OTC medicines and other non R&D-based products, which constitute the main sales of less research-intensive manufacturers, pose far smaller threats.

Table 6.3 also reports the variance–covariance matrix of residuals. Because of the recursive structure of the errors in (3), (5), (6), and (7), one can estimate the variances σ_ϵ^2, σ_θ^2, σ_δ^2, and σ_ψ^2 of the shocks ϵ, θ, δ, and ψ, and the parameters x_ϵ, y_ϵ, y_θ, w_ϵ, w_θ, and w_δ. Table 6.5 reports the variances of the shocks, and the estimated parameters x_ϵ, y_ϵ, y_θ, w_ϵ, w_θ, and w_δ computed from the variance–covariance matrix in table 6.3.

The parameter x_ϵ indicates that a unit shock ϵ to the growth rate of sales augments the growth rate of R&D by 0.37. The variance of ϵ explains about 11 percent of the total variance of R&D. News to sales, and therefore to variable profits, influences R&D growth. The interpretation suggested here is that news to sales encourages the start of new innovation projects, $_tP_{it}$.

The estimated parameter y_ϵ indicates that a unit shock to sales growth, which was interpreted to be news about new products under NDA revision or in the market for some years, raises the growth rate of capital by 0.62. The variance of ϵ explains about 28 percent of the total variance of capital. In contrast, the estimated value of y_θ indicates that θ has practically no effect on the growth of capital stock. Because of the length and uncertainty

Table 6.6. *Growth rate of market value (average across firms of the growth rate of market value in each year)*

Year	Yearly average
1968	0.0883
1969	0.1029
1970	− 0.0711
1971	0.1679
1972	0.1956
1973	− 0.1165
1974	− 0.2610
1975	− 0.0714
1976	− 0.1157
1977	− 0.1509
1978	0.1151
1979	0.0359
1980	0.1192
1981	− 0.1234
1982	0.1545
1983	0.0495
1984	0.0169
1985	0.3816
1986	0.2511
1987	0.2383
1988	− 0.0612
1989	0.1981
1990	0.1473
1991	0.2535

Notes:

Overall average:	0.0679
Average 1968–79:	− 0.0067
Average 1980–91:	0.1354

of drug development, companies do not alter their investment plans in response to unexpected successes or failures during applied research or clinical trials. Firms appear to invest in physical capital only when they are sufficiently confident about the market potential of their new compounds, i.e., typically when new products are being reviewed by the FDA or even after their initial commercialization.

Table 6.6 reports interfirm averages of the growth rate of market value in

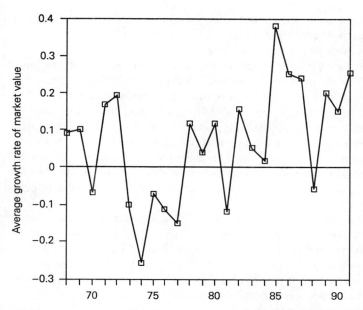

Fig. 6.2. Growth rate of market value (average across firms of the growth rate of market value in each year).

the years 1968–91. (See also figure 6.2.) The average growth of market value for 1968–79 was practically zero, whilst for 1980–91 it increased sharply (to about 13.5 percent): expected profitability in the US pharmaceutical industry increased in the 1980s.

Moreover, the shocks ϵ and θ seem to produce important interfirm differences in the growth of market value. From table 6.5, a unit shock ϵ produces a 0.85 variation in the growth of market value (w_ϵ), whilst a unit shock θ produces a variation of about 0.25 (w_θ). Together, the variances of ϵ and θ explain about 10 percent of the total variance of market value. The estimated parameter w_δ is much smaller. The unit shock δ has only a 0.04 effect on market value. To the extent that δ represents news about demand for non-R&D products, development and production of new R&D-intensive drugs are by far the most important determinant of profitability among the largest US pharmaceutical firms.

Conclusions

This chapter presented a model of the innovation process in the pharmaceutical industry. The model was estimated using data for the fourteen largest

US drug producers in the period 1968–91. This is a more comprehensive data-set than those employed by previous empirical studies of this industry, especially because of the use of a longer time series.

Two important (and interrelated) results have emerged. First, the long-run research productivity of the largest US drug corporations increased in the 1980s *vis-à-vis* the 1970s (by more than three times). Second, expected profitability in the drug industry also increased, and there were notable interfirm differences in profitability, which depend to a large extent on different research and innovation performance. Particularly, shocks to sales and technological opportunity shocks produce sizeable effects on the growth of market value of individual firms. Shocks that are idiosyncratic to capital stock, which represent news about non R&D-intensive products, have far smaller effects.

More generally, the estimated results produce enough evidence that research and innovation are the most important determinants of competitive performance and profitability among the largest US drug companies. Not only has the productivity of research increased, but it is also significantly greater than that of physical capital. Variations in the growth of capital stock that occur irrespective of variations in R&D growth have very modest effects on sales growth.

The lag structure of R&D effects on sales changed. In the 1980s, the most pronounced effect of R&D lags on sales occurred four or five years earlier (compared to one or two years in the 1970s). This suggests that the NDA review process of the FDA lengthened. In sum, while long-run research productivity has increased in the 1980s, the impact of research productivity on sales became more diluted.

The importance of research and innovation is reinforced by the fact that the market performance of high research-intensive producers has a considerable (negative) impact on the performance of rivals. The estimated impact is lower for medium research-intensive drug manufacturers, and it is fairly small for low research-intensive firms.

About 64 percent of one-lagged R&D explains current R&D. The interpretation of this finding is that only two-thirds of the projects in clinical trials in a given year survive one year later. This estimate is identical to the attrition rate estimated by Hansen (1979) using 1963–75 data, which suggests that the risks of drug development did not change after 1975.

Finally, present and past market performances have notable effects on R&D growth. The model interprets this finding as evidence that, in raising the financial capabilities of firms, market performance encourages the launch of new innovation projects. This is also consistent with the discussion in previous chapters about the cumulativeness of innovation capabilities and market performance of drug firms. Innovative firms obtain greater profits, which are used to begin new innovation projects. As shocks and other factors related to non-R&D products generate modest profit opportunities, firms with only a limited research basis appear to face greater difficulties in accumulating rents to invest money for research. This affects their ability to enter into the market for major R&D-based drugs.

Appendix: Description of data

The fourteen firms in the sample are allocated to the high, medium, and low R&D-intensive groups according to their average R&D to sales ratio in the period 1966–91. Firms with an average ratio above 8 percent are in the high group, between 5 percent and 8 percent are in the medium group, and below 5 percent are in the low group. The firms in the high group are (in parentheses, the average 1966–91 percentage R&D–sales ratio): Eli Lilly (10.1), Merck (9.6), Smithkline (9.0), Syntex (11.8), Upjohn (10.9); in the medium group: Abbott (6.6), Johnson & Johnson (5.7), Pfizer (5.7), Schering-Plough (7.6), Squibb (5.8). In the low group: American Home Products (3.7), Bristol-Myers (4.8), Sterling Drugs (3.8), Warner-Lambert (4.7).

Data for 1959–85 are from the October 1988 update of the NBER–Compustat file. The 1986–91 variables were obtained from data in *Moody's Industrial Manual* (various years). In using Moody's data, an attempt was made to replicate NBER–Compustat definitions of variables, which are reported below. For more details, see Hall *et al.* (1988). Where Moody's series were not identical to Compustat's series, the 1986 values were calculated by applying the 1986 growth rate from Moody's data to the 1985 Compustat variable. "Moody's" 1987–91 growth rates were then applied to the previous year of the series. However, differences between Compustat and Moody's series were small.

Value: The market value of the firm is equal to the sum of the value of the preference stock, the value of the common stock, the long-term debt adjusted for its age structure, and the short-term debt, less the net short-term assets (where net short-term assets are equal to current assets plus short-term debt, less the value of inventories, less current liabilities). Market value is deflated by the US fixed non-residential investment deflator.

Sales: Sales are equal to the total amount of actual billings to customers for regular sales completed during the period, reduced by cash discounts, trade discounts, and returned sales for which credit is given to the customers. Sales are deflated by the US GNP deflator.

Capital stock: The capital stock is equal to the net value of plant, plus the value of inventories and other investments of the firm (investments in unconsolidated subsidiaries, intangibles, and a miscellaneous category). The net value of plant, the value of inventories, and the value of the other investments of the firm are adjusted for inflation. Capital stock is deflated by the US fixed non-residential investment deflator.

R&D: The expenditures on research and development are the private (company-funded) expenditures on the development of new products and services. R&D expenditures are deflated by a price index for R&D goods in industry from the Battelle Research Institute (1992).

After-tax net income: After-tax net income is equal to net sales plus other incomes of the firm (interest) minus cost of products sold, other expenditures (marketing, administrative expenses, advertising, R&D, etc.), and taxes. The after-tax net income series was obtained from the Income Account Reports in *Moody's Industrial Manual* (various years). Net income is deflated by the US fixed non-residential investment deflator.

7 Complementarity and external linkages: the strategies of large firms in biotechnology*

Introduction

Chapter 3 discussed the growing importance of division of labor in pharmaceutical research and innovation. It argued that, with greater scientific intensity of pharmaceutical research, relevant knowledge for innovation can be articulated in more general and abstract forms, and hence it can be transferred more easily between organizations. This encourages division of labor among agents specializing in different segments of the drug innovation cycle.

This chapter presents empirical tests of the rising division of labor in drug innovation using data for eighty-one large US, European, and Japanese chemical and pharmaceutical corporations active in biotechnology.[1]

The analysis focuses on the linkages of large corporations with universities (and, more generally, non-profit scientific institutions), and the so-called new biotechnology firms (henceforth NBFs). There are four main types of external linkage of large firms in biotechnology: joint ventures and agreements with other firms; research agreements with universities; minority participations in NBFs; and acquisition of NBFs. This chapter tests whether these four strategies are complementary to one another – i.e., given any two of them, undertaking more of one raises the pay-off of the other. It also tests whether greater in-house scientific and technological capabilities of large companies in biotechnology (as measured by company patents) raise the marginal value of external linkages. Both hypotheses have direct relevance to the rise of a division of labor in drug innovation.

In the subsequent section the roles of universities, NBFs, and large firms in biotechnology are examined first, and this is followed by a discussion of the four strategies of external linkage. The following section presents the empirical tests. A final section summarizes the discussion, and an appendix describes the data.

Relationships between large firms and other parties in biotechnology

Division of labor among universities, NBFs, and large firms

As discussed in the previous chapters, basic and applied research in molecular biology and genetic engineering plays a prominent role in the development of biotechnology products, and particularly of new "biological" drugs.

Universities have been responsible for the initial scientific advances in this field, and they are still major repositories of fundamental knowledge and applied research in these areas. The development and commercialization of biotechnology products have also been influenced by the formation and growth of NBFs. Most NBFs were founded around the mid-1980s, and many of them were spin-offs of American universities. They were founded by groups of scientists and researchers, often in conjunction with venture capitalists, to exploit a particular discovery. The main assets of NBFs are skills and know-how in applied research. The typical output of their activities is a new protein, obtained from genetically engineered organisms, which can be potentially used for diagnostic or therapeutic purposes.

However, the synthesis of a new protein, whilst an important step in the development of new drugs or chemical products, does not exhaust the entire innovation cycle in the chemical or pharmaceutical industry. Engineering know-how is required to scale up processes from laboratory bench to full manufacturing. In the pharmaceutical industry, which covers a large fraction of present applications in biotechnology, familiarity with clinical testing and regulatory procedures is critical for innovation. Finally, commercialization assets are vital for bringing a new product to the market. Even though many NBFs have attempted to carry out the whole development process, they often lack adequate resources to go beyond the initial syntheses of new compounds (Kenney, 1986; Burrill, 1988; Chesnais, 1994).

Large "established" chemical and pharmaceutical companies have entered relatively late into biotechnology research. Many of them, however, are now investing considerable resources in this field, and they have accumulated substantial in-house scientific and technological expertise in biological sciences. Moreover, unlike universities and NBFs, they possess important downstream assets. Apart from financial capabilities for R&D, they control well-developed marketing channels. In the drug industry, they have long experience with regulatory procedures and with conducting clinical trials. They also have experience with large-scale manufacturing and bioprocessing.

In sum, universities, NBFs, and large companies are endowed with complementary assets (Teece, 1986). Thus, there are wide-ranging opportunities for collaboration, and one does observe systematic linkages among them. Universities provide large firms with access to upstream basic scientific knowledge. Research in NBFs is relatively more downstream than in universities, and relatively more upstream than product development (clinical testing, manufacturing scale-up, etc.), which is what is typically done by large firms.

The competencies and resources of universities, large firms, and NBFs also exhibit a significant degree of overlap. As suggested above, a number of large corporations have sizeable in-house research programs in biotechnology, including relatively basic scientific research programs. Likewise, universities and NBFs possess partially similar sets of resources. NBFs do perform some basic research. One reason for this is that many of them have systematic linkages of various sorts (contractual, informal, etc.) with universities. Relatedly, they hire university scientists as consultants, or they even hire professors who quit academia. Academic scientists bring in scientific expertise and help in performing upstream scientific research. Moreover, universities have been aggressive in vying for corporate funding, and they perform a good deal of applied research. From the point of view of large firms, given the difficulty in distinguishing between basic and applied research, the links with universities and those with NBFs target areas with a fairly extensive degree of overlap.

Yet, the more one moves towards the basic end of the scientific research spectrum, the better do universities provide access to resources that are not available within NBFs. At the same time, universities are not suited to perform applied research with a narrow product orientation. The closer one gets to applied research with specific products in mind, the better do NBFs supply resources that are not available within academia. One can fairly assume that the non-overlapping portions of the two sets of resources are important enough to make them sufficiently distinct, and complementary to one another.

The strategies of external linkage of large firms in biotechnology

There are four main types of external linkage that large chemical and pharmaceutical companies form with other agents in biotechnology: (1) they enter into R&D agreements with other firms; (2) they form research agreements with universities (or other non-profit scientific institutions); (3) they invest in minority participations in NBFs; (4) they acquire NBFs.[2] To a large extent, each of these four strategies pursues a particular objective of the large firms. In other words, each strategy enables the large firms to gain access to a particular set of tangible or intangible resources necessary for innovation.

Most agreements signed by large chemical and pharmaceutical producers with other companies are project-specific. They are usually agreements with NBFs, and they aim at developing and commercializing a particular discovery of an NBF in the areas of specialty chemicals, agricultural biotechnology, and, above all, pharmaceuticals.[3]

Agreements with universities tend to focus on more basic research objectives. As discussed in chapter 3, large firms finance research activities performed by academic laboratories to acquire familiarity with basic knowledge in this field. Moreover, agreements with universities are important sources for recruiting qualified scientists and researchers, and they also serve as a means by which firms can engage the services of top researchers while these researchers continue to work in the type of environment that they find most congenial.[4]

Agreements with universities also serve a more direct objective of the large firms. New biotechnology products are often intimately connected with scientific discoveries. Links with university laboratories can provide large firms with a first option on licenses – see chapter 3. This confers lead-time advantages, as firms can rapidly translate the new discoveries into commercializable products.

Through minority participations, large firms can monitor the research of NBFs. They seek familiarity with their laboratory research skills. By owning part of their capital stock, large companies can also hope to establish "preferential" linkages with their partners, which would enable them to pre-empt rivals in the commercialization of important discoveries of the NBFs. Moreover, in many cases large firms acquire part of the capital stock of a biotechnology company, and also develop formal agreements with the same company to develop a particular product. Such investments may be useful in averting problems of moral hazard, and serve as tokens of good faith.[5]

As far as acquisitions are concerned, there are two different – and in part contrary – motives for acquiring a small biotech company. On the one hand, large companies that have substantial in-house capabilities and longer experience in biotechnology, acquire NBFs specializing in particular areas of biotechnology research. Their expertise enables them to evaluate more accurately the likely contributions of the set of specialized resources that are being acquired. On the other hand, the acquisition of a biotechnology firm may represent a way of "catching-up" when large firms are relatively late entrants in this business, and they have not yet invested substantial funds in internal biotechnology R&D.[6]

In sum, not only do these four strategies each target a distinct goal of the large firms, but the strategies, and the corresponding objectives, also appear to be complementary to one another.

Agreements with universities provide the large firms with access to basic scientific knowledge. They are complementary to agreements with other firms, which focus on more downstream product-specific development. They are also synergistic with acquisitions. Whether the acquisition is carried out by a large firm with established expertise in biotechnology, or by a corporation attempting a rapid catching-up, the large company aims at internalizing a whole body of laboratory or product development capabilities. Agreements with universities are also complementary to minority participations. To the extent that the knowledge-base of NBFs relates to applied laboratory research and skills, monitoring the activities of small firms is complementary with the basic scientific knowledge of academia.

Universities and NBFs may well provide access to partially overlapping sets of resources. In addition, in the particular case of the synergy between agreements with academia and minority participations in NBFs, both strategies aim at establishing a preferential link to exploit discoveries of the partner. However, one can reiterate more explicitly the argument advanced in the previous subsection. Although one may find a "grey" area when comparing the activities of universities and NBFs, they do supply distinct tangible and intangible resources. Universities have institutional roles and objectives different from NBFs. NBFs are, after all, rent-seeking agents. Their ultimate goal is to commercialize products. Their knowledge-base must therefore involve more substantial downstream product development capabilities. In this respect, the non-overlapping portion of the resources controlled by the two agents is likely to be sufficiently strong to make interactions with NBFs complementary to agreements with universities, and vice versa.

Acquisitions of NBFs are complementary to agreements with other firms. The internalization of an entire body of laboratory and applied research knowledge is complementary to co-operative ventures to develop a specific new product. Similarly, with regard to minority participations, the addition of internal knowledge to the in-house capabilities of large firms is complementary to the goal of monitoring and establishing preferential links with other NBFs. Moreover, acquisitions are more difficult than minority participations to liquidate in the short run. Therefore, they reflect long-term objectives of the large firms. By contrast, minority participations are motivated by short-term considerations, like catching new opportunities that could rapidly lead to the commercialization of new products. Finally, minority participations enable the large firms to remain "plugged in" in ways that acquisitions typically do not allow. For example, independent NBFs have better opportunities to interact with universities on "informal" bases. Once an NBF is acquired, universities may be more reluctant to exchange information with what has then become a division of a large corporation.

Monitoring the activities and the general knowledge-base of NBFs through minority participations is complementary to joint product development agreements to implement and commercialize specific compounds. The activities of other NBFs may be useful in improving products jointly developed with other companies. Moreover, we have seen that large firms often acquire minority participations in an NBF, and then they set up formal agreements to develop a particular product.

Complementarity of external linkages in biotechnology: empirical tests

Test for complementarity

This section tests the hypothesis that the four types of external linkage discussed in the previous section are complementary. It employs data on the number of agreements with other firms (henceforth AWF), the number of agreements with universities and other non-profit scientific institutions (AWU), the number of minority participations in NBFs (PRL), and the number of acquisitions of NBFs (PRM), of eighty-one large US, European and Japanese chemical and pharmaceutical producers (thirty-one US firms, twenty-nine European firms, twenty-one Japanese firms). AWF, AWU, PRL, and PRM are the numbers of linkages established by December 1988. Data are from *Bioscan* (1988), and they are described in the appendix to this chapter along with a discussion of some of their limitations.[7]

The complementarity among AWF, AWU, PRL, and PRM cannot be tested directly since there are no available measures of the "values" of these strategies. One is thus constrained to testing an important implication of complementarity. If, for example, an increase in in-house competence from an acquisition raises the marginal value of links with universities (which is the same as saying that they are complements) it seems intuitively compelling that firms which make more acquisitions also tend to have a higher number of interactions with universities. In other words, if two strategies are complements, one would expect them to be positively correlated.

Yet, one also has to take into account the indirect feedback effects through other strategies. For instance, suppose AWU and PRM are complements, but PRL is a substitute for AWU and a complement for PRM. It is then quite possible that AWU and PRM move in opposite directions if both are more strongly related to PRM than to each other. Related to this is another problem. One cannot ignore the relationship of these strategies to other characteristics of the firm, its environment and institutional setting. It is quite possible, for instance, that AWU and PRM are positively correlated because they are both strongly correlated to a particular characteristic of the firm. Take, for instance, size. Larger firms may have a higher number of external interactions because they have greater resources, e.g. they can afford larger legal departments. Similarly, there may be institutional peculiarities specific to countries which encourage or discourage external linkages. In short, one has to control for such factors.

In Arora and Gambardella (1990) we developed a model that shows that if AWF, AWU, PRL, and PRM are complementary strategies, then the covariance between any two of these strategies, conditional upon a set of company characteristics θ, is non-negative. The model assumes that firms maximize a pay-off function of the four strategies AWF, AWU, PRL, and PRM by choosing the levels of AWF, AWU, PRL, and PRM. The pay-off also depends upon their characteristics θ. Suppose that all second-order cross-derivatives of the pay-off function with respect to any two of the four strategies are non-negative.[8] The model shows that the covariance between any two strategies, conditional upon the variables in the set θ, is non-negative. One can then test this implication of complementarity.

Essentially, the test has the following steps. First, one estimates the expected values of the conditional demands AWF(θ), AWU(θ), PRL(θ), and PRM(θ). The differences between AWF, AWU, PRL, and PRM and their expected values given θ are the values of AWF, AWU, PRL, and PRM after removing the effects of the conditioning variables. One then computes the covariances among any two of these "errors." If the strategies are complementary, the covariances are non-negative.

The AWF, AWU, PRL, and PRM equations

Before proceeding with the test, one has to define the variables in the conditioning set θ, and to make some assumption on the functional form of the conditional demands AWF(θ), AWU(θ), PRL(θ), and PRM(θ) in order to estimate their expected values.

The following variables are included in the conditioning set θ: nationality, the stock of internal knowledge of the firms in biotechnology, and size. Dummy variables were used for US, European, and Japanese firms to account for country-specific factors. The number of US patents in biotechnology, from OTAF (1987), proxies for in-house knowledge. Patent data are total number of patents applied for by 1984. As the big upsurge of co-operations in biotechnology started in the mid-1980s, this variable reflects the stock of internal knowledge before most agreements took place. It is a measure of the existing stock of knowledge. Total sales in 1985, from *Moody's Industrial Manual*, proxy for size. Table 7.1 defines the variables used in the empirical analysis, table 7.2 presents descriptive statistics. See the appendix for a fuller description of the variables in the conditioning set θ.

Table 7.1. *Definition of the variables used in the empirical analysis*

Strategies	
AWF_i	= Number of agreements with other companies of the ith firm by December 1988
AWU_i	= Number of agreements with universities and other non-profit research centers of the ith firm by December 1988
PRL_i	= Number of minority participations (share investments of less than 50 percent of the capital stock) of the ith firm by December 1988
PRM_i	= Number of acquisitions or purchases of more than 50 percent of the capital stock of the ith firm by December 1988

Variables in the conditioning set θ

CONST	= Constant
AMR_i	= Dummy variable equal to 1 if the ith firm is an American firm, and 0 otherwise
JAP_i	= Dummy variable equal to 1 if the ith firm is a Japanese firm, and 0 otherwise
P_i	= Number of US biotechnology patents of the ith firm; patents applied for by December 1984
$SALES_i$	= Total sales of the firm in 1985 (billion \$)

Table 7.2. *Descriptive statistics*

Variable	Mean	Std. dev.	Min.	Max.
AWF	9.00	6.98	0	36
AWU	1.60	2.21	0	10
PRL	1.32	1.89	0	9
PRM	0.64	1.14	0	5
P	2.44	4.96	0	27
SALES* (billion \$)	4.336	6.752	0.063	42.458

Note: Number of observations = 81 (except * number of observations = 66, as sales data not available for all European and Japanese firms).

The conditioning variables – nationality, internal knowledge, and size – are factors that determine the expected levels of the four strategies, AWF, AWU, PRL, and PRM. Country-specific institutional arrangements may facilitate the undertaking of all four strategies of external interaction. Most NBFs are USA-based, and a large fraction of the universities performing frontier research in biotechnology are US universities. Thus, US firms may find it easier to develop external linkages with these agents. The distinction between European and Japanese firms (through dummies) accounts for possible differences in industrial policies towards inter-firm co-operation and other institutional arrangements in the two areas.

Following Mowery (1981), Cohen and Levinthal (1989), Mowery and Rosenberg (1989), and Rosenberg (1990), the higher the level of internal knowledge of the large firms in biotechnology, the higher the incentives to undertake strategies of external interaction. Knowledge tends to be complex and multidimensional, particularly in fields such as molecular biology and genetic engineering. It cannot be completely internalized by individual firms. Firms with greater internal knowledge are better equipped to evaluate and exploit new knowledge generated outside of their organizational boundaries. Hence, large firms with greater internal knowledge in biological sciences are more likely to undertake all the strategies of external linkage above.

Scale is an additional factor that may account for differences in the levels of all four strategies. Larger firms may have better financial resources, they may have greater market power, or they may have some sort of economy of scale that increases the pay-offs of all or some strategies in a systematic manner.

In order to estimate the expected value of the conditional demands AWF(θ), AWU(θ), PRL(θ), and PRM(θ), one has to employ suitable estimation techniques to account for the fact that AWF, AWU, PRL, and PRM take only non-negative integer values. There are several problems with using ordinary least squares with event counts, and these arise particularly when the count variables have a small range – as with the variables employed here (see table 7.2). Ordinary least squares may lead to predicted values that are negative, which is clearly implausible with non-negative integers. Moreover, when applied to event counts, ordinary least squares produce inefficient estimators.[9]

Poisson regression analysis is a suitable technique in this case. Poisson avoids negative predicted values, and produces unbiased and efficient estimators. Poisson however has the restrictive property that the mean of the process is equal to its variance. This assumption does not appear to be plausible for our data. From table 7.2, the sample means of AWF, AWU, PRL, and PRM are smaller than the sample variances. Negative binomial was therefore used to estimate expected demands. Negative binomial is a generalization of Poisson. It allows for the variance of the process to be greater than its mean (Hausman, Hall, and Griliches, 1984; King, 1989a and 1989b).

Assume that the expected values of AWF_i, AWU_i, PRL_i, and PRM_i, where i is an index of firms, are equal to $\mu_k \equiv \exp(\beta_k \cdot \theta)$, $k = AWF$, AWU, PRL, and PRM, where β_k is a vector of parameters to be estimated. The variables in the conditioning set θ are CONST, AMR_i, JAP_i, P_i, $SALES_i$, as defined in table 7.1. They are the same for all four equations. Given the estimated parameters, the AWF-, AWU-, PRL-, and PRM-residuals are $\epsilon_k = x_k - \exp(\beta_k \cdot \theta)$, where $x_k = AWF$, AWU, PRL, PRM, and β_k is the vector of estimated parameters. The negative binomial specification estimated here assumes that the variance of the process is equal to $\mu_k \cdot \sigma_k$, where σ_k is a proportionality factor – varying between equations – to be estimated.[10] The standardized residuals are $\epsilon_k^* = \dfrac{\epsilon_k}{\sqrt{\mu_k \sigma_k}}$. One can then compute the correlation coefficients among any two of ϵ_k^*, ϵ_j^*, $k,j = AWF$, AWU, PRL, PRM. Complementarity implies that all these correlation coefficients are non-negative.

Empirical results

Table 7.3 presents the results from the negative binomial estimation of the expected values of AWF, AWU, PRL, and PRM. Table 7.4 reports the matrix of correlation coefficients for the standardized residuals of the four strategies. Tables 7.3 and 7.4 are based on a sample of sixty-six rather than eighty-one firms, because sales data for fifteen firms were not available from *Moody's* (they are all European and Japanese firms). The results are practically identical to those obtained from the entire sample of eighty-one firms, after deleting SALES from among the regressors.[11]

From table 7.4, all correlation coefficients are positive. Even after controlling for firm-specific characteristics, companies with greater propensity to undertake any one of the four strategies also show greater propensity to undertake any of the others. It thus appears that a division of labor in drug innovation is actually taking place, and it is taking fairly articulated forms. Drug companies seek access to external resources possessed by specialized agents through different means, which are underlain by different strategic goals about the target external resources that are being sought. In addition, the different strategies of external linkage are complementary, in the sense that their marginal values are synergistic.

The empirical results also offer insights about the determinants of AWF, AWU, PRL, and PRM, i.e. the effects of the characteristics θ on the expected demands for the strategies.

Scale and country-specific factors do not have a major influence on the

Table 7.3. *Results from negative binomial estimation of AWF, AWU, PRL, and PRM*

Functional form used: $E(\mathbf{x}_k) = (\boldsymbol{\beta}_k \cdot \boldsymbol{\theta})$, where $\mathbf{x}_k =$ AWF, AWU, PRL, PRM, $\boldsymbol{\beta}_k$ is a vector of parameters to be estimated, and $\boldsymbol{\theta}$ is the matrix of firm characteristics CONST, AMR, JAP, P, SALES (defined in table 7.1).
Overdispersion: The variance of the process is equal to $\mu_k \sigma_k$, $k =$ AWF, AWU, PRL, PRM, where μ is the expected value and σ is a proportionality factor. The procedure estimates δ_k such that $\sigma_k = 1 + \exp(\delta_k)$.

	Dependent variables			
	AWF	AWU	PRL	PRM
CONST	2.348	0.333	0.123	−0.135
	(0.196)	(0.328)	(0.336)	(0.344)
AMR	−0.152	0.013	0.458	−0.321
	(0.237)	(0.422)	(0.405)	(0.467)
JAP	−0.262	−0.166	−0.416	−0.469
	(0.236)	(0.418)	(0.476)	(0.486)
P	0.031	0.058	0.037	−0.012
	(0.008)	(0.014)	(0.022)	(0.036)
SALES	−0.003	0.006	−0.006	0.000
	(0.013)	(0.011)	(0.017)	(0.021)
δ_k	1.174	0.823	0.412	−0.083
	(0.253)	(0.317)	(0.318)	(0.468)
Log likelihood function	927.6	−16.9	−35.2	−54.5

Note: Number of observations = 66. Heteroskedastic consistent standard errors in parentheses.

expected value of the strategies. The sales and dummy coefficients are small, and they have low statistical significance in all four equations. A more interesting result is that the coefficient of patents is positive and statistically significant in all equations but PRM. The result for PRM is not unexpected. As argued in the previous section, acquisitions are carried out both by firms with sound in-house capabilities in biotechnology to complement their research capital in specialized fields, and by firms that are attempting to catch up.

Yet, internal knowledge is complementary to the other strategies. This offers additional support to the increasing importance of network organizations in drug innovation. One might have suspected that large firms with greater internal knowledge were more likely to adopt "go-it-alone" strate-

Table 7.4. *Correlations among the standardized residuals from negative binomial estimation of AWF, AWU, PRL, and PRM in table 7.3*

Standardized residuals: $\epsilon_k^* = \dfrac{\mathbf{x}_k - \mu_k}{\sqrt{\mu_k \sigma_k}}$, where $\mathbf{x}_k$ = AWF, AWU, PRL, PRM, μ_k is the estimated mean of the process, and σ_k is the estimated value of the proportionality factor.

Correlation coefficients				
	AWF	AWU	PRL	PRM
AWF	1.00			
AWU	0.51	1.00		
PRL	0.25	0.14	1.00	
PRM	0.34	0.46	0.18	1.00

Note: Number of observations = 66.

gies in order not to share innovation rents. In contrast, our results suggest that companies with greater internal knowledge have greater ability to extract rents from external linkages. In-house research capabilities raise the marginal value of external linkages, and these firms can take greater advantage from a division of labor in innovation.

Conclusions

This chapter tested some implications of the growing division of labor in drug research and innovation using data for eighty-one large US, European, and Japanese chemical and pharmaceutical producers. Large companies pursue four main strategies of external linkage with other parties in biotechnology. They enter into R&D agreements with other firms (mostly NBFs), they buy minority participations in NBFs, they acquire NBFs, and they develop research agreements with universities. Each type of external linkage targets a particular goal: agreements with NBFs focus on developing an early discovery of the partner; minority participations aim at monitoring the activities of NBFs; acquisitions aim at internalizing a set of specialized capabilities; and linkages with universities are formed to gain familiarity with the scientific base of this field.

The empirical results showed that firms that pursue more intensively any one of these strategies, also pursue more intensively each of the others. The four strategies are complementary. In other words, in biotechnology large firms undertake all of these strategies at once. The strategies of external linkage are also complementary with the in-house research capabilities of large firms. Drug manufacturers with greater in-house capabilities are more active in developing external linkages, which suggests that the knowledge capital of firms provides greater ability to extract benefits from external interactions.

These results are not conclusive. In particular, they do not contradict the view that extensive inter-organizational links in biotechnology are a temporary phenomenon arising from the immaturity of the technological paradigm. They can be related, however, to the discussion in the previous chapters, which showed that alliances in pharmaceutical research play an increasingly important role in the strategies of large drug manufacturers. In this respect, the empirical results discussed here do raise the question whether, in the drug industry, the innovation process is moving from full integration of R&D and marketing in large firms towards new and different organizational arrangements, in which specialized complementary assets for innovation, controlled by different types of agents, are combined.

Appendix: Description of data

The analysis used firm-level data on AWF, AWU, PRL, and PRM. *Bioscan* (1988) reports the agreements with other firms, the agreements with non-profit research institutions, the minority participations, and the acquisitions of more than 1,000 firms (large and small) active in biotechnology. The criterion employed to select the firms in the sample was that they had to be "established" chemical or pharmaceutical producers with an interest in entering the new biotechnology business. The sample consists of thirty-one US, twenty-nine European and twenty-one Japanese firms. The data cover a period of roughly ten years, ending in December 1988.

AWF_i (where i is an index of firms) is the number of agreements of each large firm in the sample with other companies. Most agreements involved joint research or development activities, although a few were of pure marketing agreements. Agreements with small biotech firms and agreements with other large firms were both included.[12] The former account for the vast majority of agreements in the sample. The agreements cover all major areas of biotechnology, particularly pharmaceuticals, specialty chemicals, and agricultural biotechnology. But pharmaceutical agreements represent the largest share of agreements in the sample.

AWU_i is the number of agreements of each large firm with a university institution or any other non-profit research center (government research labs, etc.).

PRL_i is the number of capital investments of each large firm in small or medium biotech companies that involve 50 percent or less of the capital stock of the NBFs. PRM_i is the number of capital investments in small or medium biotech companies greater than 50 percent of shares.[13] Most capital investments in the sample are either for relatively small (5–10 percent) or relatively large proportions of shares (80–100 percent). Hence, the distinction made using 50 percent of shares does not seem to introduce any particular bias. It seems to distinguish between "true" minority participations and "true" acquisitions.

Each strategy, AWU_i, AWF_i, PRL_i, and PRM_i, is defined in terms of "numbers." In other words, it is assumed that "more" of one strategy by a given firm means a "higher number" of agreements, share investments, or acquisitions. In fact, the variable that one would actually like to deal with is the total "value" of each type of strategy. But the value of such linkages is not easily observable and no good measures exist.[14]

The number of external links does provide some indication of the involvement of firms in a particular strategy of external interaction. One can think of the situation as one where corporations select a portfolio of different kinds of assets. If there are significant fixed costs of buying any particular asset (e.g., in our case, the costs of negotiating an agreement), it follows that a greater number of assets of a particular type indicates a greater valuation placed on it by the firm. Simply put, a large number of agreements of a particular sort would only arise if the firm valued those kinds of agreements highly.

Data on 1985 US firm sales are from *Moody's Industrial* (various years); for European and Japanese firms, sales data are from *Moody's International*. Not all European and Japanese firms in the sample are reported in *Moody's International*. Sales data were obtained for a total of only sixty-six firms (thirty-one US firms, seventeen European, and eighteen Japanese).

The number of US patents in biotechnology (P_i) of each firm is used as a measure of internal knowledge in this field. These data are from the OTAF (1987) data-base, which lists the institutions and the number of patents per institution granted in the US by December 1987, and applied for by 1984. As also suggested in the text, the number of patents applied for by 1984 reflect the existing stock of internal knowledge of the firms before most agreements in biotechnology took place.

A few concerns may be felt over the use of US patents to measure knowledge stock. First, patents measure knowledge and innovations that can be expressed in codified forms. This is not a major problem in biotechnology, where discoveries often take the form of new compounds. Yet, tacit capabilities play an important role as well, especially in bioprocessing. This may introduce some bias for the Japanese firms, which have superior internal skills in these activities. (See, for example, Humphrey, 1984, and Daly, 1985.)

A second concern is that US patents may introduce distortions for non-US firms. However, in biotechnology most firms patent their innovations in the USA, for the USA is the international springboard for this industry. Also, many non-US firms in the sample, especially the European firms, are major chemical and pharmaceutical multinationals with a long-standing presence in the US market.

8   Conclusions

One of the most significant events of the 1980s and early 1990s in the research-intensive, ethical drug segment of the US pharmaceutical industry has been the soaring costs of pre-clinical and clinical research. This is the result of a complex interplay of technological, economic, and institutional factors.

More stringent regulatory requirements have increased the costs of developing and marketing new drugs. At the same time, some of the most important patents of many large US drug companies have expired or will expire in the early 1990s. Companies have thus been forced to renew their product portfolios. Apart from tighter regulation, legislative interventions like the 1984 Waxman–Hatch Drug Act facilitated approval of generic versions of brand-name products. Competition from generic drugs has become more intense, with implied greater pressures on R&D returns. With longer development cycles, the effective life of drug patents, which are often applied for after pre-clinical research and before clinical trials, has diminished, thereby putting additional pressures on the expected pay-offs of R&D. (See Eisman and Wardell, 1981, Grabowski and Vernon, 1986, and Kaitin and Trimble, 1987.)

Technological factors have intensified problems. As also shown by one of the empirical results in chapter 5, drug companies face gradual exhaustion of innovation opportunities: all else being held equal, the number of patents of the largest US drug manufacturers has declined over time since the 1970s. More importantly, in the 1980s large US pharmaceutical firms faced a radical change in technological paradigm. Not only has the change occurred outside of the big firms, and primarily within scientific institutions and smaller science-based biotech firms, but it has also transformed drug innovation in ways such that it can no longer be driven only by the large companies.

The change in paradigm is revolutionizing the market structure of this industry. This is not to imply technological determinism, by suggesting that the transformation of the industry ensues only from the technological shift. The economic and institutional factors mentioned above also play important roles. However, with no radical change in its scientific and technological basis, the evolution of the industry would probably be substantially different. Large pharmaceutical firms would seek more traditional responses to new economic and institutional conditions, like imposing more rigid internal structures instead of creating flexible organizations, seeking greater internalization of resources instead of looking for external competencies, and engaging in traditional oligopolistic wars instead of taking advantage of an extended division of labor.

This book has focused on the shift in technological paradigm. In short, drug research is switching from a chemical to a biological basis. The chemical approach hinged upon scale: discovery of new compounds stemmed from systematic assays of many molecules in laboratory and clinical tests to find a few promising candidates. The biological approach hinges upon rational understanding of the functioning of the human body and the action of drugs. Researchers can make more informed choices about the entities to be tested. While scale is still important for testing molecules and for clinical trials, drug research now requires solid understanding of molecular actions and pathologies.

But the considerable advances in molecular biology and genetic engineering in the 1980s, which have given great impetus to the more rational search for new drugs, and the notable developments in the technology of experimentation (particularly, computerized drug design) are not easily translating into greater innovation opportunities. One important reason for this is that better scientific knowledge has unraveled even more clearly the complexity of problems. As shown by several examples in this book, on many occasions better scientific knowledge in pharmaceutical research has helped scientists in predicting failures rather than successes.

This has had important economic implications. Prediction of failures implies that it is more difficult to develop and commercialize drugs that are not really "good" products (in the sense of truly effective medicines). In the past, once it had been established that patients were not at great risk, many drugs were sold just because there was no compelling evidence that they were ineffective – even though they were, in fact, fairly ineffective. But now one can rationally anticipate that certain compounds will be ineffective. More drugs will be discarded at the outset of the research process, and there will be fewer "claimed" new drugs. Although the fewer new drugs will be of greater quality, it will be more difficult to obtain research and commercial successes, and hence it will be more difficult to pay back soaring investments in R&D. Only very large companies will be able to sustain the greater risks of drug development and commercialization, as they will be able to take greater advantage of economies of scale in research, production, and marketing.

This also explains the increasing consolidation of the drug industry that we have observed since the mid-1980s. Various large pharmaceutical companies merged to form giant corporations (e.g., Smithkline and Beecham, Bristol Myers and Squibb, Rhone Poulenc and Rorer, and quite a few others). Consolidation was also prompted by the experience of many major US pharmaceutical firms in the 1980s. As suggested by the case studies in chapter 4, only companies with a solid research tradition were able to benefit effectively from the growth of public scientific knowledge. Companies that tried to catch up did not really make it in becoming successful innovators.

The case studies also suggested that competitive advantages based on science and innovation exhibit self-reinforcing properties. Leading innovators produce new drugs, which generate profits that can be reinvested in research, thereby strengthening innovation capabilities. Firms lacking strong research capabilities have had greater difficulties in breaking into this virtuous spiral. Hence, many of them, even though they did attempt to become research-intensive producers, had to merge with other firms to join complementary resources in research and marketing, and to withstand the enormous competitive pressures of this industry in the 1990s.

But the US and international drug industry will not be dominated by few very large oligopolists. Another important effect is at work here. The biological approach implies that scientific creativity and highly qualified human capital, rather than scale, have become the critical resources for drug discovery. Scientific creativity and research ingenuity are more likely to be found in fairly informal organizations, with a great deal of individual autonomy, and which can be relatively small in scale. This explains not only why small to medium biotech companies have thrived in the 1980s, but also why large companies increasingly resort to their services.

Not all biotech companies that have been formed will survive. Failure is common among start-ups. Moreover, extensive formation of new biotech companies in the 1980s was clearly connected with the immaturity of the technological paradigm, and the rise of a far greater number of scientific and technological opportunities than were economically profitable and commercially feasible. But not all such companies will disappear, even when the industry starts following a more stable trajectory. Those that survive will become suppliers of new product opportunities and ideas, which they will provide to giant corporations with the considerable managerial and financial resources to cope with the increasing costs of developing and commercializing new drugs.

Relatedly, only very few biotech firms, particularly those that were capable or lucky enough to attain a major breakthrough, will become integrated pharmaceutical producers. Most of them will remain research-intensive suppliers and they will sell technical skills or research outcomes rather than finished products.

In sum, what we are seeing here are opportunities for market growth based on an extensive division of labor, in the spirit of what Allyn Young suggested about sixty-five years ago (Young, 1928). There will be small, flexibly organized, research-intensive suppliers, with comparative advantages in producing ideas, and very big firms with comparative advantages in large-scale development and commercialization. As discussed earlier, it can be hoped that the socially favorable outcome of this process will be drugs of better quality and greater expected economic pay-off.

In other words, the response to soaring drug R&D costs will not be unlimited growth in the size of firms. Drug R&D risks and costs will be so high that not even very big corporations will be able to afford them. Such soaring costs will be shared by a large number of agents, which will include large and small firms, as well as scientific institutions and public research money.

The process will not be smooth. Many small firms will fail because their skills are not sufficiently good or their ideas are not commercially feasible. Some large firms will be unable to set up a good network, and they will have to face growing competitive threats. The new trend will be particularly troublesome for medium-sized pharmaceutical firms. In the past, they could thrive either because of their over-the-counter products, or because of minor new drugs (typically drugs of lower quality and effectiveness). But now they will have to become either specialized research suppliers or marketing giants. Both types of assets are difficult to acquire in the short term. Many medium firms will be ousted from the market, or they will be forced into the less profitable segments of this business. Generic manufacturers will probably survive, especially if favored by institutional provisions like the Waxman–Hatch Act, or by weak patent protection.

The remarks made so far conform to the empirical results of chapters 5–7. Chapter 5 showed that during the 1980s the productivity of company R&D in drug discovery (proxied by the number of firm patents) increased compared to the 1970s. Consistently with the discussion in chapter 2, advances in the technology of experimentation have made laboratory testing of molecules more efficient. Also, better scientific knowledge has implied that the compounds that are actually tested are more likely to become new drugs. Chapter 5 also showed that the impact of the knowledge capital of the firms, measured by their past scientific papers, on the number of new discoveries (patents) has fallen. As discussed in chapter 2, and briefly mentioned above, growing scientific knowledge in molecular biology and genetic engineering has increased the ability to predict failures rather than successes. As a result, fewer "claimed" discoveries are made.

Chapter 6 focused on drug development and commercialization. It showed that the productivity of company R&D on sales also increased considerably in the 1980s compared to the 1970s. The empirical results also showed longer R&D lags. Among other things, this suggests more stringent regulatory requirements. Even though R&D has become a more valuable input, its returns will be realized over a longer period. The more valuable input thus requires more solid financial and other capabilities to allow for returns that will only materialize farther away in the future. For many reasons, this puts larger firms at an advantage in the large-scale development and commercialization of new drugs.

Chapter 6 also showed that competitive threats from R&D-intensive drug corporations are decidedly more significant than those from less R&D-intensive producers. Innovation appears to be the most important source of competitiveness among large US pharmaceutical companies. Relatedly, among these firms, innovation is the most important determinant of sales growth and expected future profitability, as proxied by the growth of their market value. The empirical results also indicated that increases in capital stock that are not accompanied by corresponding increases in R&D (and hence that can be interpreted as opportunities for non R&D-based products), determine only a very modest increase in sales growth and profitability.

Finally, chapter 7 looked at the division of labor among large chemical or pharmaceutical producers, small–medium biotech firms, and universities or other research institutions. The empirical results showed that large firms pursue a number of complementary strategies of external linkage with these parties, which suggests that a "true" division of labor is taking place. They form agreements with biotech firms, they invest in minority participations in biotech firms, they acquire biotech firms, and they establish agreements with research institutions. In addition, large firms with greater in-house knowledge capital in biotechnology, as measured by their patents in genetic engineering, invest more intensively in external linkages. Better in-house capabilities enhance the value of external interactions, rather than inducing companies to reinternalize the innovation cycle.

All in all, the analysis of this book suggests that while the significant expansion of the scientific and technological basis of the drug industry is opening important opportunities for socially and economically beneficial innovations, exploitation of these opportunities is by no means straightforward. The growth of knowledge has further uncovered the complexity of biochemical systems, and hence of drug innovation. At the same time, increasingly long, costly, and risky drug R&D processes, to obtain fewer, higher quality medicines, can only be accomplished by mobilizing massive financial resources.

Not even very large firms or governments can probably raise the entire set of financial resources that are nowadays necessary for drug innovation. Such resources can only be obtained by combining the financial capabilities of large firms, government (in the form of public research support), and capital markets (e.g., venture capital for biotech firms). Put differently, financial arrangements to sustain drug innovation can only stem from a division of labor. The latter would make it possible to take advantage of the economies of scale, first suggested by Young in the 1920s, that are unattainable at the level of individual firms or agents, but that can be reached at the level of industries as a whole.

In a 1993 speech, President Clinton showed concern about the large profits of US pharmaceutical companies (*ECON*, 1993b). I share his concern that market power and big business could be detrimental for social and economic efficiency, and for social justice. Yet, unlike the biotechnology industry, and many other high-tech sectors, large drug manufacturers have received little public support for their research. Sound financial returns have been necessary to keep sufficient incentives for research, and they will be even more important in the light of the rising costs of drug R&D.

In fact, the issue at stake here is not whether large drug companies make high profits, but whether, in the spirit of Schumpeter, these profits correspond to greater ability to generate important innovation, and there are no undue obstacles for competitors eroding these profits if they come up with even more important innovations. But how can one combine the needs for massive financial resources and for competitive stimuli? The only answer I can think of is to encourage the division of "innovative" labor that is unfolding in the pharmaceutical sector. This division of labor will make it possible to raise the necessary financial resources by sharing R&D costs among many parties. At the same time, it will encourage competition as it will lead to greater circulation of knowledge, greater opportunities for interaction of capabilities, and the like.

President Clinton's concern will become much more serious if the present division of tasks in the bio-pharmaceutical industry disappears, and we move back to the oligopolistic competition, and maybe collusive behavior, that characterized this industry from the 1950s. In short, the division of labor that we observe today in drug innovation has serious normative implications as well.

More generally, the rise of a division of labor in innovation is a subject of great importance for the evolution of industry structures, and its significance extends beyond the pharmaceutical sector. In many industries and activities, capitalism has exhibited, since its very beginnings, an extensive division of labor. Innovation and the production and utilization of knowledge for innovation has been a notable exception. Present industrial capitalism may be shifting from the Schumpeterian "world," in which innovation – the engine of growth – is fully internalized within large corporate structures, to a world wherein innovation, and the production and utilization of knowledge and ideas, are also the outcome of a broad division of labor. It would be useful to develop a more rigorous analysis of this issue, along with empirical studies to see whether other high-tech industries display similar patterns and similar organizations of their markets. But this is a topic for future research.

Notes

1 Introduction

1 Narin, Rosen, and Olivastro (1988) and Narin and Olivastro (1992) found a significant increase in the citations of scientific publications in US patents during the 1980s compared with the 1970s. Moreover, in the 1980s, the median age of scientific papers cited by US patents declined.

2 See Nelson and Winter (1982), De Solla Price (1984), Pavitt (1987 and 1991), Dosi (1988), Teece (1988), Mowery and Rosenberg (1989), Nelson (1990).

3 "[F]irms may conduct basic research less for particular results than to be able to identify and exploit potentially useful scientific and technological knowledge generated by universities or government laboratories, and thereby gain a first-mover advantage in exploiting new technologies" (Cohen and Levinthal, 1989, p. 593).

4 The senior officials interviewed in GUIRR (1991) also emphasized that geographical proximity plays an important role in making industry–university linkages more effective.

5 See Merton (1957), De Solla Price (1963), Ben-David (1971), Salomon (1973).

6 An important limitation of the search models discussed in this subsection is that they neglect the choices of firms about investments in basic research. Greater scientific knowledge is assumed to arise exogenously. See, however, Evenson and Kislev (1976).

7 See OTA (1984, 1988, and 1991), Sharp (1985, 1989, 1991a, and 1991b), Kenney (1986), Pisano, Shan, and Teece (1988), Sapienza (1989a and 1989b), Orsenigo (1989).

8 Indeed, pharmaceutical companies tend to abandon products that fail in clinical trials rather than trying to "correct" them. A related point is that regulatory authorities would not look favorably at products that are resubmitted for clinical tests.

9 Innovative drug companies may have greater incentives to enhance manufacturing efficiency when product patents expire, and they face price competition from generic products. (The latter are off-patent drugs sold competitively; see Thomas, 1988). However, leading pharmaceutical makers tend to abandon off-patent products to focus on new drugs. With biotechnology drugs, reductions in

manufacturing costs may become more important, as bio-processes are still very costly. (See *BTEC*, 1989.)

2 Science and innovation in pharmaceutical research

1 Carpenter (1983) examined all US patents granted in the period 1975–80. Drug patents show the highest citation rate of the scientific literature among all three-digit SIC industries, with 1.07 citations per patent. Also, academic research is far more influential in the drug industry than in other industries. See the discussion of Nelson (1988), Jaffe (1989), GUIRR (1991), and Mansfield (1991) in the previous chapter. See also NSB (1982) and Swann (1988).

2 This entails a significant increase in real terms during the 1980s. Using the US GNP deflator, 54 million dollars in 1976, 90 million dollars in 1982, 125 million dollars in 1986, and 231 million dollars in 1990, become, respectively, 97.5, 102.4, 125, and 200 million constant 1986 dollars.

3 Most compounds that look interesting in animal and other laboratory studies never even make it to clinical trial. They are either ineffective, too toxic, too difficult to produce in quantities sufficient for human testing (let alone marketing), or of such limited usefulness that the cost of development cannot be recovered. Those that show genuine promise in pre-clinical research and development face the most rigorous, costly, and time-consuming stage of drug development, evaluation first in human healthy volunteers and later – maybe – in patients who actually have the condition the drug is intended to remedy (FDA, 1988, p. 13).

4 In the nineteenth century and the early decades of this century, pharmaceutical companies engaged primarily in production and wholesale marketing. They performed little research, and new medicines were discovered by individual scientists or small groups of researchers. For instance, Smith Kline and French began as a retail drug store in Philadelphia in 1830. In the course of the century it expanded into wholesaling and manufacturing. In 1936, it still employed only 180 people, and only eight in R&D (Ganellin, 1989).

5 Schwartzman (1976, chs. 2 and 3) offers detailed accounts of these stories. See also Achilladelis (1991).

6 See *BW* (1979), Grabowski and Vernon (1982), and *ECON* (1987).

7 Glaxo's Zantac, the world top-selling drug, is another H2–antagonist anti-ulcer drug.

8 See Grabowski and Vernon (1982), *ECON* (1987), Sapienza (1987), and *FT* (1992a).

9 The observation that aspirin prevents the coagulation of blood was made very early. But as there was little knowledge about the causes of this effect, the information was not exploited to develop new drugs. The legend tells that the hemophiliac son of Nicholas II, the last Russian tsar, suffered from severe hemorrhagic pains. Doctors prescribed aspirin to soothe them. But aspirin reinforced the anti-coagulation effect, thereby worsening the pain. The shrewd Rasputin noted the correlation between aspirin and the intensification of pain, and ordered that the cure be suspended. The boy's temporary relief increased Rasputin's status at the court.

10 See *CW* (1987a), *ECON* (1988a), *NS* (1988), *NYT* (1990b).

11 Tagamet, Capoten, and Mevacor, discussed earlier, also stem from rational attempts to stimulate or inhibit human receptors.

12 Many other biotech drugs have shown diverse effects. For instance, alpha interferon, which was used to treat a rare form of leukemia and also venereal warts, is being tested against AIDS, hepatitis C and multiple sclerosis; gamma interferon, initially tested against carcinogenic disorders, is under investigation for arthritis and trauma-related infections; interleukin-2, which is under FDA review against kidney cancer, has shown promising effects against hypertension (*BW*, 1990b). Also, the increasing possibility of rational economic exploitation of different uses of drugs has encouraged the diffusion of computerized data-bases that report information about newly discovered effects of compounds. In 1991 there were thirty-one claims of new actions of known drugs (Prous, 1992).

13 By the end of the 1980s, scientists had discovered the sequence of about 7,000 proteins, and the three-dimensional structure of about 300 (*NS*, 1988). These numbers are still orders of magnitude smaller than the total number of proteins that are believed to exist in the human organism. See, for instance, *ECON* (1992).

14 Scientists have recently discovered that many receptors, when activated by an agonist, release adenosine monophosphate (AMP) inside the cell. AMP has proved to be an important substance in the mechanism that activates or inhibits the functions of cells. As a result, scientists are studying how to manipulate AMP to improve the mechanism that switches proteins on and off, and design drugs that interact with receptors in new ways (*CW*, 1987a).

15 See *CW* (1987a), *ECON* (1988a and 1988b), *BTEC* (1990), *FT* (1992b).

16 See *CW* (1987a), *ECON* (1988a), *BW* (1990b and 1991).

17 See *CW* (1987a), *BW* (1988a and 1992a), *NYT* (1990b).

18 By the early 1990s, researchers had discovered thirteen serotonin receptors, against four or five by the end of the 1980s; they expected to discover about twenty serotonin receptors by the mid-1990s (*BW*, 1992a).

19 See *NS* (1988), *C&EN* (1990), *BTEC* (1990), Olson and Goodsell (1992).

20 In the past few years, the scanning probe microscope has emerged as a third method for analyzing molecular structures. A needle whose tip is only a few atoms wide is scanned across a flat surface where a molecule is immobilized. The needle follows the contour of each atom, and traces the three-dimensional shape of the molecule (Olson and Goodsell, 1992).

21 As suggested in the previous section, although scientists have already identified the sequence of amino acids of about 7,000 proteins, they have determined the protein structure of only about 300.

22 Nova Pharmaceuticals has obtained various contracts to screen libraries of compounds of a number of large chemical and pharmaceutical companies, and of other institutions, to detect active molecules. Among others, it contracted with Eastman Kodak, GAF, and the University of Pennsylvania the screening of their libraries of, respectively, 500,000, 15,000, and 50,000 compounds (*CW*, 1987a; *CMR*, 1987a).

23 See *CW* (1987a), *ECON* (1988a), *NYT* (1988a).

24 See *ECON* (1991), *NYT* (1992c), *ECON* (1993a).

25 Whether completely computational-based or derived from X-ray crystallography or NMR data, the computational burden of these models can even strain the limits of modern supercomputers. We are talking about systems of equations that may involve more than half a million terms, and six-dimensional integrals. The search for efficient computational algorithms has therefore become critical (*Science*, 1992; *NS*, 1992).

26 See *NS* (1988), *NYT* (1988b), *BTEC* (1990), *Science* (1992), Olson and Goodsell (1992).

27 Computer visualization has also spurred the diffusion of computerized data-bases of molecular structures. Unlike researchers in many other disciplines, chemists were unable to use data-bases for many years, as data-base software could not easily handle pictures. Now many data-bases store visual information about molecules, along with information such as their categories, known therapeutic actions, etc. Difficulties persist, and data-bases normally store only pictures of small molecules, like drug compounds, and not of complex human enzymes. However, with access to such data-bases, researchers can gain useful information about various compounds without having to synthesize and test them (*FB*, 1989).

28 For instance, we saw that the FDA is retarding approval of Glaxo's drug for migraine. It rationally anticipates cardiovascular problems, even though such effects have not been observed in patients.

3 Economic implications of greater scientific intensity in drug research

1 The Levin *et al.* (1987) questionnaire survey asked 650 R&D managers in various industries to rank on a 1–7 scale the degree of protection provided by patents. The average response of drug industry managers was 6.5, the highest of all manufacturing sectors.

2 Of course, the innovator would have to apply for an IND with the FDA in order to start clinical trials. However, the FDA keeps INDs strictly confidential.

3 Clearly, there are exceptions. Glaxo's Zantac, although a second-comer in the market of H2-antagonist anti-ulcer drugs, eventually reached a higher market share than the first-comer, Smithkline's Tagamet (see next chapter). Also, the development of the so-called "me-too" drugs, i.e. products that perform essentially the same function as existing compounds, has become increasingly common (Grabowski and Vernon, 1982; Ganellin, 1989).

4 Schwartzman (1976) argues that even when universities or other scientific institutions were responsible for the discovery of new drugs, they were typically large laboratories, with characteristics very similar to industry.

5 Clearly, as pharmaceutical companies cannot fully renounce laboratory assays and animal tests, routine laboratory work is still an important part of drug discovery.

6 E.g., Paul Ehrlich and Salvarsan, Gerhard Domagk and Prontosil, Carl Djerassi and the birth-control pill, James Black and Tagamet, just to name a few. Even in the case of less important drug innovations, discovery has hinged on the work of talented researchers, who have successfully organized the activities of their

teams. Swann (1988) discusses the stories of many academic personalities who acted as general or specialist consultants for industry, and played a major role in shaping the research organization of individual firms.

7 Firms could write contracts in which scientists devote part of their time to company research, and part of it to research of their own choice wherein they would be less constrained. These contracts do exist in practice. It is also true, however, that there will always be a large overlap between the two activities. Also, there could be conflicts of interest. By and large, more stimulating research topics are also more likely to yield commercial results. While scientists would like to use their "unrestricted" time for such topics, firms may force them to use their "restricted" time.

8 For more details on university–industry research collaborations in the pharmaceutical industry, see, among others, NSB (1982), OTA (1984, 1988, and 1991), Kenney (1986), D. Smith (1991).

9 As shown by table 3.1, preferential access to discoveries is often a formal clause of research contracts (rights to companies on discoveries). See also Kenney (1986). Apart from formal clauses of the contract, agreements with universities entail that companies have easier and quicker access to research findings (preview of papers, discussion with faculty, etc.), with implied lead-time advantages.

10 As scientific research gains more economic value, not only will companies have greater incentives to keep academic findings from rivals, but the scientists themselves could become more secretive because of the greater pecuniary rewards that they can derive from "selling" their research outcomes, particularly on an exclusive basis. (See Dasgupta and David, 1994.)

11 However, as Gluck (1987) also recognized, it is not clear whether industry sponsorship helped faculty in publishing more, or companies selected more renowned faculty members who published more and were more dedicated to academic activities.

12 Similarly, faculty members at Washington University could apply for Monsanto research grants only after revealing all their consultancies with other companies (Kenney, 1986).

13 I wish to thank Paul David for this point.

14 In the early 1980s, about 150 firms conducted research and produced patented drugs in the USA. However, the twenty largest firms accounted for 80 percent of US industry sales, and 98 percent of patented drug sales (Thomas, 1988).

15 Stock prices of biotech companies plunged around 1987–88. However, since then, they have risen again (OTA, 1991).

16 Henderson's (1993) empirical findings show that even when they invest in the new technology, incumbents are less productive than the new entrants.

17 Biotech companies and large firms have also engaged in research races. For instance, in the case of super-aspirin discussed in chapter 2, discovery of the genetic structure of platelet receptors has prompted intensive research efforts in both large established firms (Merck, Smithkline-Beecham, Hoffmann La Roche), and in some biotech companies (Cor Therapeutics, Centocor). Each company, whether large or small, hopes to be the first to produce an important breakthrough (*WSJ*, 1992).

18 Even nylon, probably the most important invention originating from within Du Pont, resulted from the work of one researcher, Wallace Carothers, who worked almost in isolation within the company. In the early 1930s, Carothers clarified various theoretical aspects of polymer chemistry, and discovered neoprene, the first synthetic fiber, and then nylon. Only after such discoveries did Du Pont invest considerable resources in large-scale development and manufacturing of the new products. See Smith and Hounshell (1985) and Hounshell and Smith (1988).

19 Relatedly, as will also be discussed in the next section, larger firms can shift the risks of early research activities to their innovative suppliers. They can acquire only those research outcomes that achieved some initial success, and save the costs of internal investments in projects that will eventually fail.

20 As argued earlier, it was also more costly for smaller firms to acquire development and commercialization assets using external capital markets.

21 A related, "historical" explanation is that, in the early twentieth century, before they developed extensive in-house research assets, pharmaceutical companies were manufacturers and distributors of drugs. Thus, commercial capabilities pre-existed investments in research. It was then natural that they used their own commercial capabilities to market their research products.

22 Computerized visualization of molecular structures has greatly enhanced the opportunities of transferring scientific information in biochemistry. On many occasions, one can simply deliver the image of receptors or drugs. See Lenoir and Lecuyer (1992) and Cambrosio, Jacobs, and Keating (1993).

23 This explains why biotech companies are looking very seriously at the present turmoil about patentability of biological material, and they are pushing for strong protection (see for instance *FT*, 1992b). They realize that this can have vital consequences for their opportunities for growth, and even for their survival.

24 Even though they may have a preferred linkage with one corporation, or they have been acquired by one corporation, biotech companies normally have relationships with many large firms. See for instance Burrill and Lee (1991).

25 The computer industry is an important historical precedent. The industry now features an established "division of innovative labour" between large hardware makers and software companies. See, among others, Torrisi (1995).

26 ICI is carrying out a similar reorganization. See *CW* (1990) and *ECON* (1990).

4 In-house scientific research and innovation: case studies of large US pharmaceutical companies

1 This is not unconnected with the fact that a few top executives of the company come from academia. Roy Vagelos, Merck's CEO, was Dean of the Biological Chemistry Department at Washington University before joining Merck in 1975 as Director of Research. Alfred Albert, who directed the Mevacor project (see below), was also hired from Washington University in 1975.

2 Recently, Merck issued a new research award (Scientific Award of the Board of Directors) to be bestowed for major scientific findings in areas related to

pharmaceuticals. The prize includes a $50,000 grant to a school chosen by the winner.

3 *BW* (1987) reports about a top Merck scientist who spends 10–20 percent of his company time doing independent research at the National Cancer Institute.

4 Sankyo, a Japanese pharmaceutical company, was also carrying out research on anti-cholesterol drugs concurrently with Merck. The two companies engaged in a major race to market a new anti-cholesterol drug during the 1980s. However, Sankyo's compound proved to be less successful than Merck's lovastatin. Particularly, Sankyo's molecule caused tumors in laboratory animals, which slowed down the project (*BW*, 1987).

5 See *BW* (1988d), *BS&C* (1989d), *NYT* (1992a and 1992b).

6 Eli Lilly is thus responsible for two of the seven biotechnology-based human therapeutics approved for marketing in the US during the 1980s. The other five are: alpha-interferon, OKT-3 (a monoclonal antibody that prevents kidney transplant rejection), hepatitis B vaccine, tissue plasminogenactivator, and erythropoietin (EPO) (*CW*, 1989b).

7 The leading institution was the University of California with thirty-four patents (OTAF, 1987).

8 See *BW* (1988a and 1992a) and *NYT* (1990b).

9 Eli Lilly's ability to capitalize on new advances in molecular biology and cell receptors is not limited to Prozac. In chapter 2, we saw that the human growth hormone resulted from rational understanding that dwarfism is caused by under-production of the hormone. Eli Lilly is also investigating the effects of the growth hormone on aging. Eli Lilly's scientists noted that the effects of aging also depend upon reduced secretion of the hormone (*BW*, 1990b; *NYT*, 1990g).

10 Lilly's 1986 acquisition of Hybritech, a small research-intensive company specializing in diagnostics, exemplifies the shortcomings of its stiff bureaucratic control. Lilly insisted on reviewing even minor decisions of the acquired company. Hybritech's original management left, thereby emptying the company of a significant portion of its human capital value (*BW*, 1992b).

11 See table 3.1.

12 Before the merger, the companies were considering the possibility of entering into a joint venture to sell Pravachol (*WSJ*, 1989d).

13 Sir James Black, the scientist responsible for the discovery of Tagamet, left Smithkline in 1973. He said: "I left because, once I know the problems are solved in principle, I quit. And I'm happy to quit, once I know they are solved in principle" (Sapienza, 1987, p. 5).

14 Syntex also produces Anaprox, another non-steroidal anti-inflammatory drug based upon a slightly different version of the Naprosyn compound, naproxen sodium.

15 The stories of our one-drug companies suggest that even the commercialization of just one important new product may be not enough to consolidate long-run research capabilities.

16 See *BS&C* (1989i), *NYT* (1989a and 1990a), *CW* (1989d), *Time* (1990).

5 Scientific research and drug discovery: an econometric investigation

1 See the discussion in chapter 1 about search models in innovation, and references therein.

2 Hence, not only may papers "cause" patents (in a Granger-causality sense), but they may also be "caused" by pre-clinical discoveries.

3 Halperin and Chakrabarti define elite scientists to be people cited in the *Directory of American Men and Women of Science*.

4 In (7) v_0 was replaced by v_{-1} for consistency of notation. The value at the beginning of a period is equivalent to the value at the end of the previous period.

5 For γ this is obvious, while for δ simply take its derivative with respect to θ. To show that $0 < \delta < 1$, notice that $\phi - (\phi - 1)\theta > (\phi - 1)(1 - \theta)$ implies that $\phi(1 - \theta) > -1 + \phi(1 - \theta)$ (which is a true statement), and both the numerator and denominator of δ are positive numbers. Moreover, $\phi - (\phi - 1)\theta > 0$, as it implies that, with $0 < \theta < 1, \phi > (\phi - 1)\theta$. Also, $\phi - (\phi - 1)\theta > 1$, for, with $0 < \theta < 1$, $(\phi - 1) > (\phi - 1)\theta$. Hence, $0 < \gamma < 1$.

6 In (8) a time trend was used but, unlike (7), no squared time trend was used. In the empirical estimation, a squared time trend had a significant effect in (7), while it was statistically insignificant in (8).

7 In the course of the empirical analysis various measures for $(v_{-1} - q)$ were tried, such as the log of market value divided by the stock of physical capital and/or a measure of the research stock, and/or a measure of the advertising stock of the company. The results did not change.

8 The reason why x_{-1} in the fourth term of (8) was replaced, but not x_{-1} in the fifth term of (8), is that the former enters equation (8) after substituting ϵ_{-1} from the one-period lagged expression of patents. (See previous section.) In other words, this is as if one replaces x with (7) in the patent equation for the current period, and x_{-1} with (7) lagged one period in the patent equation for the previous period; and then one substitutes ϵ_{-1} in the present patent equation from the patent equation in the the previous year.

9 I would like to thank Ashish Arora for this point.

10 Estimation of (7)–(8) for 1968–91 with structural differences in all parameters is not equivalent to separate estimation of (7)–(8) in the two subsamples because of non-linearities in the parameters. However, as shown by table 5.4, results in the two cases are very similar.

11 Chapter 2 discussed the example of Abbott's development of a renin inhibitor: computer simulation enabled researchers to discard a number of candidate molecules just by observing on the computer that their geometrical structure did not fit the target chemical in the human body. Similarly, some new serotonin drugs are expected to have undesired side-effects even though they have not shown such effects in patients.

12 The file also contains 1980 and 1981 patent applications, but they are incomplete.

13 It is relevant to state here that equations (7) and (8) were also estimated using 1968–86 data, with a distinction between the two subperiods 1968–77 and 1978–86. This was done to avoid use of the 1987–91 patent data. The magnitude of

some estimated parameters changed slightly. However, the overall results were equivalent to the 1968–91 estimation, and the discussion of empirical results in the text is in full accord with the 1968–86 estimation.

14 *Science Citation Index* adds new journals every year from which papers are collected. A constant journal set thus provides a consistent basis.

15 Papers in *Science Citation Index* were collected under company names, and for their subsidiaries that were important research performers. In two cases (Bristol-Myers and Johnson & Johnson), the companies acquired important research-intensive biotech firms in the 1980s. For these companies, the papers of the acquired concerns after the acquisition year were included. This is justified by the fact that their knowledge capital had then become part of the knowledge capital of the parent. It is further justified by the fact that the patents of the parent companies exhibited a small jump after the acquisitions. This suggests that either the patents of the acquired company also became patents of the parent company, or that the acquisitions helped in some way to increase the research productivity of the parents (or both).

6 A model of the innovation cycle in the pharmaceutical industry

1 See figure 2.1. See also Hansen (1979), Wardell (1979), Grabowski and Vernon (1982), Wardell, May, and Trimble (1982), US DoC (1984), and Kaitin, Richard, and Lasagna (1987).

2 See, for example, Grabowski, Vernon, and Thomas (1978) and Kaitin, Richard, and Lasagna (1987).

3 "Negative" sales shocks can be important as well. Reports about unexpected adverse reactions and other undesired effects of drugs are very common, especially when drugs are used by many people in the market (see, among others, FDA, 1988). They can have serious consequences for sales and profits, and therefore inhibit investments in new innovation projects or in physical capital.

4 The number of projects P_{it} includes all projects of firms in applied research or clinical trials; it does not include projects in the NDA revision stage of the FDA.

5 For example, in 1986 the FDA received over 53,000 reports of adverse reactions to drugs; this represents a small percentage of the 2.3 billion prescriptions filled annually (FDA, 1988). However, some of these reports were quite serious. Moreover, a recent investigation reported that 102 out of 198 drugs approved for marketing between 1976 and 1985 showed side-effects serious enough to warrant withdrawal from the market or major changes in their labels (*NYT*, 1990f).

6 See chapter 2.

7 The parameter β is equal to the sum of the derivatives of sales at time t with respect to R&D at $t-2$, $t-3$, $t-4$, ..., ∞. This follows from the fact that the summation of $\exp(-\lambda)\cdot(\lambda^{\tau-2}/(\tau-2)!)$, for τ from 2 to ∞, is the sum of Poisson probabilities over the range.

8 In other words, z_{iGt-1}, G = H, M, L, is equal to the average of $\log(NY)$ at $t-1$ for all firms in the H, M or L group, provided that, for the group to which the ith firm belongs, the average for that group does not include $\log(NY_i)$.

9 Estimation results change only trivially when varying the number of R&D lags.
10 If δ is a demand shock for non R&D-based products, it does not affect R&D, as is evident from equation (5). Moreover, it was assumed that δ_{it} does not have direct effects on current sales (see equation (3)). It only affects sales at $t+1$ through the capital stock K_{it}.
11 The error structure of (6) follows from the first-order conditions of the optimization problem if one assumes that the user cost of capital a_{it} depends upon ϵ_{it}, θ_{it}, and δ_{it}.
12 See also Griliches, Hall, and Pakes (1988), Lach and Schankerman (1989), and Hall and Hayashi (1989).
13 Clearly, it is also assumed that the errors ϵ, θ, and δ are persistent over time, i.e. their autoregressive coefficient is close to 1.
14 In principle, given the form of equation (7), the dependent variable of the value equation, after taking differences from time means, should be regressed over a constant constrained to be equal to 0. In order to maintain flexibility in the estimation, this constant was not imposed. However, the estimated value of the constant was very close to 0, and it was statistically insignificant.
15 Using the likelihood ratio test, the four sales lags in (5) are jointly significant.

7 Complementarity and external linkages: the strategies of large firms in biotechnology

* This chapter draws upon joint work with Ashish Arora. See Arora and Gambardella (1990).
1 The term "biotechnology" is used as commonly denoted in a number of technical reports and economic articles (e.g., OTA, 1984, 1988, and 1991; Humphrey, 1984; Daly, 1985; Olson, 1986; Pisano, Shan, and Teece, 1988). While drugs represent the bulk of new biotechnology products, the latter also include specialty chemicals, and animal and plant agricultural products. In fact, the empirical analysis of this chapter also covers data and firms in areas other than biopharmaceuticals. This was done in order to enlarge the size of the sample. However, biopharmaceutical products account for the largest share of activities in the data-set. (See also the section on empirical tests below.)
2 See OTA (1984), Daly (1985), Kenney (1986), Sharp (1987 and 1989), Roberts and Mizouchi (1988), Pisano, Shan, and Teece (1988), *NYT* (1988c), and Sapienza (1989a and 1989b).
3 In biotechnology, one also observes a few agreements between large established corporations. This is particularly true of agreements between large American and Japanese firms. Major examples include Abbott–Dainippon, Merck–Shionogy, Monsanto–Mitsubishi, Schering-Plough–Suntory, Upjohn–Chugai Pharmaceuticals (*Bioscan*, 1988). These agreements relate either to the supply of specialized equipment, or materials such as cell lines, or to marketing agreements in each other's national territories.
4 Kenney (1986) suggests that a "preferential access" to trained manpower is an important reason for university–corporate linkages in biotechnology.
5 For instance, in 1986, American Home Products bought 13.5 percent of the

shares of California Biotechnology, and in the same year the two companies signed a formal agreement to develop and commercialize cardiovascular drugs, veterinary products, and drug delivery systems. Similar examples include Abbott and Amgen, American Cyanamid and Cytogen, Johnson & Johnson and Cytogen, Smithkline-Beckman and Amgen, and Smithkline-Beckman and Synbiotics. See *Bioscan* (1988).

6 For example, in 1986 Eli Lilly acquired Hybritech to internalize specialized capabilities in monoclonal antibodies. Eli Lilly is one of the most research-intensive drug companies in the USA. In the same year, Bristol-Myers, a less research-intensive producer, and a late entrant in biotechnology, acquired Genetic Systems and Oncogen to establish in-house expertise in the new field. (See also chapter 4.)

7 The bulk of the US and European companies in the sample are pharmaceutical firms. The sample also includes major US and European chemical producers with important stakes in pharmaceuticals (e.g. Monsanto, Du Pont, Hoechst, and Bayer). The Japanese companies are more diversified. They are typically firms with activities in pharmaceuticals and in other chemical-based fields, particularly food and agricultural products.

8 This is precisely the definition of complementarity, namely that the marginal value of any strategy rises with the level of any other strategy.

9 For more details on the problems associated with using ordinary least squares with event counts, see Hausman, Hall, and Griliches (1984), and King (1988 and 1989a).

10 It is assumed that $\sigma_k > 1$ for all k's, i.e. the negative binomial process estimated here allows only for overdispersion of the data.

11 Also, OLS and Poisson regressions produced similar results.

12 An agreement involving more than one firm was counted once for each large firm. However, these were rare.

13 Joint ventures, which in most cases represent purchases of 50 percent of a company jointly established with another partner, are classified as agreements with firms and not as capital investments.

14 Using stock price variations for each firm in a small time period centered around the announcement of each agreement or capital investment is one possibility. However, stock prices may vary for a number of reasons other than those we are interested in. Moreover, the sample includes US, Japanese, and European firms; thus, stock price variations might introduce biases due to inter-country differences in the efficiency of the stock market.

References

Books and papers

Abbreviations
ADL   Arthur D. Little Inc.
CSE&PP   Committee on Science, Engineering, and Public Policy
FDA   Food and Drug Administration
GUIRR   Government University–Industry Research Roundtable
NSB   National Science Board
OTA   Office of Technology Assessment
OTAF   Office of Technology Assessment and Forecast
PSI&TA   Panel on Scientific Interfaces and Technological Applications
US DoC   US Department of Commerce

Achilladelis, B. (1991), "The Dynamics of Technological Innovation: The Sector of Antibacterial Medicine," mimeo, Stanford University, Stanford CA.

Ängård, E. (1991), "Knowledge Management in Industry and the Universities," in B. Durie (ed.), *Success and Creativity in Pharmaceutical R&D*, IBC Technical Services, London.

Arora, A. (1991), "Transferring Tacit Knowledge in Technology Transfer: How Can Intellectual Property Rights Legislation Help the Industrializing Countries?," Working Paper 91–35, The Heinz School, Carnegie Mellon University, Pittsburgh PA.

Arora, A. and A. Gambardella (1990), "Complementarity and External Linkage: The Strategies of the Large Firms in Biotechnology," *Journal of Industrial Economics*, 37(4), pp. 361–79.

(1992), "Public Policy Towards Science: Picking Stars or Spreading the Wealth?," Working Paper #23, Istituto di Scienze Economiche, University of Urbino, Italy.

(1993a), "New Trends in Technological Change: The Use of General and Abstract Knowledge in Industrial Research," *Rivista Internazionale di Scienze Sociali*, 100(3), pp. 259–77.

(1993b), "Division of Labor in Inventive Activity," Working Paper 93–3, The Heinz School, Carnegie Mellon University, Pittsburgh PA.

180   References

(1993c), "The Division of Innovative Labor in Biotechnology," Working Paper 93–30, The Heinz School, Carnegie Mellon University, Pittsburgh PA.

(1994a), "Evaluating Technological Information and Utilizing It," *Journal of Economic Behavior and Organization*, 24(1), pp. 91–114.

(1994b), "The Changing Technology of Technical Change: General and Abstract Knowledge and the Division of Innovative Labour," *Research Policy*, 23(5), pp. 523–32.

Arrow, K. (1962), "Economics of Welfare and the Allocation of Resources for Invention," in National Bureau of Economic Research, *The Rate and Direction of Inventive Activity*, Princeton University Press, Princeton NJ.

(1983), "Innovation in Large and Small Firms," in J. Ronen (ed.), *Entrepreneurship*, Lexington Books, D. C. Heath and Co., Lexington MA.

Arthur D. Little Inc. (ADL) (1988), *An Assessment of the Pharmaceutical Industry*, Technomic Publishing Co., Lancaster MA.

Ayanian, R. (1975), "The Profit Rates and Economic Performance of Drug Firms," in R. Helms (ed.), *Drug Development and Marketing*, American Enterprise Institute, Washington DC.

Baily, M. (1972), "Research and Development Costs and Returns: The US Pharmaceutical Industry," *Journal of Political Economy*, 80(1), pp. 70–85.

Baker, W. (1986), "The Physical Sciences as the Basis for Modern Technology," in R. Landau and N. Rosenberg (eds.), *The Positive Sum Strategy*, National Academy Press, Washington DC.

Battelle Research Institute (1992), *Probable Levels of R&D Expenditures in 1993: Forecasts and Analysis*, Battelle Research Institute, Columbus OH.

Ben-David, J. (1971), *The Scientist's Role in Society*, University of Chicago Press, Chicago.

Bioscan (1988), *The Biotechnology Corporate Directory Service*, Oryx Press, Phoenix AZ (April and December editions).

Bioscan (1992), *The Biotechnology Corporate Directory Service*, Oryx Press, Phoenix AZ (August edition).

Blumenthal, D., M. Gluck, Louis K. Seashore, and D. Wise (1986), "Industrial Support of University Research in Biotechnology," *Science*, 231, pp. 242–5.

Braun, E. and S. MacDonald (1978), *Revolution in Miniature*, Cambridge University Press, Cambridge.

Brown, A. (1982), "Can the Gene Splicers Survive Commercial Success?," *Chemical Business*, 67 (July 26), pp. 9–16.

Brownlee, O. (1979), "Rates of Return to Investment in the Pharmaceutical Industry: Survey and a Critical Appraisal," in R. Chien (ed.), *Issues in Pharmaceutical Economics*, Lexington Books, D.C. Heath, Lexington MA.

Burrill, G., with the Arthur Young High Technology Group (1988), *Biotech 89: Commercialization*, Mary Ann Liebert Inc., New York.

(1989), *Biotech 90: Into the Next Decade*, Mary Ann Liebert Inc., New York.

Burrill, G. and K. Lee (1991), *Biotech 92: Promise to Reality*, Ernst & Young, San Francisco.

Cambrosio, A., D. Jacobi, and P. Keating (1993), "Ehrlich's 'Beautiful Pictures' and the Controversial Beginnings of Immunological Imagery," paper presented at the Science, Technology and Economics Workshop, Department of Economics, Stanford University, Stanford CA, February 16.

Carpenter, M. (1983), "Patent Citations as Indicators of Scientific and Technological Linkages," paper presented at the Annual Meeting of the American Association for the Advancement of Science, Detroit MI, May 30.

Chandler, A.D.,Jr. (1977), *The Visible Hand*, Harvard University Press, Cambridge MA.

Chesnais, F. (1994), "Technological Cumulativeness, the Appropriation of Technology and Technological Progressiveness in Concentrated Market Structures," in F. Arcangeli, P. A. David, and G. Dosi (eds.), *The Diffusion of Innovation: Modern Patterns in Introducing and Adopting Innovations*, vol. I, Oxford University Press, Oxford, forthcoming.

Chien, R. and R. Upson (1980), "Returns to Drug Industry Common Stocks: An Alternative Measure of Economic Profitability," *Managerial and Decision Economics*, 1 (December), pp. 172–8.

Clarkson, K. (1977), *Intangible Capital and Rates of Return*, American Enterprise Institute, Washington DC.

(1979), "The Use of Pharmaceutical Profitability Measures for Public Policy Action," in R. Chien (ed.), *Issues in Pharmaceutical Economics*, Lexington Books, D.C. Heath and Co., Lexington MA.

Clymer, H. (1969), "The Changing Costs and Risks of Pharmaceutical Innovation," in J. Cooper (ed.), *Economics of Drug Innovation*, American University, Washington DC.

Cohen, W. and R. Levin (1989), "Empirical Studies of Innovation and Market Structure," in R. Schmalensee and R. Willig (eds.), *Handbook of Industrial Organization*, vol. II, Elsevier Science Publishers (North Holland), Amsterdam.

Cohen, W. and D. Levinthal (1989), "Innovation and Learning: The Two Faces of R&D," *Economic Journal*, 99, pp. 569–96.

Cohen, W., R. Florida, and R. Goe (1992), "University–Industry Research Centers in the United States," report to the Ford Foundation, Center for Economic Development, Carnegie Mellon University, Pittsburgh PA.

Comanor, W. (1965), "Research and Technical Change in the Pharmaceutical Industry," *Review of Economics and Statistics*, 47(2), pp. 182–90.

(1986), "The Political Economy of the Pharmaceutical Industry," *Journal of Economic Literature*, 24(3), pp. 1178–1217.

Committee on Science, Engineering and Public Policy (CSE&PP) (1983), "Opportunities in Chemistry," in *Research Briefings 1983*, National Academy Press, Washington DC.

Cox, J. and A. Styles (1979), "From Lead Compound to Product," *R&D Management*, 9(2), pp. 125–30.

Cusumano, J. (1992), "Creating the Future of the Chemical Industry: Catalysis by Molecular Design," in J. Thomas and K. Zamarev (eds.), *Catalysis in the 21st Century*, Blackwell Scientific Publications, New York.

Daly, P. (1985), *The Biotechnology Business*, Francis Pinter, London.

Dasgupta, P. and P. David (1987), "Information Disclosure and the Economics of

Science and Technology," in G. Feiwel (ed.), *Arrow and the Ascent of Economic Theory*, New York University Press, New York.

(1994), "Towards a New Economics of Science," *Research Policy*, 23(5), pp. 487–521.

Dasgupta, P. and J. Stiglitz (1980), "Uncertainty, Industrial Structure and the Speed of R&D," *Bell Journal of Economics*, 11, pp. 1–28.

David, P. (1991), "Reputation and Agency in the Historical Emergence of the Institutions of 'Open Science,'" mimeo, Stanford University, Stanford CA.

David, P. and J. Stiglitz (1979), "Analysis of Factors Affecting the R&D Choices of Firms," Research Memorandum #232, Center for Research in Economic Growth, Stanford University, Stanford CA, March.

David, P., D. Mowery, and E. Steinmueller (1992), "Analyzing the Economic Payoffs from Basic Research," *Economics of Innovation and New Technologies*, 2(4), pp. 73–90.

De Solla Price, D. (1963), *Little Science, Big Science*, Columbia University Press, New York.

(1984), "The Science/Technology Relationship, the Craft of Experimental Science and Policy for the Improvement of High Technology Innovation," *Research Policy*, 13(1), pp. 3–20.

Di Masi, J. (1991), *The Cost of Innovation in the Pharmaceutical Industry: New Drug R&D Cost Estimates*, Pharmaceutical Manufacturers Association, Washington DC.

Di Masi, J., R. Hansen, H. Grabowski, and L. Lasagna (1991), "Cost of Innovation in the Pharmaceutical Industry," *Journal of Health Economics*, 10, pp. 107–42.

Dosi, G. (1988), "Sources, Procedures, and Microeconomic Effects of Innovation," *Journal of Economic Literature*, 26(3), pp. 1120–71.

Drews, J. (1992), "Pharmaceutical Industry in Transition," *Drug News and Perspectives*, 5(3), pp. 133–8.

Eberhardt, J., J. Young, P. Molton, and J. Dirks (1991), "Technological Advancements in Instrumentation: Impacts on R&D Productivity," draft report, Pacific Northwestern Laboratory, Richland WA.

Eisman, M. and W. Wardell (1981), "The Decline in Effective Patent Life of New Drugs," *Research Management*, 24(1), pp. 18–21.

Evenson, R. and Y. Kislev (1975), *Agricultural Research and Productivity*, Yale University Press, New Haven CT.

(1976), "A Stochastic Model of Applied Research," *Journal of Political Economy*, 84(2), pp. 265–81.

Food and Drug Administration (FDA) (1988), "From Test Tube to Patient: New Drug Development in the United States," *FDA Consumer* (special report), Dept. of Health and Human Service, HHS Publication # (FDA) 88–3168, January.

Friedman, J. and Associates (1973), *R&D Intensity in the Pharmaceutical Industry*, Jesse Friedman and Associates, Washington DC.

Ganellin, C. (1989), "Discovering New Medicines," *Chemistry and Industry*, 2 (January), pp. 1–7.

Gibbons, M., and R. Johnston (1974), "The Roles of Science in Technological Innovation," *Research Policy*, 3(5), pp. 220–42.

Gluck, M. (1987), "University-Industry Relationships in Biotechnology: Implications for Society," Ph.D. thesis, Harvard University, Cambridge MA.

Gomory, R. and R. Schmitt (1988), "Science and Products," *Science*, 240 (May 27), pp. 1131–32 and 1203–4.

Government University–Industry Research Roundtable (GUIRR) (1991), *Industrial Perspectives on Innovation and Interactions with Universities*, National Academy Press, Washington DC.

Grabowski, H. (1968), "The Determinants of Industrial Research and Development: A Study of the Chemical, Drug, and Petroleum Industries," *Journal of Political Economy*, 76(2), pp. 292–305.

(1989), "An Analysis of US International Competitiveness in Pharmaceuticals," *Managerial and Decision Economics*, 10 (special issue), pp. 27–33.

Grabowski, H. and J. Vernon (1981), "The Determinants of R&D Expenditures in the Pharmaceutical Industry," in R. Helms (ed.), *R&D Process: Economic Factors*, American Enterprise Institute, Washington DC.

(1982), "The Pharmaceutical Industry," in R. Nelson (ed.), *Government and Technical Progress*, Pergamon, New York.

(1983), *The Regulation of Pharmaceuticals: Balancing the Benefits and Risks*, American Enterprise Institute, Washington DC.

(1986), "Longer Patents for Lower Imitation Barriers: The 1984 Drug Act," *American Economic Review*, 76(2), pp. 195–8.

(1990), "A New Look at the Returns and Risks to Pharmaceutical R&D," *Management Science*, 36(7), pp. 804–21.

Grabowski, H., J. Vernon, and L. G. Thomas (1978), "Estimating the Effects of Regulation on Innovation: An International Comparative Analysis of the Pharmaceutical Industry," *Journal of Law and Economics*, 21(1), pp. 133–163.

Griliches, Z. (1957), "Hybrid Corn: An Exploration in the Economics of Technological Change," *Econometrica*, 25(4), pp. 501–22.

(1958), "Research Cost and Social Returns: Hybrid Corn and Related Innovations," *Journal of Political Economy*, 66(4), pp. 419–31.

(1960), "Hybrid Corn and the Economics of Innovation," *Science*, 205 (July 29), pp. 275–80.

(ed.) (1984), *R&D, Patents, and Productivity*, University of Chicago Press, Chicago.

(1986), "Productivity, R&D, and Basic Research at the Firm Level in the 1970s," *American Economic Review*, 76(1), pp. 141–54.

Griliches, Z., B. Hall, and A. Pakes (1988), "R&D, Patents, and Market Value Revisited: Is There a Second (Technological Opportunity) Factor?," Working Paper #2624, National Bureau of Economic Research, June.

Hall, B. and F. Hayashi (1989), "Research Development as an Investment," mimeo, National Bureau of Economic Research, Stanford University, Stanford CA, February.

Hall, B., C. Cummins, E. Laderman, and J. Mundy (1988), "The R&D Master File Documentation," user documentation, National Bureau of Economic Research, Stanford University, Stanford CA, October.

Halliday, R., S. Walker, and C. Lumley (1992), "R&D Philosophy and Management in the World's Leading Pharmaceutical Companies," *Journal of Pharmaceutical Medicine*, 2, pp. 139–54.

Halperin, M. and A. Chakrabarti (1987), "Firm and Industry Characteristics Influencing Publications of Scientists in Large American Companies," *R&D Management*, 17(3), pp. 167–73.

Hansen, R. (1979), "The Pharmaceutical Development Process: Estimates of Development Costs and Times and the Effects of Proposed Regulatory Changes," in R. Chien (ed.), *Issues in Pharmaceutical Economics*, Lexington Books, D.C. Heath and Co., Lexington MA.

Hausman, J., B. Hall, and Z. Griliches (1984), "Econometric Models for Count Data with an Application to the Patents–R&D Relationships," *Econometrica*, 52(4), pp. 909–38.

Hayashi, F. (1982), "Tobin's Marginal q and Average q: A Neoclassical Interpretation," *Econometrica*, 50(1), pp. 213–24.

Henderson, R. (1993), "Underinvestment and Incompetence as Responses to Radical Innovation: Evidence from the Photolithographic Alignment Equipment Industry," *Rand Journal of Economics*, 24(2), pp. 248–70.

Henderson, R. and K. Clark (1990), "Architectural Innovation: The Reconfiguration of Existing Product Technologies and the Failure of Established Firms," *Administrative Science Quarterly*, 35(1), pp. 9–30.

Holmstrom, B. (1989), "Agency Costs and Innovation," *Journal of Economic Behavior and Organization*, 12(3), pp. 305–27.

Hounshell, D. and J. Smith (1988), *Science and Corporate Strategy: Du Pont R&D 1902–1980*, Cambridge University Press, Cambridge.

Humphrey, A. (1984), "Commercializing Biotechnology: Challenge to the Chemical Engineer," *Chemical Engineering Progress*, December, pp. 7–12.

Jaffe, A. (1989), "Real Effects of Academic Research," *American Economic Review*, 79(5), pp. 957–70.

Jensen, E. (1987), "Research Expenditures and the Discovery of New Drugs," *Journal of Industrial Economics*, 36, pp. 83–95.

(1988), "The Determinants of R&D Expenditures in the Ethical Pharmaceutical Industry," Working Paper 87/8, Hamilton College, Clinton NY, June.

Jewkes, J., D. Sawers, and R. Stillerman (1958), *The Sources of Invention*, Macmillan, London.

Kaitin, K. and G. Trimble (1987), "Implementation of the Drug Price Competition and Patent Term Restoration Act of 1984: A Progress Report," *Journal of Clinical Research and Drug Development*, 1, pp. 263–75.

Kaitin, K., B. Richard, and L. Lasagna (1987), "Trends in Drug Development: The 1985–86 New Drug Approvals," *Journal of Clinical Pharmacology*, 27, pp. 542–8.

Kenney, M. (1986), *Biotechnology: The University–Industry Complex*, Yale University Press, New Haven CT.

King, G. (1988), "Statistical Models for Political Science Event Counts: Bias in Conventional Procedures and Evidence for the Exponential Poisson Regression Models," *American Journal of Political Science*, 32(3), pp. 838–63.

(1989a), *Unifying Political Methodology: The Likelihood Theory of Statistical Inference*, Cambridge University Press, Cambridge.

(1989b), "Event Count Models for International Relations: Generalizations and Applications," *International Studies Quarterly*, 33(2), pp. 123–47.

Kline, S. and Rosenberg, N. (1986), "An Overview of Innovation," in R. Landau and N. Rosenberg (eds.), *The Positive Sum Strategy*, National Academy Press, Washington DC.

Koenig, E. (1983), "A Bibliometric Analysis of Pharmaceutical Research," *Research Policy*, 12(1), pp. 15–36.

Kuznets, S. (1966), *Modern Economic Growth*, Yale University Press, New Haven, CT.

Lach, S. and M. Schankerman (1989), "Dynamics of R&D and Investment in the Scientific Sector," *Journal of Political Economy*, 97(4), pp. 880–904.

Landau, R. (1990), "Chemical Engineering: Key to the Growth of Chemical Processing Industries," *American Institute of Chemical Engineers Symposium Series*, 86(274), pp. 9–39.

Landes, D. (1969), *The Unbound Prometheus*, Cambridge University Press, Cambridge.

(1991), "Homo Faber, Homo Sapiens: Knowledge, Technology, Growth and Development," European Association of Research on Industrial Economics, Annual Meeting, Ferrara, Italy, September 3–5.

Lasagna, L. and W. Wardell (1975), "The Rate of New Drug Discovery," in R. Helms (ed.), *Drug Development and Marketing*, American Enterprise Institute, Washington DC.

Lederman, L. (1984), "The Value of Fundamental Science," *Scientific American*, 251(5), November, pp. 40–7.

Lenoir, T. and C. Lecuyer (1992), "Visions of Theory," mimeo, Department of History, Stanford University, Stanford CA.

Levin, R., A. Klevorick, R. Nelson and S. Winter (1987), "Appropriating the Returns from Industrial Research and Development," *Brookings Papers on Economic Activity*, #3, pp. 783–831.

Link, A. (1981), "Basic Research and Productivity Increase in Manufacturing: Additional Evidence," *American Economic Review*, 71(5), pp. 1111–12.

(1982), "An Analysis of the Composition of R&D Spending," *Southern Economic Journal*, 51(2), pp. 342–9.

(1985), "The Changing Composition of R&D," *Managerial and Decision Economics*, 6, pp. 125–8.

Madison, J. (1989), *Eli Lilly: A Life, 1885–1977*, Indiana Historical Society, Indianapolis.

Mansfield, E. (1980), "Basic Research and Productivity Increase in Manufacturing," *American Economic Review*, 70(5), pp. 863–73.

(1981), "Composition of R&D Expenditures: Relationship to Size, Concentration and Innovation Output," *Review of Economics and Statistics*, 62(4), pp. 610–14.

(1986), "Patents and Innovation: An Empirical Study," *Management Science*, 32(2), pp. 173–181.

(1991), "Academic Research and Industrial Innovation," *Research Policy*, 20(1), pp. 1–12.

Mansfield, E., M. Schwartz, and S. Wagner (1981), "Imitation Costs and Patents: An Empirical Study," *Economic Journal*, 91, pp. 907–18.

Mansfield, E., J. Rapoport, A. Romeo, E. Villani, S. Wagner, and F. Husic (1977), *The Production and Application of New Industrial Technology*, Norton, New York.

Merton, R. (1957), "Priority in Scientific Discovery," *American Sociological Review*, 22(4), pp. 635–59.

Moody's Industrial Manual (various years), Moody's Investor Service Inc., New York.

Moody's International Manual (various years), Moody's Investor Service Inc., New York.

Mowery, D. (1981), "The Emergence and Growth of Industrial Research in American Manufacturing 1899–1945," Ph.D. thesis, Stanford University, Stanford CA.

(1983), "Economic Theory and Government Technology Policy," *Policy Sciences*, 16, pp. 27–43.

(1988), "Collaborative Ventures between US and Foreign Manufacturing Firms: An Overview," in D. Mowery (ed.), *International Collaborative Joint-Ventures in US Manufacturing*, Ballinger, Cambridge MA.

Mowery, D. and N. Rosenberg (1982), "The Commercial Aircraft Industry," in R. Nelson (ed.), *Government and Technical Progress*, Pergamon, New York.

(1989), *Technology and the Pursuit of Economic Growth*, Cambridge University Press, Cambridge.

Mueller, W. (1962), "The Origins of Basic Inventions Underlying Du Pont's Major Product and Process Innovations, 1920 to 1950," in National Bureau of Economic Research, *The Rate and Direction of Inventive Activity*, Princeton University Press, Princeton NJ.

Narin, F. and D. Olivastro (1992), "Status Report – Linkage between Technology and Science," *Research Policy*, 21(3), pp. 237–49.

Narin, F. and R. Rozek (1988), "Bibliometric Analysis of US Pharmaceutical Industry Performance," *Research Policy*, 17(3), pp. 139–54.

Narin, F., E. Noma, and R. Perry (1987), "Patents as Indicators of Corporate Technological Strength," *Research Policy*, 16(2–4), pp. 143–55.

Narin, F., M. Rosen, and D. Olivastro (1988), "Patent Citation Analysis: New Validation Studies and Linkage Statistics," in A. van Raan, A. Nederhof, and H. Moed (eds.), *Science Indicators: Their Use in Science Policy and their Role in Science Studies*, DSWO Press, Amsterdam.

National Science Board (NSB) (1982), *University–Industry Research Relationships*, US Government Printing Office, Washington DC.

Nelson, R. (1959), "The Simple Economics of Basic Scientific Research," *Journal of Political Economy*, 67(2), pp. 297–306.

(1961), "Uncertainty, Learning and the Economics of Parallel Research and Development Efforts," *Review of Economics and Statistics*, 43(3), pp. 351–64.

(1962), "The Link between Science and Invention: The Case of the Transistor," in

National Bureau of Economic Research, *The Rate and Direction of Inventive Activity*, Princeton University Press, Princeton NJ.

(1982), "The Role of Knowledge in R&D Efficiency," *Quarterly Journal of Economics*, 97(3), pp. 453–70.

(1986), "Institutions Supporting Technical Advance in Industry," *American Economic Review, Proceedings*, 76(2), pp. 186–9.

(1988), "Institutions Supporting Technical Change in the United States," in G. Dosi *et al.* (eds.), *Technical Change and Economic Theory*, Francis Pinter, London.

(1990), "Capitalism as an Engine of Progress," *Research Policy*, 19(3), pp. 193–214.

(1994), "Institutions Generating and Diffusing New Technologies," in F. Arcangeli, P. David, and G. Dosi (eds.), *The Diffusion of Innovation: Modern Patterns in Introducing and Adopting Innovations*, vol. I, Oxford University Press, Oxford, forthcoming.

Nelson, R. and N. Rosenberg (1993), "American Universities and Technical Advance in Industry," Working Paper #342, Center for Economic and Policy Research, Stanford University, Stanford CA, March.

Nelson, R. and S. Winter (1982), *An Evolutionary Theory of Economic Change*, Harvard University Press, Cambridge MA.

Office of Technology Assessment (OTA) (1984), *Commercial Biotechnology: An International Analysis*, US Congress, OTA-BA-218, US Government Printing Office, Washington DC.

(1988), *New Developments in Biotechnology: US Investments in Biotechnology*, US Congress, OTA-BA-360, US Government Printing Office, Washington DC.

(1991), *Biotechnology in a Global Economy*, US Congress, OTA-BA-494, US Government Printing Office, Washington DC.

Office of Technology Assessment and Forecast (OTAF) (1987), *Technology Profile Report: Genetic Engineering*, US Patents and Trademark Office, Office of Document Information, Washington DC.

Olson, A. and D. Goodsell (1992), "Visualizing Biological Molecules," *Scientific American*, 265 (November), pp. 76–81.

Olson, S. (1986), *Biotechnology: An Industry Comes of Age*, National Academy Press, Washington DC.

Orsenigo, L. (1989), *The Emergence of Biotechnology: Institutions and Markets in Industrial Innovation*, Francis Pinter, London.

Pakes, A. (1985), "On Patents, R&D, and the Stock Market Rate of Return," *Journal of Political Economy*, 93(2), pp. 390–409.

Panel on Scientific Interfaces and Technological Applications (PSI&TA) (1986), *Scientific Interfaces and Technological Applications*, National Academy Press, Washington DC.

Pavitt, K. (1987), "The Objectives of Technology Policy," *Science and Public Policy*, 14(4), pp. 182–8.

(1991), "What Makes Basic Research Useful," *Research Policy*, 20(2), pp. 109–19.

(1992), "Some Foundations for a Theory of the Large Innovating Firm," in G.

Dosi, R. Giannetti, and P. Toninelli (eds.), *Technology and Enterprise in a Historical Perspective*, Clarendon Press, Oxford.

Pisano, G., W. Shan, and D. Teece (1988), "Joint Ventures and Collaboration in the Biotechnology Industry," in D. C. Mowery (ed.), *International Collaborative Ventures in US Manufacturing*, Ballinger, Cambridge MA.

Polanyi, M. (1967), *The Tacit Dimension*, Doubleday Anchor, Garden City, NY.

Predicasts Index (1983–1988), US Companies, vol. II, Predicasts Inc., Cleveland OH.

Prous, J. (1992), "The Year's New Drugs," *Drug News & Perspectives*, 5(2), pp. 93–101.

Roberts, E. and R. Mizouchi (1988), "Inter-Firm Technological Collaborations: The Case of Japanese Biotechnology," Working Paper #2034–88, Sloan School of Management, MIT, Cambridge MA.

Rosenberg, N. (1976), *Perspectives on Technology*, Cambridge University Press, Cambridge.

(1982), *Inside the Black Box*, Cambridge University Press, Cambridge.

(1985), "The Commercial Exploitation of Science by American Industry," in K. Clark, R. Hayes, and C. Lorenz (eds.), *The Uneasy Alliance: Managing the Productivity–Technology Dilemma*, Harvard Business School Press, Boston MA.

(1987), "The Relations between Science and Technology in the XX Century," paper presented at the conference on *Technology and Enterprise in a Historical Perspective*, Terni, Italy, October 1–4.

(1990), "Why Do Firms Do Basic Research?," *Research Policy*, 19(2), pp. 165–74.

(1992), "Scientific Instrumentation and University Research," *Research Policy*, 21(4), pp. 381–90.

Rosenbrock, H. (1988), "Engineering as an Art," *AI & Society*, 2(4), pp. 315–20.

Rothschild, M. and J. Stiglitz (1970), "Increasing Risk I: A Definition," *Journal of Economic Theory*, 26(2), pp. 225–43.

Rullani, E. and S. Vaccà (1987), "Scienza e Tecnologia nello Sviluppo Industriale," *Economia e Politica Industriale*, 14, pp. 3–41.

Salomon, J. (1973), *Science and Politics*, Macmillan, London.

Sapienza, A. (1987), "The Paradox of a Successful Drug Discovery: The Story of Tagamet," mimeo, Harvard School of Public Health, Harvard University, Cambridge MA.

(1989a), "Technology Transfer: An Assessment of the Major Institutional Vehicles for Diffusion of US Biotechnology," *Technovation*, 9(4), pp. 463–78.

(1989b), "R&D Collaboration as a Global Competitive Tactic – Biotechnology and the Ethical Pharmaceutical Industry," *R&D Management*, 19(4), pp. 285–95.

Scherer, F. and D. Ross (1990), *Industrial Market Structure and Economic Performance*, 3rd edn., Houghton Mifflin, Boston MA.

Schnee, J. (1972), "Development Costs: Determinants, and Overruns," *Journal of Business*, 45(3), pp. 347–74.

Schumpeter, J. (1942), *Capitalism, Socialism and Democracy*, Harper and Row, New York.

Schwartzman, D. (1975), "Pharmaceutical R&D Expenditures and Rates of Return," in R. Helms (ed.), *Drug Development and Marketing*, American Enterprise Institute, Washington DC.

(1976), *Innovation in the Pharmaceutical Industry*, Johns Hopkins University Press, Baltimore MD.

Science Citation Index (various years), Institute for Scientific Information, Philadelphia.

Sharp, M. (1985), *The New Biotechnology: European Governments in Search of a Strategy*, Sussex European Paper #15, SPRU, University of Sussex, Brighton, UK.

(1987), "Europe: Collaboration in the High Technology Sectors," *Oxford Review of Economic Policy*, 3(1), pp. 52–65.

(1989), "Collaboration and the Pharmaceutical Industry – Is it the Way Forward?," DRC Discussion Paper #71, SPRU, University of Sussex, Brighton, UK.

(1991a), "Pharmaceuticals and Biotechnology: Perspectives for the European Industry," in C. Freeman, M. Sharp, and W. Walker (eds.), *Technology and the Future of Europe*, Francis Pinter, London.

(1991b), "Technological Trajectories and Corporate Strategies in the Diffusion of Biotechnology," in E. Deiaco, E. Hornell, and G. Vickery (eds.), *Technology and Investment: Critical Issues for the 1990s*, Francis Pinter, London.

Shelley, J. (1991), "The Ocean and the Bucket," in B. Durie (ed.), *Success and Creativity in Pharmaceutical R&D*, IBC Technical Services, London.

Smith, A. (1982), *The Wealth of Nations* [1776], Penguin Books, Harmondsworth, UK.

Smith, J. and D. Hounshell (1985), "Wallace H. Carothers and Fundamental Research at Du Pont," *Science*, 229 (August 2), pp. 436–42.

Smith, D. (1991), "Industry Sponsorship of Academic Research – the Alliance between Oxford and Bristol Myers Squibb," in B. Durie (ed.), *Success and Creativity in Pharmaceutical R&D*, IBC Technical Services, London.

Smith, W. (1991), "Molecular Mechanisms of Aspirin Action," *Drug News and Perspectives*, 4(6), pp. 362–6.

Soete, L., B. Verspagen, P. Patel, and K. Pavitt (1989), "Recent Comparative Trends in Technology Indicators in the OECD Area," paper presented at the International Seminar on Science, Technology and Economic Growth, OECD, Paris.

Spangenberg, J., R. Starmans, Y. Bally, B. Breemhaar, F. Nijhuis, and C. Van Dorp (1990), "Prediction of Scientific Performance in Clinical Medicine," *Research Policy*, 19(3), pp. 239–55.

Stauffer, T. (1975), "Profitability Measures in the Pharmaceutical Industry," in R. Helms (ed.), *Drug Development and Marketing*, American Enterprise Institute, Washington DC.

Steinmueller, E. (1987), "Microeconomics and Microelectronics: Economic Studies of Integrated Circuit Technology," Ph.D. thesis, Stanford University, Stanford CA.

Stigler, G. (1961), "The Economics of Information," *Journal of Political Economy*, 69(3), pp. 213–25.

Swann, J. (1988), *Academic Scientists and the Pharmaceutical Industry: Cooperative Research in the XX Century America*, Johns Hopkins University Press, Baltimore MD.

Sylos Labini, P. (1992), "Capitalism, Socialism and Democracy, and the Large Firms," in F. Scherer and M. Perlman (eds.), *Entrepreneurship, Technological Innovation and Economic Growth: Studies in the Schumpeterian Tradition*, University of Michigan Press, Ann Arbor.

Taylor, C. and A. Silberston (1973), *The Economic Impact of the Patent System: A Study of the British Experience*, Cambridge University Press, Cambridge.

Teece, D. (1986), "Profiting from Technological Innovation," *Research Policy*, 15(6), pp. 285–305.

(1988), "Technological Change and the Nature of the Firm," in G. Dosi *et al.* (eds.), *Technological Change and Economic Theory*, Francis Pinter, London.

Thomas, L.G. (1987), "Regulation and Firm Size: FDA Impacts on Innovation," First Boston Working Paper FB-87-24, Boston MA, September.

(1988), "Multifirm Strategies in the US Pharmaceutical Industry," in D. C. Mowery (ed.), *International Collaborative Ventures in US Manufacturing*, Ballinger, Cambridge MA.

Torrisi, S. (1995), "The Organization of Innovative Activities in European Software Firms," Ph.D. thesis, University of Sussex, Brighton, UK.

US Department of Commerce (US DoC) (1984), *A Competitive Assessment of the US Pharmaceutical Industry*, US Government Printing Office, Washington DC.

Vaccà, S. (1986), "L'Economia delle Relazioni tra Imprese: Dall'Espansione Dimensionale allo Sviluppo per Reti Esterne," *Economia e Politica Industriale*, 13, pp. 3–41.

Vane, J. (1964), "A Plan for Evaluating Potential Drugs," in D. Laurence (ed.), *Evaluation of Drug Activities – Pharmacokinetics*, Academic Press, London.

Vernon, J. and P. Gusen (1974), "Technical Change and Firm Size: The Pharmaceutical Industry," *Review of Economics and Statistics*, 56(3), pp. 294–302.

Vincenti, W. (1990), *What Engineers Know and How they Know it*, Johns Hopkins University Press, Baltimore MD.

Virts, J. and J. Weston (1980), "Returns to Research and Development in the US Pharmaceutical Industry," *Managerial and Decision Economics*, 1(3), pp. 103–11.

Wardell, W. (1979), "The History of Drug Discovery, Development and Regulation," in R. Chien (ed.), *Issues in Pharmaceutical Economics*, Lexington Books, D.C. Heath and Co., Lexington MA.

Wardell, W., M. May, and G. Trimble (1982), "New Drug Development by United States Pharmaceutical Firms," *Clinical Pharmacology and Therapeutics*, 32, pp. 407–17.

Wiggins, S. (1981), "Product Quality Regulation and New Drug Introductions: Some Evidence from the 1970s," *Review of Economics and Statistics*, 63(4), pp. 615–19.

(1983), "The Impact of Regulation on Pharmaceutical Research Expenditures: A Dynamic Approach," *Economic Inquiry*, 21(1), pp. 115–28.

(1987), *The Cost of Developing a New Drug*, Pharmaceutical Manufacturers Association, Washington DC.

Wildasin, D. (1984), "The q Theory of Investment with Many Capital Goods," *American Economic Review*, 74(1), pp. 203–10.

Williamson, O. (1985), *The Economic Institutions of Capitalism*, Free Press, New York.

Winter, S. (1984), "Schumpeterian Competition in Alternative Technological Regimes," *Journal of Economic Behavior and Organization*, 5(3–4), pp. 287–320.

Young, A. (1928), "Increasing Returns and Economic Progress," *Economic Journal*, 38, pp. 527–42.

Periodicals, trade publications, and related items

Abbreviations

BS&C	*Bear, Sterns & Co. Inc.*
BTEC	*Bio/Technology*
BW	*Business Week*
C&EN	*Chemical Engineering News*
CMR	*Chemical Marketing Reporter*
CW	*Chemical Week*
ECON	*Economist*
FB	*Forbes*
FT	*Financial Times*
JC	*Journal of Commerce*
MAN	*Medical Advertising News*
MKTLTR	*Marketletter*
NS	*New Scientist*
NYT	*New York Times*
UST	*USA Today*
WSJ	*Wall Street Journal*

Bear, Sterns & Co. Inc. (1988), "Pharmaceutical Product Trends," November 29, Bear, Sterns & Co. Inc. Investment Research, New York.

(1989a), "Squibb Corp.," January 13, Bear, Sterns & Co. Inc. Investment Research, New York.

(1989b), "Pharmaceutical Product Trends," February 3, Bear, Sterns & Co. Inc. Investment Research, New York.

(1989c), "Warner-Lambert," February 10, Bear, Sterns & Co. Inc. Investment Research, New York.

(1989d), "Merck & Co.," February 17, Bear, Sterns & Co. Inc. Investment Research, New York.

(1989e), "American Home Products," February 24, Bear, Sterns & Co. Inc. Investment Research, New York.

(*BS&C*) (1989f), "Pharmaceutical Product Trends," March 1, Bear, Sterns & Co. Inc. Investment Research, New York.

(1989g), "Smithkline Beckman," April 7, Bear, Sterns & Co. Inc. Investment Research, New York.

(1989h), "Upjohn," April 14, Bear, Sterns & Co. Inc. Investment Research, New York.

(1989i), "Pharmaceutical Industry Review," April 26, Bear, Sterns & Co. Inc. Investment Research, New York.

Bio/Technology (1989), "Downstream Processing," August, pp. 777–82.

(1990),"Non-Protein Engineering: Small Drug Design," February, pp. 105–7.

Business Week (1979), "Eli Lilly: New Life in the Drug Industry," October 29, pp. 134–45.

(1986), "Monstanto's College Alliance is Getting High Marks," May 12, pp. 33–4.

(1987), "The Miracle Company," October 19, pp. 84–90.

(1988a), "Fighting Depression with One of the Brain's Own Drugs," February 22, pp. 156–8.

(1988b), "Smithkline's Case of Ulcers," October 10, pp. 40–1.

(1988c), "How Glaxo's Eager Beavers Chewed Up Tagamet's Lead," October 10, p. 40.

(1988d), "Don't Look Back Squibb – A Giant is Gaining on You," October 10, pp. 68–76.

(1988e), "Why Generics May Not Give Syntex a Migraine," October 10, p. 76.

(1988f), "Drugs: What's in a Name Brand? Less and Less," May 12, pp. 172–6.

(1989), "Will Relief for Lab Animals Spell Pain for Consumers?," October 30, p. 43.

(1990a), "Rhone-Poulenc Finds Its American Connection," February 5, p. 39.

(1990b), "The Many Personalities of Gene-Spliced Drugs," July 30, pp. 68–9.

(1991), "The Search for Superdrugs," May 13, pp. 92–6.

(1992a), "Racing to Unlock the Secrets of Serotonin," November 9, pp. 56–7.

(1992b), "Lilly Looks for a Shot of Adrenalin," November 23, pp. 70–2.

Chemical and Engineering News (1990), "Use of Mathematical Modeling for Biochemical Systems Increases," January 22, pp. 18–20.

Chemical Marketing Reporter (1986), "Bristol Myers Opens a New Research Center in Connecticut," June 30, p. 5.

(1987a), "Nova Screens the Chemical Library of the Pennsylavania State University," April 27, p. 9.

(1987b), "Merck Expects its R&D to Produce a Continuous Flow of New Drugs," November 16, p. 9.

Chemical Week (1987a), "RT Speeds Screening for New Drugs," April 15, pp. 19–20.

(1987b), "Self-Assembling Drugs Hit the Spot," June 17, p. 22.

(1988a), "A New Team in Three-Dimensional Drug Design," May 11, p. 17.

(1988b), "Robots and Information Management Systems Take Hold in the Laboratory," July 20, pp. 32–5.

(1988c), "Syntex Prepares for the Future," July 20, pp. 40–1.

(1989a), "Technology Moves Forward in the Chemical Industry," Special Report, March 29, pp. 30–47.

(1989b), "Biotechnology: On the Rebound and Heading for a Boom," September 27, pp. 31–2.

(1989c), "Magic Bullets, Better Drugs, Growing Markets," September 27, pp. 92–4.

(1989d), "Merck and Du Pont jointly Develop and Market Drugs to Treat Heart Disease and High Blood Pressure," October 11, p. 6.

(1989e), "Automating the Chemical Processing Industry," special report, October 25, p. 16 and pp. 20–37.

(1990), "ICI Focuses on Leading Edge Research," April 11, p. 22.

Economist (1984), "Why investors are losing the biotechnology bug," August 12, p. 89.

(1986), "More Than a One-Drug Wonder?," December 20, pp. 87–8.

(1987), "Molecules and Markets," special survey on the pharmaceutical industry, February 7.

(1988a), "Super Nova," January 9, pp. 62–3.

(1988b), "A Survey of Biotechnology," special survey on biotechnology, April 30.

(1989), "The Money-Guzzling Genius of Biotechnology," May 13, pp. 69–70.

(1990), "Reshaping ICI," April 28, pp. 21–3.

(1991), "The Silver Shotguns," December 14, pp. 83–4.

(1992), "The End of the Beginning," October 24, pp. 85–7.

(1993a), "Drug Discovery by Numbers," January 23, pp. 88–9.

(1993b), "Drug Companies: Golden Pills," March 20, pp. 77–8.

Financial Times (1989a), "Biotechnology," special survey on biotechnology, May 12.

(1989b), "Pharmaceuticals," special survey on the pharmaceutical industry, November 6.

(1992a), "Gambling on a Gut Reaction," May 19, p. 16.

(1992b), "Of Mice, Men and Money," June 3, p. 12.

First Boston (1988), "Drug Industry Statistical Overview," First Boston Inc., Boston.

Forbes (1987), "Where Research Rules," February 23, pp. 128–9.

(1989), "Etch-a-Drug," June 12, pp. 154–5.

Journal of Commerce (1988), "Bristol Myers and Yale Set R&D Co-operation Agreement," March 10, p. 9B.

Marketletter (1991), "MCE's 19th Annual Pharmaceutical Conference," June 17, p. 7.

(1992), "Global Markets and Factors of Success," March 30, p. 1.

Medical Advertising News (1987), "Top 50 Pharmaceutical Companies," special survey, September 1.

New Scientist (1988), "Computers Picture the Perfect Drug," June 16, pp. 54–7.

(1992), "The Shape of Proteins to Come," May 9, p. 16.

New York Times (1988a), "Beyond White Rats and Rabbits," February 28, p. F1 and pp. F8–F10.

(1988b), "Advances in Drugs, Courtesy of Computers," August 3, p. C5.

(1988c), "Drug Makers Try Biotech Partners," September 30, pp. C1–C2.

(1989a), "Du Pont, Merck, Set Drug Pact," September 29, p. C1 and p. C4.

(1989b), "New Drug from Chinese Tree is Found to Shrink Colon Tumors in Mice," November 24, p. A12.

(1990a), "US Biotechnology Leader to Sell Swiss 60% Stake," February 3, p. 1 and p. 21.

(1990b), "The Intriguing Potential of Molecular Switches," February 4, p. F8.

(1990c), "New Antidepressant is Acclaimed but not Perfect," March 29, p. B8.

1990d), "Reducing Blood Pressure Reduces Risk to the Heart," April 10, pp. B5–B6.

(1990e), "In Clinical Trials Some Contend Big is Beautiful," April 15, p. E5.

(1990f), "Dangers of Some New Drugs Go Undetected, Study Says," May 27, p. Y10.

(1990g), "More Gilding for Lilly as New Drug Stars," July 17, p. C1 and p. C9.

(1992a), "Prostate Drug's Effects Cited," June 22, pp. B5–B6.

(1992b), "New Drug Approved for Merck," June 23, p. B1 and p. C2.

(1992c), "New Drugs by Process of Elimination," October 6, p. C1 and p. C5.

Science (1992), "The Ascent of Odorless Chemistry," April 17, pp. 306–8.

Scrip (1991a), "Sandoz' Biotech Discovery Initiative," March 20, p. 7.

(1991b), "Ciba Geigy – A Flotilla rather than a Supertanker," May 24, p. 15.

Time (1990), "The Price Isn't Right," January 8, pp. 56–7.

USA Today (1987), "Merck Would Like to Have the Leading Laboratory in Every Aspect of Medicine," December 27, p. 1B.

Wall Street Journal (1987a), "Rorer Aims to Become a Top Drug Firm," April 13, p. 6.

(1987b), "Star Performer: Hypertension Drug Boosts Squibb but also Stirs Criticism of Promotional Efforts," May 28, p. 1 and p. 5.

(1987c), "Search for New Drugs Focuses on Organisms Under the Sea," July 24, p. 19.

(1988a), "Bristol-Myers Boosts Laggard Drug Research Group," February 16, p. 14.

(1988b), "Smithkline Stops Tests of an Ulcer Drug That Was to Back Up Flagging Tagamet," November 14, p. B4.

(1989a), "Drop In Tagamet Sales is Putting Smithkline in Danger of Takeover," January 13, p. 1 and p. 5.

(1989b), "Global Drug Industry Appears to Be Headed for Big Consolidation," April 13, p. 1 and p. 5.

(1989c), "Biotech Start-Ups are Increasingly Bred just to be Sold," July 19, p. B2.

(1989d), "Bristol-Myers and Squibb Agree to Merge in a Stock Swap Valued at $11.52 Billion," July 28, p. A3.

(1992), "Super Aspirin's Promise Exemplifies Value of Biotech," February 24, p. B3.

Index

AB Astra, 70, 88
Abbott Laboratories, 38, 49, 122, 144, 175, 177–8
academia, 45–6, 55–7, 59–60, 81, 86, 148, 150
ACE, *see* angiotensinogen-converting enzyme
acquisitions, 92, 98, 101, 146, 150–1, 153, 159
Adalat, 24
adjustment costs, 110
adrenaline, 22
aeronautics, 2
Affymax, 35, 63
Agouron Pharmaceuticals, 89
agreements, research, 48–55, 59
Ahlquist, Raymond, 22
Ajinomoto, 66–7
Albert, Alfred, 173
alliances, 17, 81, 91, 101
alpha blockers, 22
ALZA, 63, 70, 73
American Cyanamid, 49, 178
American Home Products (AHP), 49, 83–4, 101–4, 122, 144, 177
Amgen, 66, 178
Anaprox, 174
angiotensinogen-converting enzyme (ACE), 85, 87, 93–4
animal tests, 18, 24, 34, 37–9, 44, 56–7, 90, 128
Ansaid, 99
appropriability, 43, 55–8, 60
  of scientific research, 4–6
aspirin, 26
asymmetric information, 55, 76
attrition rate, 21, 40, 125–6, 142
  survival rate, 137
Axid, 88–9

Battelle, 53, 145
Bayer, 24, 26, 73, 178
Beckman Instruments, 98
Beecham, 98, 102, 104, 163
beta blockers, 22
Biogen, 51, 63, 66, 70
biotechnology, 7, 9, 17, 57–8, 65, 88, 92, 103, 146–60, 165–6
  drugs, 18, 28–9
  firms (NBFs), 16–7, 34–5, 61–2, 78–81, 101, 103, 146–60, 161, 163, 165–6
Black, James, 25, 45, 97–8, 171, 174
Bovet, Daniel, 22
Bristol-Myers, 24, 31, 49–50, 83–4, 87, 92–5, 101, 103–4, 122–3, 144, 163, 176, 178
Brown, Michael, 87
Bryson, Vaughn, 90–1
Buspar, 93

California Biotechnology, 177
California Institute of Technology, 51, 53
capital stock, 124, 127, 129–30, 133–6, 139, 142, 144–5, 165
Capoten, 24–5, 85, 87–8, 93–5, 170
Cardene, 100
Carothers, Wallace, 1, 173
Ceclor, 24, 89
Celltech, 70, 73
Centocor, 91–2, 172
Centoxin, 91–2
Cetus, 35
chemical reactions, 26
Chiron, 35, 64, 66–7, 70
Chugai Pharmaceuticals, 177
Ciba-Geigy, 24, 31, 62–5, 81, 99
clinical studies, 93
clinical tests, 37, 44, 52, 55, 57, 161
clinical trials, 14–5, 18–21, 24, 28–9, 37–40,

195

clinical trials (*cont.*)
44–5, 57, 61, 79, 83, 85, 88, 93, 106,
108–9, 114, 119, 125, 130, 134, 137,
140, 142, 147, 161
Columbia University, 49, 50–1, 53
commercialization, 4–5, 14, 17, 20, 28, 52,
57, 61, 76–8, 91–2, 95, 101, 103–4, 106,
125, 133, 139–40, 147, 149–50, 162,
164–5
competition, 4, 9, 14, 17, 126–7, 132
computers, 7, 16, 42
computational power, 26, 33
computer science, 3
computer simulation, 3–4, 117, 119
computerized drug design, 13, 36–9, 41,
46, 121, 162
in drug research, 32–9
Connaught Biosciences, 103
Cor Therapeutics, 26, 172
crystallography, X-ray, 3, 32–3, 36–7, 56,
171
Cytogen, 178

Dainippon, 177
Dale, Henry, 22
discovery by design, 21–41, 86, 89
division of labor, 16–7, 61–81, 91–2, 101,
104, 146–8, 155, 157, 162, 164–7
Djerassi, Carl, 171
Domagk, Gerhard, 22, 171
Drews, Jurgen, 81
drug development, 17, 39, 45, 56, 61, 82, 88,
91, 93, 103, 125–8, 133, 138, 140, 142,
162, 165
drug design, 56, 94
and computers, 36–9, 41
rational, 30
drug discovery, 17, 21–41, 43–4, 56, 61, 63,
78, 79, 86, 106–21, 163–4
rational method of drug research, 23, 28,
162
drug industry, 37, 48
drug innovation cycle, 14, 18–21, 124, 146
drugs, 7–8, 13–15, 18–23, 25–6, 28–30, 32,
35–7, 39–41, 42–3, 45, 47, 62, 78–9,
82–3, 85, 88, 91, 93, 98, 100–1, 103,
106, 119–20, 125–7, 129–30, 139, 143,
147, 162–5
different applications, 14, 25
prediction of failures, 32, 39–40, 119,
121, 162, 165
Du Pont, 9, 58, 62, 76, 70, 104, 173, 178
Duke University, 51, 70
Duncan, William, 45, 97–8

Eastman Kodak, 104, 170
economies of scale, 44, 78, 99, 154, 163, 166

Ehrlich, Paul, 21, 27, 171
electronics, 1, 3, 9, 39
Eli Lilly, 24, 28, 31, 50–1, 82–4, 88–92, 97,
103–4, 122–3, 144, 174, 178
experimental observations, 3, 21–2, 24, 26,
33, 42, 78
experimentation, 11–13, 28, 40–1, 42, 118
121, 162, 164
experimental techniques, 29
experimentation technologies, 13–14, 17,
38, 41, 112, 114, 118
laboratory, 40
experiments, 2, 8, 15, 32–3, 77, 118
hit-and-miss, 23, 33, 41
laboratory, 38
physical, 3–4
simulation of, 3–4
and theory, 2–4, 24
trial-and-error experiments, 1, 29

first-mover advantages, 5, 28, 43, 47
Food and Drug Administration (FDA),
19–20, 31–2, 87–8, 91, 93, 100–1, 125,
130, 142, 169–71, 176

Genentech, 28, 53, 64, 67, 104
General Electric, 9
generics
generic drugs, 161
generic manufacturers, 90, 100, 164
generic medicines, 126
generic producers, 99
generic products, 95, 99–100
genetic engineering, 13, 16, 18, 27, 29, 30,
41, 56, 61–2, 78, 89, 92, 147, 154, 162,
165
Genetic Systems, 92, 178
Genetics Institute, 59
Genzyme, 67, 73
Glaxo, 24, 31–2, 88, 90, 95, 98, 169, 171
Goldstein, Joseph, 87
growth hormone, 27, 89

Harvard University, 58, 67, 82
Hoechst, 58–9, 71, 178
Hoffmann La Roche, 62, 66–8, 81, 104, 172
Houghten Pharmaceuticals, 35
human insulin (Humulin), 88–9
Hybritech, 174, 178

IBM, 9
ICI, 24, 71, 85, 88, 173
IG Farbenindustrie, 22
in vitro, 34
in vivo, 34
Institut Merieux, 103
Institut Pasteur, 22, 50

instrumentation, 2–3, 13, 16, 42, 98
instruments, 3, 8, 117
  advanced, 26
  scientific, 32–9
integration, 61–2, 92
Investigational New Drug Exemption
  (IND), 19–20, 37, 108, 125, 128, 171

Janssen Pharmaceutica, 90
Johns Hopkins University, 53
Johnson & Johnson, 50, 71, 104, 122, 144,
  176, 178
joint ventures, 146

knowledge, 1–2, 4–5, 8, 11–13, 15, 23–30,
  34, 36, 42–4, 46–7, 56, 78–9, 81, 90, 94,
  106–7, 114, 118–19, 146–8, 150–2, 154,
  157, 160, 164–7
  academic, 59
  basic, 4–5, 11–12, 23, 33, 109, 148
  external, 5, 17, 43, 82, 94, 107
  external scientific, 46–7
  knowledge capital, 106–11, 114–15,
    120–1, 158, 164–5
  outside, 15, 47
  public, 4, 9, 15–16, 23, 43, 90, 110
  scientific, 13, 17, 18, 21–2, 25–6, 34, 43–4,
    47, 60, 78, 82, 94, 109–10, 114, 117–18,
    120–1, 150, 162–4
  theoretical, 32, 42
Kramer, Alex, 81
Kuznets, Simon, 1

laboratory search, 21
laboratory trials, 24
learning, 5–6, 14, 28, 43, 47, 77–9
licenses, 48–55, 92, 100, 149
life sciences, 29–30, 38, 41, 42
Link, Max, 81
linkages, 9–10, 16–17, 48, 56, 80, 86, 109
  external, 17, 48, 80, 104, 146–60, 165
Losec, 85, 88
lovastatin, 87

Maalox, 102–3
Marion Laboratories, 104
market value, pharmaceutical firms, 107,
  109, 112–13, 122, 124, 127–8, 134–5,
  140–1, 142, 144, 165
marketing, 46, 49, 51, 64, 66–7, 70–1, 73–5,
  83, 87, 89, 91–6, 98–9, 101–5, 147, 161,
  163
Marx, Karl, 1
Massachusetts General Hospital, 51–2,
  58–9, 70
Max Planck Institute, 50
MB 693, 22

Merck, 24–6, 50–1, 62, 70–2, 83–8, 90, 97,
  103–4, 122, 144, 172–4, 177
Merrell-Dow, 68, 104
Mevacor, 24–5, 85–8, 93, 170
minority participations, 146, 148–51, 153,
  159, 165
minoxidil, 25
MIT, 8, 49–51
Mitsubishi, 177
molecular biology, 13, 16, 18, 27, 29–30, 41,
  56, 61–2, 78, 92, 147, 154, 162, 164
Monsanto, 51, 54–5, 58, 172, 177–8
moral hazard, 76

Naltraxone, 25
Naprosyn, 24, 99–100, 174
naproxen, 99
National Cancer Institute, 50, 54, 174
National Institute of Health, 49, 52, 90
NBF, *see under* biotechnology
networks, 61, 80–1, 92, 156, 164
  distribution, 61
  neuronal, 3
  of agreements, 63–75
  scientific, 16, 48, 59, 109
New Drug Application (NDA), 19, 88, 91,
  93, 101, 125, 128, 130–1, 134, 137, 142,
  176
"not-invented-here," 91
Nova Pharmaceuticals, 34, 170
Novascreen, 34
nuclear magnetic resonance (NMR), 3, 33,
  36–7, 56, 171

Ohio State University, 52
Oncogen, 92, 178
one-drug companies, 83, 94–5, 99–100, 103
Oregon State University, 52
over-the-counter (OTC), 63, 71, 99, 101–2,
  126

papers, 55, 97–8, 107–8, 110–15, 120–1,
  123, 164
Parfet, William, 81
patents, 5, 7, 43–4, 48, 56, 68, 76, 79,
  99–100, 106–8, 111, 113–15, 119–22,
  146, 152–3, 156, 160, 161, 164–5
  applications for, 106, 108, 112, 122–3
  citations of, 120
peer evaluation, 45, 86
Pennsylvania State University, 52
Pepcid, 85, 88
Pfizer, 54, 62, 73–5, 83, 122, 144
pharmaceutical industry, 13–17, 28–9, 39,
  48, 59, 61, 77–8, 80, 83, 106, 108, 125,
  128, 133, 136, 141, 147, 161
platelets, 26

Pravachol, 94–5, 174
Primaxin, 85
Prinvil, 85, 88, 94
Procter & Gamble, 99
Prodiac, 85
Prontosil, 22, 171
Proscar, 85, 88
Prozac, 31, 89–90, 174
publications, 9, 47, 57, 97, 106–7, 109, 114, 123
Purdue University, 52, 54, 72

Questar, 87, 93

R&D, 1, 4–7, 11, 14, 17, 19–21, 49–52, 54, 63–4, 66–7, 70–4, 77, 96, 100, 102–4, 112–13, 122–8, 130–9, 141–5, 147–9, 158, 161–2, 164–6, 169, 176–7
receptors, 30, 36, 37, 39, 43, 47, 79, 90
    cell, 27–32, 34–5
    platelet, 26
    protein, 27–32
    receptor technology, 27–32, 34
    receptor structure, 26, 43, 47, 78
    serotonin, 31, 90
    similarity of, 29
recombinant DNA (rDNA), 51–3, 64, 70, 72
renin, 38, 93
Repligen, 72, 91
research, 1–3, 5–7, 9–10, 14–17, 21–2, 28, 32, 40, 42, 44–55, 58, 61–2, 64–7, 69–72, 73, 76–8, 80–1, 82–3, 86–92, 94–8, 100–5, 119–21, 126, 131, 136, 138–9, 142–3, 145, 149, 156, 162–4, 166
    applied, 8–13, 16, 20, 22, 38, 41, 44, 55, 58, 62, 76, 78, 106, 117–18, 121, 125, 132, 140, 147, 149–50
    applied laboratory, 14, 38, 106, 121, 150
    basic, 4–6, 8, 11, 15, 18, 24, 43–4, 46, 55, 76, 132, 147–9
    clinical, 108, 127, 161
    experimental, 32, 43, 77
    in-house, 2, 9, 15, 78, 83–105, 148, 157
    in-house scientific, 15, 46, 83–105
    laboratory, 111–12, 117, 149
    pharmacological, 25
    pre-clinical, 18, 44, 108, 125, 127, 133, 161
    public, 10, 57, 90, 164, 166
    scientific, 3, 5–6, 11, 15, 30, 42–8, 55, 57, 82, 94, 97–8, 103–4, 106, 148
research collaborations, 48–55, 57–61, 92
research openness, 16, 46–8
research opportunities, depletion of, 108, 111, 114, 120–1, 161

Revlon, 102
Rhone-Poulenc, 102–4, 163
Robins, 101–2, 104
Rogaine, 25
Rorer, 83–4, 102–4, 163

Salvarsan, 21, 26, 29, 171
Sandoz, 81
Sankyo, 174
Schering-Plough, 49, 52, 68, 122, 144, 177
Schumpeter, Joseph, 1
science, 5–6, 9–10, 13–16, 29, 39–41, 43, 56, 60, 82–3, 103, 154, 161
    and innovation, 1–5, 15, 163
    as a source of economic value, 4–13
    experimental, 4, 18, 39
scientific capital, 106–7
scientific community, 8–11, 41, 46–7, 56, 82, 86, 109
scientific creativity, 10, 16, 44–6, 59, 83, 163
scientific institutions, 4, 9, 30, 43, 48, 55–7, 79, 161, 164
screening, 23, 42, 44, 78
    chemical, 21–2
    laboratory, 18, 22
    random, 13
    screening technologies, 34–6
Scripps Clinic, 50, 52
search theory, 41
    in innovation, 11–13
    search models, 107
Searle, 55
Selectide, 35
serendipity, 100, 108, 111, 120–1
serotonin, 43, 89–90
    serotonin drugs, 30–2, 90
Shionogy, 177
Shockley, William, 1
side-effects, 27–9, 31–2, 39–40, 95, 130
Smith, Adam, 1
Smith, George, 34
Smithkline, 24, 26, 52–3, 72, 88, 90, 95–8, 102–4, 122, 144, 163, 169, 171–2, 174, 178
software, 3, 9
specialization, 17, 92, 101, 104
Squibb, 24–5, 50, 53, 57, 83–5, 87, 92–5, 101, 103–4, 122, 144, 163
Stanford University, 49, 52, 54
Sterling Drugs, 53, 104, 122, 144
sunk costs, 61
Suntory, 177
super-aspirins, 26, 43
survival rate, *see under* attrition rate
Synaptic Pharmaceutical, 90–1
Synbiotics, 178

Syntex, 24, 53, 68, 83–4, 99–101, 103, 122, 144, 174

Tagamet, 24–5, 45, 88, 95–8, 170–1, 174
technological community, 8–11
technological opportunities, 5–7, 13, 43, 55, 136
  technological opportunity shock, 127–9, 142
Tenormin, 24
theories, 6, 33, 42
  and experiments, 2–4, 24
  theoretical models, 36
Tolrestat, 101
transaction costs, 55
trial, pre-clinical, 40
trial and error, 11, 23, 32, 36–7, 40–1, 42
trial-and-error tests, 33

universities, 5, 16–17, 49–54, 57, 61, 86, 92, 165
  in biotechnology, 146–60
  educational and research functions, 6–8
  restrictions to academic freedom, 57–61
  university–industry linkages, 48, 56–8, 61
  university institutions, 34
  university research, 55–59

University College, London, 54
University of Auckland, 54
University of California, 26, 174
University of Cambridge, 52
University of Chicago, 49
University of Göteborg, 54
University of Kansas, 53
University of Oxford, 53, 57
University of Pennsylvania, 170
Upjohn, 25, 53–4, 81, 83, 99, 122, 144, 177

Vagelos, Roy, 173
Vane, John, 93
Vasotec, 24, 85, 87–8, 94
Voltaren, 24, 99

Warner-Lambert, 54, 83, 122, 144
Washington University, 34–5, 51, 55, 58, 172–3
Waxman–Hatch Drug Act, 161, 164
Wealth of Nations, 1

Yale University, 50, 92
Yamanouchi Pharmaceuticals, 100

Zantac, 24, 88, 95, 98, 169, 171
Zocor, 88